Edith Maier

Activity Theory for Intercultural Human-Computer Interaction

Edith Maier

Activity Theory for Intercultural Human-Computer Interaction

A Theoretical Framework for Investigating Intercultural Issues in Computer-Mediated Information and Communication

Südwestdeutscher Verlag für Hochschulschriften

Impressum/Imprint (nur für Deutschland/ only for Germany)
Bibliografische Information der Deutschen Nationalbibliothek: Die Deutsche Nationalbibliothek verzeichnet diese Publikation in der Deutschen Nationalbibliografie; detaillierte bibliografische Daten sind im Internet über http://dnb.d-nb.de abrufbar.
Alle in diesem Buch genannten Marken und Produktnamen unterliegen warenzeichen-, marken- oder patentrechtlichem Schutz bzw. sind Warenzeichen oder eingetragene Warenzeichen der jeweiligen Inhaber. Die Wiedergabe von Marken, Produktnamen, Gebrauchsnamen, Handelsnamen, Warenbezeichnungen u.s.w. in diesem Werk berechtigt auch ohne besondere Kennzeichnung nicht zu der Annahme, dass solche Namen im Sinne der Warenzeichen- und Markenschutzgesetzgebung als frei zu betrachten wären und daher von jedermann benutzt werden dürften.

Verlag: Südwestdeutscher Verlag für Hochschulschriften Aktiengesellschaft & Co. KG
Dudweiler Landstr. 99, 66123 Saarbrücken, Deutschland
Telefon +49 681 37 20 271-1, Telefax +49 681 37 20 271-0, Email: info@svh-verlag.de
Zugl.: Vienna, University of Vienna, PhD Thesis, 2005

Herstellung in Deutschland:
Schaltungsdienst Lange o.H.G., Berlin
Books on Demand GmbH, Norderstedt
Reha GmbH, Saarbrücken
Amazon Distribution GmbH, Leipzig
ISBN: 978-3-8381-0647-2

Imprint (only for USA, GB)
Bibliographic information published by the Deutsche Nationalbibliothek: The Deutsche Nationalbibliothek lists this publication in the Deutsche Nationalbibliografie; detailed bibliographic data are available in the Internet at http://dnb.d-nb.de.
Any brand names and product names mentioned in this book are subject to trademark, brand or patent protection and are trademarks or registered trademarks of their respective holders. The use of brand names, product names, common names, trade names, product descriptions etc. even without a particular marking in this works is in no way to be construed to mean that such names may be regarded as unrestricted in respect of trademark and brand protection legislation and could thus be used by anyone.

Publisher:
Südwestdeutscher Verlag für Hochschulschriften Aktiengesellschaft & Co. KG
Dudweiler Landstr. 99, 66123 Saarbrücken, Germany
Phone +49 681 37 20 271-1, Fax +49 681 37 20 271-0, Email: info@svh-verlag.de

Copyright © 2009 by the author and Südwestdeutscher Verlag für Hochschulschriften Aktiengesellschaft & Co. KG and licensors
All rights reserved. Saarbrücken 2009

Printed in the U.S.A.
Printed in the U.K. by (see last page)
ISBN: 978-3-8381-0647-2

Table of Contents

List of Tables and Figures vi

1 Introduction 1
   1.1 Background to research 1
      1.1.1 Role of researcher in the Project 1
      1.1.2 Research context and 'field' environment 2
   1.2 Research issues 4
      1.2.1 The problem with defining culture 4
      1.2.2 Intercultural factors in the research context 5
      1.2.3 The problem with defining context 6
   1.3 The search for an overarching theoretical framework 9
   1.4 Contents of chapters 11

2 Terminological Issues 16
   2.1 Definition of terms in human-computer interaction 16
      2.1.1 Localisation 16
      2.1.2 Internationalisation 17
      2.1.3 Globalisation 18
      2.1.4 Intercultural *versus* cross-cultural 18
   2.2 Definition of terms in the eLearning field 19
      2.2.1 eLearning, online learning or blended learning? 19
      2.2.2 CMC, CBI or CAI? 20
   2.3 The principles of knowledge management 20
      2.3.1 Knowledge management directions 21
      2.3.2 Intellectual capital 21
   2.4 Definition of key terms 22
      2.4.1 Knowledge 22
      2.4.2 Data, information and knowledge 23
      2.4.3 Explicit and tacit knowledge 23
   2.5 The knowledge management process 24
      2.5.1 Knowledge base and building blocks 24
      2.5.2 Human and cultural issues 25
      2.5.3 Measuring knowledge management 26
      2.5.4 Knowledge management and eLearning 27
   2.6 Knowledge management framework 28
   2.7 Summary 29

3 The Problem of Defining Culture 30

3.1 Introduction 30
3.1.1 Psychological approaches to the concept of culture 31
3.1.2 Attempts at defining culture 32

3.2 Concepts and models for identifying cultural differences 33
3.2.1 Culture as mental software 33
3.2.2 Critique of Hofstede's approach 35
3.2.3 Critique from an anthropological point of view 37
3.2.4 Culture as an object of knowledge management 38
3.2.5 Cultural standards 39
3.2.6 Cultural mental models and schemas 40

3.3 Summary 41

4 Literature Survey and Recent Developments 42

4.1 Introduction 42

4.2 Cultural factors in the realm of usability 42
4.2.1 Brief overview of the literature on internationalisation and localisation 43
4.2.2 Current trends and key issues in intercultural usability engineering 44
4.2.3 Relevant publications in internationalisation, localisation and globalisation 49

4.3 Current trends and key issues in eLearning 52
4.3.1 Learning management systems and learning objects 53
4.3.2 Recent publications in eLearning 54
4.3.3 Cultural factors in the eLearning literature – a topic of benign neglect? 56

4.4 Computer-supported collaborative work and communities of practice 57

4.5 Summary 59

5 Theories and Models in Human-Computer-Interaction 61

5.1 Introduction 61

5.2 Cognitive ergonomics 62
5.2.1 Role of culture 62
5.2.2 Critique 63

5.3 Situated action 64
5.3.1 Role of culture 64
5.3.2 Critique 65

5.4 Distributed cognition 66
5.4.1 Role of Culture 67
5.4.2 Critique 67

5.5 Activity theory 68

    5.5.1   Role of Culture 69

    5.5.2   Critique 69

  5.6   *The use of cultural models in human-computer interaction* 70

  5.7   *Summary* 76

6 Theories and Models in eLearning 78

  6.1   *Introduction* 78

  6.2   *Brief historical outline of learning theories with reference to computer-based instruction* 79

  6.3   *Metaphors of learning* 81

  6.4   *Approaches in the field of eLearning* 82

    6.4.1   Modellers *versus* non-modellers 83

    6.4.2   Instructivists *versus* constructivists 83

    6.4.3   Individualistic *versus* communicative or sociocultural theories 84

  6.5   *Towards a theory of eLearning* 84

    6.5.1   Engagement Theory 86

    6.5.2   Pedagogical models 87

  6.6   *Theoretical approaches, concepts and models and the role of culture* 90

  6.7   *Cultural models and their application to learning and teaching* 91

    6.7.1   Applying cultural models to eLearning studies 94

  6.8   *Activity theory as an integrative framework* 95

7 The Quest for a Theoretical Framework 98

  7.1   *Introduction* 98

  7.2   *Reasons for choosing activity theory as a theoretical framework* 99

  7.3   *The main tenets and principles of activity theory* 102

    7.3.1   Hierarchical structure of activity 103

    7.3.2   Object-orientedness / Environment 103

    7.3.3   Internalisation/externalisation 104

    7.3.4   Mediation by tools 105

    7.3.5   Development 106

  7.4   *Unifying concepts* 107

  7.5   *Discussion of relevant publications* 110

    7.5.1   Application of activity theory to HCI studies 110

    7.5.2   Application of activity theory to eLearning studies 112

    7.5.3   Activity theory and collaborative and communal aspects 113

  7.6   *Summary* 114

8 Methodology ... 116

8.1 Introduction ... 116

8.2 Defining culture-specific usability requirements ... 117

8.2.1 Adapting evaluation methods to different cultures ... 118
8.2.2 Cultural factors in the research environment ... 119

8.3 Methodological tools of activity theory ... 121

8.4 Ethnographic research in an activity theory framework ... 123

8.4.1 Problems with ethnographic research ... 124

8.5 Usability testing ... 126

8.5.1 General principles of usability ... 127
8.5.2 Usability testing methods and techniques ... 128

8.6 Methods for data analysis ... 132

8.7 Summary ... 134

9 Practical Implementation ... 137

9.1 Organisational context for the empirical study ... 137

9.2 Ethnographic research related to training ... 139

9.2.1 Investigating course organisation and development ... 140
9.2.2 Description of case study – the VEMD prototype ... 144

9.3 Usability testing ... 146

9.3.1 Heuristic evaluation through experts ... 147
9.3.2 End-user tests ... 148

9.4 Preparation of empirical data for analysis ... 150

9.5 Summary ... 151

10 Analysis ... 152

10.1 An activity theoretical analysis ... 153

10.1.1 The internal structure of the activity ... 153

10.2 Results of ethnographic research ... 154

10.2.1 The importance of professional culture ... 154

10.3 Structured description of training ... 155

10.3.1 Strategies and goals of training ... 155
10.3.2 Organisational context of training activity ... 160
10.3.3 Learning, cognition and interaction ... 165
10.3.4 Transformation and development ... 172

10.4 The role of cultural factors ... 175

10.4.1 Strategies and goals ... 176

	10.4.2	Organisational context 176
	10.4.3	Learning, cognition and interaction 177
	10.4.4	Transformation and development.. 181
10.5		*Contradictions 185*
	10.5.1	Strategies and goals of training 185
	10.5.2	Strategies and goals.. 186
	10.5.3	Organisational context 187
	10.5.4	Learning, cognition and interaction 187
	10.5.5	Transformation and development.. 188
11	**Conclusions**	**.. 189**
11.1		*Why activity theory? 189*
11.2		*Recommendations and guidelines... 190*
	11.2.1	Guidelines for usability testing 191
	11.2.2	Recommendations for the development of eLearning materials 192
	11.2.3	The accommodation of cultural factors.. 194
	11.2.4	Recommendations concerning methodology 196
12	**References**	**.. 199**
12.1		*Literature.. 199*
12.2		*Internet Resources 207*

List of Tables and Figures

Figure 1: Extended Activity Triangle 104

Figure 2: Extended Activity Triangle (adapted) 135

Figure 3: Interview questions for instructors 142

Figure 4: Evaluation of interactive aspects 150

Figure 5: Training Activity System 197

List of Tables

Table 1: Spiral of knowledge creation 109

Table 2: Comparison of ethnographic research methods 126

Table 3: General usability guidelines by Nielsen 128

Table 4: Adaptation of Hofstede's cultural dimension of Power Distance
to instructor – trainee relations 131

Table 5: Roles and tasks involved in course development 163

Table 6: Cultural differences with regard to user interface design 179

1 Introduction

1.1 Background to research

The research for this thesis was conducted within the framework of a transnational European project called Enhancing Knowledge Management in Enterprises (ENKE), co-funded by the European Commission under the Information Society Technologies Programme (IST-2000-29482). The Project[1] started in September 2001 and ended in October 2003 and focused on the definition and application of a comprehensive framework for introducing and enhancing knowledge management (KM) in organisations and the development and implementation of two technology-based knowledge management applications for two entirely different industrial sectors.

1.1.1 Role of researcher in the Project

I was responsible for coordinating and managing the Project on behalf of my employer, the Centre for Knowledge and Information Management at the Donau-Universität Krems. The Centre was the only academic partner in the Project Consortium.

Within the Consortium, the Centre had been allocated the task of ensuring that human, social and cultural factors would be duly taken into account in the development and implementation of the various applications. This task was largely inspired by the increasing awareness among experts that although information and communication tools played an important role in KM applications, their successful and efficient use very much depended on the motivation of employees. The Centre was also responsible for coordinating the work package concerned with demonstrations and assessment, which involved defining criteria for measuring the performance of KM approaches and tools and, subsequently, analysing and evaluating the demonstrations carried out by the partners and preparing a synthesis of the project work done.

As far as the validation of the functional requirements was concerned, the Centre was expected to suggest any non-technical measures, including ergonomic, cognitive or social measures, which would have to accompany the implementation of the KM tool(s) at the partners' sites. In addition, we defined the features required for the KM tools in terms of user-friendliness or usability. The partners in the Project also realised that human, social and cultural factors would have to be taken into account long before the validation stage (as originally foreseen in the official Description of Work) and at all levels (analysis of user requirements, development and design, implementation and evaluation) for the applications to succeed.

An additional factor, which was not explicitly considered in the project proposal, but soon came to the foreground when the actual work began, was the importance of the multicultural dimension in one of the two applications, namely the Web-based training modules to be developed at the site of

---

[1] Throughout this study, whenever the term "project" is capitalised, it refers to the ENKE Project, which served as the major source of data for this investigation.

the French industrial partner, a major international helicopter producer. As far as the other partner was concerned, the KM application was directed at a more culturally homogeneous group of project leaders who needed access to a vast array of widely distributed, unstructured and diverse information resources.

The Learning Management System, the platform which would integrate the Web-based training modules, however, had to cater for a culturally very diverse range of customers from more than a hundred countries. Although all trainees were expected to be proficient in English and share the same professional context, it could be assumed that their different cultural values, traditions and attitudes would have an influence on their understanding of and their cognitive approach to the training content.

Early on in the Project, it came to be recognised by all involved – the partners, the project officer of the European Commission and the reviewers assigned to the Project by the Commission – that the innovative contribution made by the Project would consist to a considerable degree in its taking into account of intercultural factors, something not yet done in similar EU initiatives in the fields of KM and eLearning. The integration of cultural diversity into knowledge capture and transfer activities was therefore considered an important contribution that this Project and the research carried out in connection with the Web-based training application, in particular, could deliver for the advancement of both KM and eLearning.

This turn of events led to an extension of my role. I came to realise that the Project offered an ideal opportunity for combining the different strands of my professional background – i.e. applied languages, anthropology and information science, in particular, human-computer interaction (HCI). Furthermore, I realised that the research questions involved indeed merited in-depth treatment and that there did not seem to be any ready answers or proven and well-established solutions dealing with these questions. Exchanges with other researchers at conferences as well as my survey of recent publications showed a serious lack of both a unifying terminology and theoretical framework.

This is why I decided to apply for study leave so as to be able to concentrate fully on conducting the research and user trials required by the Project and, at the same time, to gather the data for my thesis. The Consortium also felt that the quality of the research in connection with the Project would benefit greatly if the outcome were theoretically well-founded as a result of being embedded in and accompanied by a doctoral study.

1.1.2 Research context and 'field' environment

Conducting the research related to the various Project activities and tasks involved several months of working on-site in the training centre of the French industrial partner, Eurocopter, an international helicopter producer with headquarters in Marignane near Marseilles. The training centre, or 'Campus', as it is called, is at the heart of a worldwide network of thirteen training centres at company subsidiaries around the globe, which together form the Eurocopter Training Academy. The centres vary greatly in size from 17 instructors in the US subsidiary to one instructor in some of the smaller ones.

The Marignane Campus comprises a total of 32 instructors and 16 classrooms equipped with smartboards and PCs (a total of 105). Of the 32 instructors, seven specialise on avionics, thirteen on mechanics and twelve on pilot courses, both ground and flight. Instructors spend an average of about 80% of their time in the classroom which leaves little time for information exchange with other instructors, thinking about and developing new courses and reflecting on pedagogic or didactic issues.

Apart from courses for pilots, technicians and avionic specialists, the Campus also organises specialised courses on logistics and other related topics such as engines, hydraulic or electrical systems, as well as the use of autopilot and simulation systems. Courses tend to be type rating, i.e. training on a particular aircraft, conversion or refresher courses; so far no *ab initio* courses, i.e. courses for beginners, are offered.

The company's participation in the Project was motivated by its wish to reduce the time and cost spent on course development and to respond to growing customer demand for eLearning. This was to be achieved by efficiently organising the information (documents, files, images, simulations, etc.) required for course building by means of an information or KM system[2]. This, in turn, was considered a prerequisite for developing a learning management system, a platform for computer-based or Web-based training modules which would allow trainees to study certain portions of the teaching content at home. It was clear from the outset, however, that eLearning would never replace, but only supplement on-site training. For instance, it could help achieve more homogeneous groups in terms of *a priori* knowledge, one of the most important success factors for training purposes.

In conjunction with the instructors and the Project management, the decision was taken to develop a prototype application, namely a Web-based training module of the VEMD (Vehicle and Engine Multifunctional Display). This module would allow future or potential customers, especially those who had been trained on aircraft without more advanced or sophisticated semi-automatic indicating and recording systems, to acquire a basic knowledge of the VEMD before coming to the Campus and, thus, allow them to start off on an equal footing with their fellow students. Other important factors in the selection of the VEMD for the pilot system included the facts that it is installed on the company's most popular helicopters – which together account for more than 60% of the total of machines sold in 2002 – and that it is a relatively self-contained unit.

---

[2] See the chapter on Terminological Issues for a differentiation between information and knowledge management.

1.2 Research issues

1.2.1 The problem with defining culture

As was to be expected, the problem of defining 'culture' raised its head at an early stage of the research. Did 'cultural' factors refer to national, organisational or domain aspects? Basing the selection of informants or interviewees on purely national criteria or country of origin when analysing user requirements, for example, soon proved unsatisfactory. Requirements seemed to be influenced more by profession, i.e. mechanics or pilots, as well as by whether trainees had a military or a civil background.

This observation was confirmed by the research carried out at the second industrial partner's site, where although the majority of the members of the pilot group shared the same nationality, their different requirements were also strongly influenced by their professional roles, e.g. the needs and expectations of project managers differed greatly to those of administrators or management.

Given my training in anthropology, I was familiar with the myriad attempts to define the notoriously complex and slippery notion of culture. Rather than enter into and contribute to a probably fruitless discussion, I tried to limit, or rather adapt, it to the task in question and define it in the context of information processing and management to assess whether and to what extent culture could be considered a design variable in the construction of a KM or eLearning system.

This implied looking at the following issues and trying to find answers to questions such as:

- To what extent does culture (national, organisational, domain) influence the way people seek and use information?
- How is 'usability' defined in this context? Do we mean performance, user satisfaction or some other criterion we had not thought of?
- Once we have defined the usability criteria, how can they be measured?
- Culture is mediated by many factors including contextual factors such as training or work environment, individual factors such as gender, age, professional experience, computer usage, etc. which all have an impact on information use and knowledge exchange. How – if at all - do these change the effect of cultural background on information use? We assumed, for instance, that it would make a difference whether a mechanic accessed an information system in the field to find a solution to a particular maintenance problem or whether he was interested in obtaining general maintenance information whilst following a training session.
- What methods are best suited for studying cross-cultural differences in information seeking and knowledge exchange?

- What design dimensions should be considered in eLearning systems? Can general user interface design aspects such as language, images and content organisation also be applied to eLearning or KM systems?
- What new or additional dimensions – e.g. relevance, interactivity, involvement, community, novelty, etc. – do we need to consider?

I decided that for the purposes of this study the most adequate approach to culture was that expressed by Holden in his book on cross-cultural management (2002). He defines culture as the "infinitely overlapping and perpetually redistributable habitats of common knowledge and shared meaning" (p. 316). He posits cross-cultural management as a form of KM and examines how cultural diversity can be transformed into organisational knowledge. Rather than regard cultural differences as obstacles that need to be overcome, he considers them as enriching and as a potential source of innovative ideas.

This emphasis on practical solutions greatly echoed the on-site challenges I faced during the study. Furthermore, Holden's perspective on culture is founded to a great extent on very detailed case studies, all of them situated in multinational corporate environments dominated by modern information and communication technologies. His work provides an array of new concepts, models and insights that proved very helpful to orient my investigations in a similar environment.

Holden's approach is also more capable of accommodating the very dynamic, constantly shifting nature of modern organisations and is far more adapted to the globalised or rather globalising world of international computer-mediated activities and networks. Traditional approaches based on the concept of culture as essence and difference have limited explanatory value for this type of research since they tend to be intrinsically linked to language, nationality and ethnicity. These notions no longer play the kind of role accorded to them by anthropologists in the nineteenth and twentieth centuries and prove inadequate when studying today's multinational organisations. Even though cultural orientation systems that are acquired early in life continue to have a strong influence on human beings throughout their lives, they are insufficient to account for behaviour differences in learning situations, for instance, where factors such as profession, status or corporate culture play a major role. Furthermore, when it comes to the actual design of products such as Web-based training modules, we also need a precise understanding of work objectives and work contexts.

1.2.2 Intercultural factors in the research context

Despite being a large multinational group with offices all over the world, the corporate culture of the French partner in the Project was very much shaped by French traditions, language and business conventions. Similarly, German working practices, language and culture strongly influenced corporate culture at the German partner, with its international offices expected to adapt to fit.

This is why the discourse and perspective on cultural factors has several facets. Firstly, the information I gathered in the course of interviews and the tacit knowledge I obtained through participant observation was filtered through my own cultural background, which is shaped by having lived and worked primarily in a German-speaking (Austria) and an Anglo-Saxon, English-speaking environment (15 years in England and Ireland).

Given my anthropological training, I was sensitive to the possible misinterpretations or misunderstandings which could arise from this cultural gap. One way of counteracting bias or distortion is to discuss and crosscheck findings with other experts such as interpreters or colleagues who have been exposed to both cultural environments. They can serve as a useful correcting agent and help throw light on puzzling data. Consequently, the fact that my colleague at the German partner's site was British, had a background as a professional translator and had lived in a German-speaking country for 17 years, proved highly beneficial for discussion purposes.

Secondly, the corporate culture was very different from the organisational environments I was familiar with. Whereas my work experience up to that time was largely gained in small, non-profit organisations, such as universities, museums and libraries, the research setting was that of a big company with around 6000 employees. Most of my interlocutors – instructors, software designers and developers – as well as my Project partners on-site had been trained in or gained their work experience in military environments dominated by a strongly hierarchical structure. This also applied to a considerable portion of the end-users, i.e. the trainees.

Thirdly, the information gathered from the trainees, who – in line with the principles of participatory design – were involved right from the start, had to be crosschecked with the French instructors to ascertain whether my interpretations of what was said or of what could be observed in the classroom coincided with their interpretations. Thus, over the course of time, a complex and intricate web of meanings and interpretations evolved, which in turn required continuous examination and re-examination.

1.2.3 The problem with defining context

In addition to the cultural aspects, the notion of 'context' proved to be a veritable Pandora's Box and opening this box lifted the lid on an endless string of questions. When analysing the requirements for the Project application, it soon emerged that the need to 'contextualise' the design of computer-based systems was far from straightforward. Was this tantamount to taking into account the physical environment in which a system was to be used or did it imply detailed accounts of how people perform the activities such as knowledge exchange or learning which we intended to support?

Should our considerations be extended to a wider context and include, for example, the Training Academy with its worldwide network of training centres? Or should it simply be restricted to the Campus? What about the firm as a whole? There was no doubt that decisions taken at Board level had an impact on the training policy and the strategic orientation of the Campus. The success of the KM applications as defined by the Project obviously depended to a large extent on whether their objectives were in line with company objectives. Management support, for instance, would be essential for any KM or eLearning initiative to succeed.

Should we take into account the developments at the site of Eurocopter's German partner company, where various similar initiatives, especially in the computer-based training sector, were underway? After all, one of the aims of the merger between the French and German companies over ten years ago had been to exploit the synergies resulting from sharing experiences and solutions.

Furthermore, one could well argue that customers, suppliers, competitors and national Governments (e.g. as sponsors of new programmes) also played a role in the formulation of strategy. Indeed, it was largely in response to customer demand that the decision to develop the computer-based/Web-based modules was conceived and incorporated into the corporate agenda.
Apart from these wider contextual factors, the design of the computer-based training modules would also be influenced by a host of factors associated more specifically with the actual eLearning endeavour.
For instance, according to the Project's Description of Work, the Learning Management System was to be designed in line with AICC guidelines[3]. Which actual guidelines would be used? All of them (there is a total of 9 guidelines) or just those concerning Web-based training or icon or graphic presentation?

Further questions or issues immediately related to the development of Web-based training modules, which had to be clarified, included:

- What is the extent of interactivity required for the training modules?
- Will the courseware have to include any (official) certification features?
- Is any importation of learning content from third parties envisaged?
- Define compulsory and optional features for the Learning Management System.
- To what extent and how are contextual and community features going to be integrated in the Learning Management System?
- To what extent will Eurocopter instructors be able or allowed to develop and/or update Learning Objects?
- Which tasks will be sub-contracted?

---

[3] The Aviation Industry Computer-Based Training Committee (AICC) is an international association of training professionals and has developed guidelines for the development, delivery and evaluation of computer-based training and related training technologies, e.g. for computer-mediated instruction interoperability (extended in 1998 to include Web-based technologies) or navigation icons to help standardise the student user components or interfaces.

- How will the KM and eLearning systems be integrated with existing intranet solutions, data repositories and/or document management systems?
- Will there be one central person responsible for the content or will this task be delegated to each individual course manager or trainer? The latter scenario could raise issues of consistency, duplication of efforts, etc.
- Will the instructors be involved in the design and/or development of the KM and/or Learning Management System?

All the above questions or issues can be subsumed under the heading contextual factors, which have come to play an increasing role in HCI studies and, by extension, in its practical application areas such as usability engineering.

1.2.3.1 The methodological implications of a contextual design approach

The emphasis on context including social, cultural and human factors has encouraged the use and incorporation of techniques, methods and theories from anthropology, sociology and social psychology, to name but a few of the disciplines which deal with such factors. Ethnographic techniques such as participant observation and interviews have become widely recognised as a good way of gathering contextual information.

Studies inspired by an ethnographic orientation focus on building up an understanding of work or activity as it occurs *in situ*. This orientation eschews employing a prior theoretical stance to the subject of study, focusing instead on the details of the situation-specific practices through which work (or activity) is achieved by participants as a recognisable social accomplishment.

A major challenge posed by an ethnographic approach is how to generalise from ethnographic studies in order to provide guidance for system designers and other users? How can we build up a repository of design knowledge based on extraction and comparison of findings across studies? How can we study context so that it is useful for designers? They tend to look for analysis methods for evaluating the impact of design decisions and information that proposes actual designs rather than general guidelines.

On the other hand, how can we alleviate the fact that most existing guidelines lack a theoretical underpinning and thus suffer from fragmentation and incoherence and tend to refer to very specific settings and situations? At the same time, there are many systems whose interfaces have not been the object of explicit design or were not developed with the help of research into HCI approaches (such as cognitive ergonomics), but which nevertheless serve their users well enough. Why do they work so well?

1.3 The search for an overarching theoretical framework

Given the complex and intricate web of interactions and interrelations between the different aspects of the Project work, the quest for a theoretical framework to provide guidance and orientation in my research endeavours increased in importance. The theoretical framework would have to supply concepts and models both for HCI and learning and teaching approaches and would also have to provide for the specific requirements encountered in a virtual environment. At the same time, it had to be able to embrace human, social and (inter)cultural factors, cope with computer-mediated collaboration processes and take into account the environment or context in which activities such as learning and teaching occur.

The more deeply I delved into the various major approaches in HCI research – especially with regard to the influence of cultural factors – the more I realized that none of them could do justice to the diverse facets involved in my research. First of all, not all of them take cultural factors into account. Indeed, they hardly figure at all in cognitive ergonomics or human factors engineering, which still influence a great deal of usability studies and methods and tend to concentrate on the man-machine dyad. Consequently, some of the more recent approaches such as situated action, distributed cognition and activity theory seemed more suited to the Project work because they incorporated the impact and importance of context and thus of social and cultural factors.

Situated action states that every course of action depends in essential ways upon its material and social circumstances. The embeddedness of the user in a specific (cultural) context and a framework of reference is recognised, but the approach does not provide tools or models with which to describe them, especially if they go beyond the immediate situation. The emphasis is on the emergent, contingent and improvisatory nature of situations, which makes abstraction or generalisation very difficult and does not allow for a longer time horizon. Motives and goals are seen as post-hoc rationalisations, not as conditions for action.

Distributed cognition posits a system goal and has proved useful in analysing work practices that span specific situation contexts and extend to a community of individuals. According to its promoters, it focuses on whole environments and helps to understand interactions between people and technologies. However, people and technologies or artefacts are seen as conceptually equivalent and both are considered 'agents' in a system. In contrast, activity theory regards them as basically asymmetrical.

Activity theory is a set of basic principles that constitute a general conceptual system rather than a highly predictive theory and, being a dynamic and systemic approach, it can cope with a rapidly changing environment. Activity theory traces its roots back to psychological perspectives in the Soviet Union and now supports studies in developmental psychology and educational technology around the world. It also provides a broad framework for describing the structure, development and context of computer-supported activities and a foundation on which HCI researchers might base common discourse and from which they can derive tools for design and evaluation (see Kaptelinin and Nardi 1999).

Although distributed cognition and activity theory are close in spirit and both portray themselves as integrated frameworks for HCI studies, I eventually opted for activity theory as the preferred framework. It is from this approach that we can derive models and concepts for analysing cultural and historical structures in usability engineering and for the dynamic processes in man-computer interaction or computer-mediated activity.

The value of activity theory for contextual studies of HCI has been convincingly described and it has increasingly been applied to practical applications, including the development of educational software (Bellamy 1996). According to Engeström, Engeström and Suntio (2002), an activity theory framework can be used as a tool to implement new teaching-learning approaches and for analysing the processes of computer-supported collaboration in general.

Given its integrative nature and goal-based structure, activity theory appeared a more promising conceptual approach to deal with cultural issues in usability and online training. It offers a unified framework for looking at the use of computers as tools to achieve certain goals and for exploring the issues connected with these activities. It also helps us overcome the shortcomings of the information processing models prevalent in cognitive science, which have dominated in HCI research.

However, the path leading up to activity theory was anything but straightforward. It was the need to find answers and solutions to the practical questions and difficulties encountered in the course of the Project work which served as the driving force. Consequently, as described above, the challenge to find a theoretical framework that could embrace all the diverse aspects, guide the researcher when analysing the use of information and communication technologies in cross-cultural eLearning contexts and provide suitable tools for analysing the empirical data became the main focus of my research interests.

In addition to the reasons given above, this shift of focus can also be attributed to the following factors and considerations:

- the fact that a unifying approach had to be found within the Project to accommodate the two separate industrial applications,
- the requirement imposed by the financing body, i.e. the European Commission, that the results should be transferable to other projects and
- the fact that an increasing number of comparable projects in the realm of KM and eLearning appeared to be struggling with similar problems and had failed to find a solution.

For all these reasons, the quest for theoretical concepts and tools that would allow abstraction and generalisation came to look like a very worthwhile and highly topical and timely endeavour. As a result, although the original focus on the impact of intercultural factors on information presentation and representation continued to play a role in both the practical and theoretical work, the shift in focus as it crystallised in the course of several months, emphasised the theoretical framework.

In many ways, this resulted in an asynchronous process between practice and theory. Or rather, practice became the driving force behind theory and served to provide information for the theoretical investigations. As a result, the theoretical insights lagged behind the empirical research and could either no be taken into account or could only be taken into account to a limited extent in the actual Project work.

This, however, is not such an unusual state of affairs. Kuutti in his article on "Activity Theory as a Potential Framework for Human-Computer Interaction Research" (1996) refers to the "well-known gap between research results and practical design" (p. 19). Design guidelines tend to be derived from practical experience and not based on a specific underlying theory.

This study therefore is the outcome of a thinking process, which was triggered by:
- issues raised by working practices and problems encountered in the field,
- the shortcomings of existing approaches and
- the requirement to produce results which would be transferable to similar applications and projects.

It also meant that although the user trials, expert reviews and demonstrations of the prototype were conducted largely in line with Project requirements, the main result of this study, i.e. a theoretical framework which could accommodate the whole range of research questions as described above, could not be incorporated at the actual Project stage because the practical work followed its pre-designed course and was subject to the strict time constraints imposed by the general project design.

Thus, the relevance of this study lies mainly in its contribution to a growing body of research trying to cope with the increasingly interdisciplinary and intercultural nature of present-day computer-mediated activities in global or globalising corporate environments.

1.4 Contents of chapters

The Introduction outlines the background for this study and discusses my role in the Project that provided the data for my investigations. It also describes the environment in which the research took place, both in terms of the tasks surrounding it as well as the organisational context.

It also describes how the research context raised issues and questions not anticipated at the outset and gradually led to a shift in emphasis: whereas the study originally focused on the impact of intercultural factors on usability in KM and eLearning applications, the quest for a theoretical framework which would be able to accommodate the widely disparate parts of this highly interdisciplinary research came to dominate the research endeavour.

The second chapter discusses Terminological Issues and clarifies terms such as internationalisation, globalisation, intercultural and cross-cultural as well as concepts such as eLearning *versus* online learning. It also outlines the differences between data, information and knowledge and the characteristics of tacit and explicit knowledge.

The chapter then provides a short introduction to the key issues in KM including the building blocks of KM defined by Probst et al (1999). It explores key concepts in KM such as organisational change and culture, human and cultural issues as well as the various methods and criteria available to measure the success of KM. It then goes on to discuss the relations between KM and information technology (IT) as well as those between KM and eLearning and concludes with a brief outline of the KM framework developed as part of the Project.

The third chapter starts by looking at the problem of defining culture and introduces the different psychological theoretical approaches to this problem. It then investigates the related concepts and models for identifying and analysing cultural differences, among them the cultural dimension model proposed by Hofstede, the best known of the 'interculturalists'.

This is followed by a critique of Hofstede's model of culture as mental software and a presentation of alternative models such as the notion of cultural standards developed by Thomas and Holden's KM approach to cross-cultural activities. It is argued that the latter provides a new conceptual framework for dealing with culture in a world of global networks and multicultural teams and is therefore better suited to the environment under study.

The fourth chapter combines a survey of recent developments and publications on the issues of cultural factors in connection with usability, learning and teaching. This state-of-the-art *cum* literature survey illustrates the ongoing influence of the concept of cultural dimensions derived from Hofstede in both these fields. At the same time, it also highlights its shortcomings, since in most cases findings do not confirm the hypotheses derived from this essentialist approach.

Firstly, I briefly outline recent developments in usability studies, which are characterised by the increasing attention given to contextual factors. The role of cultural factors in the design of user interfaces is dealt with mostly in the literature on internationalisation and globalisation. The issue of usability is further narrowed down to the particular usability concerns relating to Websites as well as interactive and community features.

Discussions of cultural aspects in learning and teaching – when such do occur – are still permeated by references to Hofstede, but are also influenced by the work of Trompenaars, Clyne and Galtung. Various studies applying the models found in all the above are examined. Their findings on the whole do not seem to corroborate the hypotheses formulated on the basis of these approaches.

The literature survey highlights the lack of any coherent theoretical underpinning and the shortcomings of the existing approaches when it comes to studies that go beyond the confines of an individual discipline.

Chapter 5 presents four major approaches in the area of HCI: cognitive ergonomics, situated action, distributed cognition and activity theory. Their main characteristics, shortcomings and the extent to which they take into account cultural factors are discussed. Based on a comparison of the different approaches, it is concluded that activity theory provides a wider theoretical basis for studies of computer-mediated activity than cognitive psychology or situated action, as it can accommodate both social interactions and cultural factors as well as higher-level goals and values.

Activity theory can provide the disparate approaches to HCI with a common vocabulary for issues emerging in the study of technology usage. Furthermore, it is argued that it is not exclusive of other approaches, but can serve as a backbone for analysis supplemented and enriched with concepts from other perspectives.

Chapter 6 discusses theories and models in eLearning and sets out by giving a brief historical outline of learning theories with reference to computer-based instruction. Various metaphors of learning – knowledge acquisition, participation and knowledge creation – and their links to the different 'camps' in the eLearning field or instructional technology community are explored. These include modellers *versus* non-modellers, advocates of instructivist *versus* constructivist theories and individualist *versus* communicative or sociocultural theories.

Whereas in most approaches culture appears to be a topic of benign neglect, the sociocultural approaches inspired by Vygotsky, one of activity theory's founding fathers, pay particular attention to cultural factors. They stress the social, situated nature of all activity and the importance of collaboration and interaction.

The chapter then outlines four pedagogical models – Authentic Learning Context, Collaborative Learning, Progressive Inquiry Model and Problem-based Learning – which influence the debate on eLearning. After discussing various studies that have applied cultural models to eLearning, activity theory is proposed as an integrative framework.

The Quest for a Theoretical Framework that underlies the discussion of the various theoretical approaches, models and concepts culminates in chapter 7, which brings together the different strands of the discussion on the role of cultural factors and the importance of context, community and interaction in both HCI studies and eLearning.

After briefly outlining the common trends in HCI and eLearning, the chapter explains why activity theory is more appropriate than other approaches as an overarching approach to deal with the complex issues involved in interdisciplinary research into computer-mediated activities. The chapter then presents the main tenets, concepts and principles of activity theory such as the hierarchical structure of activity, object-orientedness or environment, internalisation/externalisation and, above all, the mediation of activity by tools or artefacts and development.

Finally, various studies that have applied activity theory in both HCI and eLearning are discussed, including studies focusing on collaborative and community aspects. These testify to the remarkable adaptiveness of activity theory and demonstrate how it can be combined with other approaches.

The following chapter (8) discusses the methodological implications of activity theory and the main requirements that can be deduced from applying it, such as adequate duration of study, contextualisation and a mix of different methods, for the various dimensions of the present study.

Chapter 8 begins with a discussion of the various methodological approaches suggested for identifying and capturing cultural factors, especially with regard to user interfaces and eLearning platforms. It then describes the activity checklists that present the theoretical structure of activities in an operational form and support the researcher in the move from theory to practice. These can serve as a tool for orienting and guiding research as well as for analysing, interpreting and reflecting on the empirical data.

The next section examines the use of ethnographic methods such as participant observation, interviews and focus group discussions for capturing the context in which computer-based systems (will) operate. It explores both the benefits and the problems of ethnographic research, including the difficulties of generalising the findings, formalising the data and the personal bias of the researcher. As far as usability testing is concerned, the general principles involved are discussed, including participatory and iterative design, i.e. the involvement of users from an early stage onwards in the development process. The usability section then explores the different types of usability tests, in particular systematic reviews conducted with experts (heuristic evaluation) and end-user testing.

The principles of the participatory design approach also apply if a product or application is directed at an international user group. It is argued that trying to understand critical incidents or breakdowns in intercultural situations is the most appropriate technique for identifying the impact of cultural factors.
Finally, grounded theory is proposed as a method for analysing empirical data. It aims less at verifying existing hypotheses and more at conceiving new models or approaches which can be derived from the available data.

The chapter on Practical Implementation describes how I gathered the contextual data by means of ethnographic research. Given the KM orientation of the Project, the research was strongly influenced by KM concepts, which are in turn closely linked with eLearning. The information on the organisational environment and course development was captured mostly through attending courses and interviewing key actors. Through immersion in the environment, a comprehensive picture of the training activity, including the different roles involved in course development, emerged over time.

The chapter then illustrates how usability testing was planned and carried out and describes the questionnaires and focus group discussions that were organised to clarify issues raised by the tests.

Expert reviews were conducted with the prototype application, the VEMD module, whereas end-user tests were restricted to a quiz with exam questions to investigate the interactive features of the future eLearning module.

In chapter 10, the empirical data gathered by means of the different methods are analysed. With the help of grounded theory and the activity checklist for evaluation, the data are structured and organised and eventually integrated into a wider activity theory framework. The chapter begins by discussing how the attempt to classify students' behaviour in the classroom according to the prevailing cultural models proved unsatisfactory.

By means of the checklist for evaluation, the contextual data are structured into four areas that outline the space of context, namely Strategies and goals of training, Organisational context of training, Learning, cognition and interaction, and Transformation and development.

The following section deals with the role of cultural factors in training and is based on the analysis of the usability test results. As proposed by grounded theory, categories and concepts are derived from the data collected to identify the factors that influence the requirements for the development of eLearning materials.

Finally, the contradictions that can be observed in the training system are explored. In activity theory, these are seen as a source of development and change. With regard to eLearning, several emerging themes are discussed, such as attitude to authority or task *versus* relationship orientation. These may be relevant in the transfer of existing materials into an online environment and will have to be taken into consideration in the practical implementation.

In the final chapter – Conclusions – the findings are summarised and translated into a series of recommendations and concrete guidelines for usability testing, developing eLearning materials, accommodating cultural factors and methodology.

Though the main focus of this study is on training and course development, its scope goes well beyond the development of eLearning training materials to encompass the exchange and transfer of knowledge and information as a whole, with training being just one aspect of this activity.

I conclude that activity theory is an extremely flexible framework that can be combined with concepts and models derived from other approaches depending on the particular environment or organisational context in which activities take place.

2 Terminological Issues

Before embarking on the survey of literature and recent developments in HCI and eLearning, I have incorporated a section on terminological issues. The lack of consistency and/or differentiation in the use of terms such as internationalisation and globalisation, intercultural and cross-cultural, eLearning, online learning, CMC, CBI, etc. often bedevils discussions on these topics. Rarely do authors agree on a single definition of a term, if they indeed even bother to explain the terms they use at all. But despite, or rather because of the lack of consensus, I consider it essential to make it clear what definition(s) I have decided to adopt for the most relevant terms so as to avoid misunderstandings and ambiguities.

The second part of this chapter is dedicated to a brief introduction to the key issues in KM to establish a common understanding of these issues. Since the Project which served as the basis for the empirical study concerned enhancing KM in enterprises, the term itself as well as the concepts that are associated with it, continually crop up in the discussion. This is why it is important to clarify the terminology, concepts and issues used in connection with KM, present the main building blocks of KM and finally arrive at a general framework that underlies the whole treatment of this topic.

Furthermore, in the discussion on the various approaches to defining culture, the reader will be confronted with Holden's KM approach to cross-cultural management. As this study has strongly been influenced by his approach, this introduction to KM serves as a foundation for discussing Holden's contribution.

2.1 Definition of terms in human-computer interaction

2.1.1 Localisation

The literature on this subject contains a variety of definitions. Synonyms include customisation, adaptation and the abbreviation L10N[4]. Localisation is normally seen as the process of adapting a product to suit the language, conventions and market requirements of a target audience other than the one for which the product was originally developed. To make it accessible and acceptable, it has to be 'infused' with a specific cultural context.

Many large software companies, especially those from the United States, the largest exporter of software in the world, earn a substantial part of their revenues from sales outside their home country. This is why the adaptation of their products to diverse international markets has become a major challenge and requires careful planning. With the high costs and risks involved, it is paramount to ensure successful, effective and efficient adaptation.

---

[4] The abbreviation L10N uses the first and last letters of the English word localisation and inserts the amount of the total number of characters in between them.

One of the best books in this area was written by Hoft (1995) and, although it was written primarily for practising professionals, it also makes reference to cultural models for collecting information and researching international variables about target users. She defines this as "the process of creating or adapting an information product for use in a specific target country or specific target market" (p. 11) and distinguishes between different degrees: general localisation focuses on superficial cultural differences, whereas radical localisation focuses on cultural differences below the surface, those that affect the way users think, feel and act. Choosing between the two is a business decision based on balancing the economic goals of a company with a cultural understanding of the target users.

Radical localisation would also address learning styles and culturally specific examples. The difference may be so radical that it results in multiple information products.

2.1.2 Internationalisation

Internationalisation is sometimes referred to as a separation of form from function and creation of a core product. The point here is that it is much easier to localise a product that is not embedded in the cultural context of its creators. The product, e.g. the software code, must be generic enough to accept many variations and cultural contexts. The Digital Equipment Corporation (1992)[5], for example, defines internationalisation as a two-step process that includes product localisation. An international product is seen as consisting of four components, one of which is generic, while the other three are the market-, user- and country-specific components that are subsequently localised. According to Digital, localisation is most effectively performed on an internationalised product with a modular design.

Hoft's definition (1995:18-9) largely coincides with Digital's approach to internationalisation. She describes internationalisation as "the process of re-engineering an information product so that it can be easily localised for export to any country in the world. An internationalised information product consists of two components: core information and international variables."

According to Hoft, international variables identify superficial and deep cultural differences. They can influence the page design, the writing style, the cultural content of graphics and/or examples and the language in which the localised product is printed. Internationalisation involves isolating and researching these variables to discover where in the information product general localisation needs to be performed. Hoft investigates deeper cultural differences by using the international variables identified in various models of culture.

---

[5] Jones, S, Kennelly, C., Mueller, C., Sweezey, M., Thomas, B., and Velez, L. (1992). *The Digital Guide to Developing International User Information*. Digital Press, p. 2.

2.1.3 Globalisation

According to Hoft a global product is "something that has universal appeal and that can be understood and used by anyone, anywhere" (p. 23). She regards it as a relative concept that is defined by the success of products that can be used in multicultural and multilingual environments without modification.

Microsoft has a somewhat different definition. A global product is seen as having:
- A core world-wide feature set
- Market-/country-specific localisation as appropriate
- Interoperability between the various language versions

However, with this definition, a global product is no different from a product that has been internationalised and subsequently localised. A more accurate definition is provided by Digital, i.e. "a product that functions properly in a usage environment that includes users throughout the world."[6]

Hoft (1995:24) gives the following definitions:

> A *global product* is one that can be used successfully in several target markets without modification of any kind.
> *Globalisation* is the process of creating a product that can be used successfully in many cultural contexts without modification.

Perhaps, she continues, this is comparable to the process of creating a universally intuitive product. According to Hoft, globalisation is achievable to some degree, but only by way of performing a thorough user analysis, building an international team that is truly representative of all the target markets and doing multinational usability studies on all information products.

For the purposes of this study I have by and large adopted Hoft's definitions because they are clear and unambiguous and have found wide recognition in the field of international technical communication and HCI.

2.1.4 Intercultural *versus* cross-cultural

According to Merriam-Webster dictionary, the term 'cross-cultural' can be defined as dealing with or offering comparison between two or more different cultures or cultural areas. 'Intercultural' refers to communication or interaction among people of different cultures. Efforts in intercultural training and communications usually aim to bridge the differences and eliminate bias among culturally

---

[6] See entry in the glossary in the Digital Guide (see previous footnote).

diverse populations. Quite often the terms 'cross-cultural' and 'intercultural' are used interchangeably or even synonymously with the related term 'multicultural' (Limaye and Victor 1995). In general, however, the term 'cross-cultural' tends to imply a comparative dimension, whilst the term 'intercultural' is usually more concerned with interactions between people representing different cultures.

Holden (2002), for example, gives the following reasons for opting for cross-cultural as the preferred generalising term:

> In the UK and USA there is no doubt that the term 'cross-cultural' prevails over 'intercultural' with respect to the international activities of managers. On the other hand, the term 'intercultural' has wide currency in several European languages, but it is clear that *interculturel* (French) and *interkulturell* (German) do not exclude the comparative dimension more strongly implied in the word 'cross-cultural'. (p. xviii)

Over the years, Holden has also come to the conclusion that most people who talk about intercultural management tend to focus on interpersonal communication across barriers of language and culture, whilst the management dimension gets lost by the wayside.

Based on this distinction, I prefer the term 'intercultural' factors and their impact on usability and learning and teaching when talking about the case study underlying this research, since my attention focused primarily on the interactions between trainees and instructors when observing classroom behaviour. However, when looking at the influence of cultural factors on learning and teaching approaches in general, the comparative dimension tends to be in the foreground. Similarly, when discussing how people from different cultural backgrounds perceive and evaluate Websites, the emphasis is on the comparative perspective, and therefore 'cross-cultural' is more appropriate. But there are occasions in this study when the two terms may for all practical purposes be considered synonymous.

2.2 Definition of terms in the eLearning field

2.2.1 eLearning, online learning or blended learning?

In the eLearning Action Plan of the European Commission (2001:2), eLearning is defined as "the use of new multimedia technologies and the Internet to improve the quality of learning by facilitating access to resources and services as well as remote exchanges and collaboration."

Since the term 'multimedia' excludes very simple, but highly efficient exchange and collaboration tools (such as electronic mail or listservers for mailing lists), I have adopted the more general and neutral definition given by the educational scientist Nichols. In his paper "A theory for eLearning", Nichols (2003) defines eLearning as "the use of various technological tools that are either Web-based, Web-distributed or Web-capable for the purposes of education" (p. 3). Online learning is described as "education that occurs only through the Web, that is, it does not consist of any physical learning materials issued to students or actual face to face contact" (*ibid.*). According to Nichols, online learning is therefore tantamount to the use of eLearning tools in a distance education mode using the web as the only medium for all student learning and contact.

Since in our own Project it was always envisaged to combine face-to-face and distance approaches, I have opted for the term 'eLearning' whenever I refer to the research context and activities related to the development of the Web-based training modules. This type of approach is also called 'mixed-mode', 'blended' or 'resource-based learning', as a resource base of content materials and learning activities is usually made available to students, including eLearning modules.

2.2.2 CMC, CBI or CAI?

Nichols' definition of eLearning coincides to a large extent with the concept of computer-mediated communication (CMC), which now appears to be the prevailing paradigm in the eLearning area. Whereas the earlier type, known as Computer Based Instruction (CBI), focused on the interaction between the student and computer drills, tutorials or simulations, with CMC the primary form of interaction is between students and instructors, mediated by the computer. CBI usually implies individualised (self-study) learning, while CMC involves facilitation by a teacher or tutor.

CAI (computer-aided instruction) seems to be the preferred term in France, at least in the corporate and research context that surrounded the Project, to describe computer-mediated learning. However, it is sometimes applied in a very restricted sense to denote the actual materials including simulations used by instructors.

In this study, eLearning and/or computer-mediated learning/teaching are used interchangeably because the latter is also the term preferred in publications based on an activity theory approach (e.g. Nardi 1996).

2.3 The principles of knowledge management

The following introduction to KM reflects the thinking which influenced the Project that served as a source of empirical data for the present study. In the course of the Project, the thinking of the Project team on KM issues evolved and changed in line with the requirements of real-life situations and applications, the questions that emerged and the insights gained through experience and practice. This led to the creation of a common framework for the successful implementation of KM.

KM is a relatively new discipline that is developing rapidly in the marketplace and attracting much attention. It has emerged from the recognition that one of the most important corporate assets is the experience and expertise in every employee's mind and the realisation of the need to try to manage (i.e. access, capture and share) this intellectual capital. In fact, the choice of the term 'KM' is often considered to be unfortunate as knowledge resides in people's brains and therefore cannot be easily saved and/or managed.

KM is an extremely complex, interdisciplinary issue with enormous potential and can mean many things to different people. However, following the initial hype and negative publicity in the mid-1990s generated by the limited success or even failure of many initial KM projects (generally solutions based on information technology (IT), which did not take human factors into the equation), experts began to realise that KM was not just about technology and IT solutions; it was far more about people, culture and human behaviour. The enormous importance attached to KM is demonstrated in the huge number of books and papers still being published almost weekly on this subject.

One of the main roles of KM is to mobilise knowledge, i.e. to create, encourage and maintain a culture and environment in which people are able to innovate, share, learn and use knowledge for the benefit of the organisation and the people who work in it. The creation of a knowledge environment can require a change in corporate values and culture, in the way people work and their work patterns. This environment must provide people with easy access both to each other and to relevant data and information resources.

2.3.1 Knowledge management directions

Sveiby, one of the pioneers of KM, makes the differentiation between 'IT-Track' and 'People-Track' KM in an article published in 1996. He describes IT-Track KM as the management of information and sees the supporters of this type of KM as often having a computer and/or information science background. They consider knowledge as objects that can be identified and handled in information systems. According to Sveiby, People-Track KM, on the other hand, deals with the management of people, and practitioners of this field come usually from philosophy, psychology, sociology and/or business and management backgrounds. They consider knowledge to be processes, i.e. a complex set of dynamic skills, know-how etc. that is constantly changing. However, as mentioned above, the importance of the human and cultural aspects of KM is now widely considered to outweigh that of any chosen IT solution(s).

2.3.2 Intellectual capital

The increasing relevance of knowledge and intellectual capital as a competitive factor is constantly gaining importance, together with the recognition that organisations must find ways of making use of the knowledge stored in the heads of their employees. KM is thus often described as the art of creating value from intangible assets.

The first attempts to document these assets were carried out by the Swedish company SKANDIA, who published their first Annual Report Intellectual Capital in 1993. Some possible indicators used to indicate knowledge assets include experience and expertise, customer relationships, market reputation, use of IT, patents, etc.

However, unlike financial assets, there are currently no real tools available for defining and measuring intellectual capital and knowledge resources. Therefore, effective KM must aim to provide such tools by including methods and possibilities for analysing, auditing and managing corporate intellectual capital.

2.4 Definition of key terms

There still appears to be much confusion as to what 'knowledge' actually is and here the experts choose to differ. However, it was considered essential to the success of our Project (or indeed to any KM initiative) to define a common understanding of knowledge in the (Project) context. Similarly, it is essential to clarify the main terms for the purpose of this study to avoid misunderstandings and create a common ground for author and readers.

There are numerous definitions of knowledge but the common thread that runs through them all is the concept that knowledge is intrinsically linked with people. Indeed some experts go so far as to claim that knowledge can neither be stored nor managed. However, this was not the opinion of the Project team, which aimed to provide a working definition of knowledge in its particular context and a framework for its effective management and storage.

Knowledge is often described as information in context to produce an actionable understanding. However, everyone provides his/her own context and decides what constitutes data, information and knowledge for themselves.

2.4.1 Knowledge

Davenport and Prusak (2000) describe knowledge as:

> "...a fluid mix of framed experience, values, contextual information and expert insight that provides a framework for evaluating and incorporating new experiences and information. It originates and is applied in the minds of the knowers. In organizations, it often becomes embedded not only in documents or repositories but also in organizational routines, processes, practices, and norms." (p. 5)

Probst et al (1999) provide the following definition:

> Knowledge is the entirety of experience and abilities used by individuals to solve problems. This includes both theoretical insight and practical day-to-day rules and instructions for action. Knowledge is based on data and information, yet in

contrast to these is always linked to people. It is construed by individuals and represents their expectations on cause-effect correlation. (p. 46)

2.4.2 Data, information and knowledge

Very often, data and information are assumed to be the same thing as knowledge. However, these are not interchangeable concepts and effective KM needs to understand the fundamental differences between these elements.

Davenport and Prusak (2000:5) contend that "Most people have an intuitive sense that knowledge is broader, deeper and richer than data or information." Probst et al (1999) support this and describe the difference between characters, data, information and knowledge as a process of enrichment:

CHARACTERS + Syntax → DATA + context
→ INFORMATION + linking → KNOWLEDGE

They also differentiate between individual and collective knowledge bases and see competitive advantage arising primarily from the expertise of competent employees (i.e. in the transformation from data into information and knowledge).

Data and information management systems are often key sources in organisational KM. However, the best data and information management systems are of little use if the information they contain is not put to use and effective KM must ensure that this happens.

2.4.3 Explicit and tacit knowledge

The KM movement recognises a difference between explicit and tacit knowledge. Explicit knowledge can be codified, stored, transmitted and shared. It includes what we know that we can express in words (e.g. the exact steps in a process, regulations and guidelines). Tacit knowledge is what we do not know that we know and includes know-how, judgement, experience, feelings, values, etc.

Nonaka and Takeuchi (1995) describe explicit knowledge as that which:

"... can be expressed in words and numbers and can be easily communicated and shared in the form of hard data, scientific formulae, codified procedures or universal principles." (p. 8)

They define tacit knowledge as "... something not easily visible and expressible. Tacit knowledge is highly personal and hard to formalise, making it difficult to communicate or share with others. Subjective insights, intuitions and hunches fall into this category of knowledge." (*ibid.*)

Most IT-based KM initiatives deal only with explicit knowledge, as this is often readily available and can be codified (i.e. in the form of documents), thus making it 'manageable'. This is an excellent starting point for KM activities and the effect and achievement in successfully doing so should by no means be underestimated. However, KM must go beyond that and address the more complicated issue of tacit knowledge. Indeed, it is the managing of tacit knowledge that is the bigger challenge to KM efforts and where its mastery will bring higher benefits.

2.5 The knowledge management process

There are no individual solutions available for KM and the key lies in how an individual organisation approaches KM. Ideally, it can build on existing systems and provide appropriate tools for the organisation in question. An effective way to do so is to identify a specific, existing problem and orient initial KM activities around that problem. Indeed, there is no point in introducing KM if there is no concrete reason for doing so.

These activities can then serve as a base from which to expand KM activities across the organisation. Most experts agree that initial KM activities should not try to provide a solution to all issues in one go. KM must also include criteria for measuring its success and be effectively communicated to all involved.

2.5.1 Knowledge base and building blocks

To manage knowledge effectively, a common understanding of what is meant by knowledge and what constitutes the organisational knowledge base must first be reached. It is also considered important to identify and evaluate what knowledge is critical to success and how that knowledge is spread across the organisation.

Probst et al (1999) see the organisational knowledge base as being made up of the individual and collective knowledge available to an organisation to be used in completion of its tasks. This includes data and information resources (internal and external databases, Intranets, best practices, yellow pages, etc.). They have defined six building blocks of KM:

- **Knowledge identification** (includes establishing an overview of internal/external data, information and expertise)
- **Knowledge acquisition** (includes, for example, possibilities for drawing on the expertise in customer and partner relationships)
- **Knowledge development** (how is new knowledge created, how does the organisation itself deal with new ideas and make use of the creativity of its employees)

- **Knowledge distribution/sharing** (one of the most essential parts of the process - what should be distributed to whom and when, also the processes of dissemination of existing knowledge within the organisation)
- **Knowledge application/use** (the real goal and purpose of KM is the productive use of organisational knowledge for the benefit of the organisation)
- **Knowledge storage** (includes the selection process of what should be stored and must also take in the aspects of continual updating, i.e. removal of out-of-date information; requires the efficient use of modern technologies).

2.5.2 Human and cultural issues

Once it has been established and accepted that knowledge resides in the heads of people, it then follows that KM itself must also essentially be about people issues and cultural issues must play a key role in all KM initiatives.

Sveiby (1996) notes that "the key to unlocking the value of knowledge is **People**."

He continues:
> The 'People-Track', although old in its theory origins, is still in its infancy when it comes to KM applications. It is the most promising because the issues are about how to maximize the ability of an organization's people to creating new knowledge and how to build environments conducive to sharing of knowledge. (p. 2)

2.5.2.1 Collaboration

To create a collaborative, knowledge-sharing environment, it is essential to make a visible connection between sharing knowledge and practical business goals. People have to see the reason behind and the need for KM in their daily work. Most people have more than enough work to do and will not willingly take on the additional workload of exchanging knowledge just for the sake of it – they have to somehow (be made to) recognise the benefits of doing so to themselves and the organisation. Indeed, many organisations do not even call such initiatives 'KM' to avoid unnecessary resistance to something new.

The important aspects of knowledge sharing (language, activities, Intranet, etc.) must match the style and culture of an organisation. However, KM should avoid imposing too many rules on knowledge sharing activities. It is also important to encourage 'soft' technologies for knowledge sharing, such as meeting spaces for knowledge exchange, discussion, shared learning and problem solving. Knowledge sharing also emphasises the need for effective communication flow and documentation.

2.5.2.2 Teams, communities of practice and networks

Teams are usually formed by management and are a group of people selected to work on a joint project or task. They are often made up of people with the different skills needed to achieve the project goals. They generally last until the project is finished and they have achieved their goals. The results produced by a team are generally documented at various stages of the project and are an important source of collaborative knowledge.

Communities of practice, on the other hand, are generally formed by groups of volunteers. The term was introduced by Wenger (2000) to demonstrate a shift from the authority of position to the authority of knowledge. No one forces the members to join or participate in a community of practice and they are generally formed around a common interest and passion for a particular subject. Some communities may have stated goals, their main purpose and function is not to produce deliverables, but to learn together. They need a coordinator who plays a key role in the development of the community and will generally last as long as the common thread exists and members still feel they can learn from and with each other.

Communities of practice are now very common throughout all kinds of organisations and are an extremely powerful form of KM – both as enablers of knowledge creation and as an important source of knowledge flow. It is often said that the best ideas are formed in informal situations. KM must look to provide the time and space for such innovation. This could include the creation or promotion of informal knowledge areas (e.g. coffee rooms, chat areas, etc.) or the creation of idea boards in the Intranet.

The way knowledge is currently shared in an organisation is extremely important for KM initiatives. Many informal networks have grown over a long period of time (e.g. weekly night out, groups that meet for lunch, sports teams, etc.) and have worked successfully in the past without formal incentives or sanctions. KM must look to build on these networks, without over formalising them. Any attempts to exclude their relevance from KM initiatives would be counter-productive.

2.5.3 Measuring knowledge management

Since one of the main reasons for introducing KM is to increase corporate value, organisations need to also introduce methods of measuring the impact and success of KM measures and of normative, strategic and operative knowledge goals. KM measures take up resources and time and must therefore prove their worth. Traditional accounting methods are not suitable for measuring knowledge and there is increasing evidence that they do not capture the full value of an organisation. However, there are currently no real tried-and-tested measurement methods available. One of the challenges of effective KM is the establishment of appropriate ways of measuring whether or not goals are being met.

2.5.3.1 Information audit

An information audit is an important step in enabling an organisation to understand the information and knowledge that it needs to drive and develop its business. An information audit highlights the information and knowledge currently available in the organisation and helps to determine knowledge gaps. It helps to create awareness of the importance of knowledge, information and KM and to build an information and knowledge strategy. The decisions made when planning and conducting an audit must be based on the nature, goals and drivers of an organisation.

2.5.3.2 Balanced scorecard

The balanced scorecard is a method of measuring performance by linking an organisation's mission and strategy to specific measures. It is made up of four perspectives of measurement: financial, customer, internal business process and learning and growth. Strategic use of the balanced scorecard links measurement to strategy and business objectives and provides information on the success of a strategy. The balanced scorecard emphasises information in context for an actionable understanding.

2.5.3.3 Intellectual capital

KM recognises the value of knowledge and approaches for measuring intellectual capital attempt to give it value. One method for measuring intellectual assets is the Intangible Assets Monitor introduced in the early 1990s by Sveiby, which differentiates between three categories of assets: human competence, external structure and internal structure.

2.5.4 Knowledge management and eLearning

There are obvious links between eLearning and KM since one of the goals of both practices is to get the right knowledge and information to the right people. However, where eLearning has focused on delivering courses and testing performance, KM takes a keen interest in capturing the knowledge.

A combination of both these factors is a desirable aim and efforts need to be made to integrate eLearning programmes with existing and planned KM initiatives, thus giving trainees access to existing knowledge bases and resources. There must also be a focus on other aspects of learning (e.g. in communities, through experience and/or conversation) and on introducing input from eLearning applications into KM applications.

In an ideal world, KM and eLearning would share the same infrastructure, thus avoiding the need for users to learn two completely different systems. This would also lead to trainees being in a position to share their knowledge more quickly. This should be assisted by widespread adoption of broadband technologies, to provide the performance needed to deal with some of the human aspects of training (e.g. discussions with instructors and other trainees).

2.6 Knowledge management framework

One of the aims of the Project was to provide a proposal and general set of guidelines for enhancing KM in enterprises. The actual issues involved differ for every KM implementation, for every organisation and indeed even for different groups/departments within an individual organisation. Whilst the general description of KM given above aims to include as many relevant issues as possible, not all of them need to be addressed in every KM implementation.

The definition of a common KM framework for the Project was preceded by an analysis of several framework models, including one developed by another EU-funded project, the European KM Forum (EKMF), creator of one of the most popular information and exchange platforms for KM. This was adopted because it appeared to include all the aspects considered necessary by the Project consortium for successful implementation of KM.

The EKMF framework consists of eight interlinked modules designed to support both the innovativeness of the system and secure the reuse of existing knowledge within the system on the other. These modules are:

- KM strategies
- Human and Social KM issues
- KM organisational aspects
- KM processes
- KM technologies
- Leadership
- KM performance measurement and
- KM business cases and implementation aspects.

Although the framework was felt to be complete and highly useful for the implementation of KM, it was also criticised for number of points, for example, the lack of distinction between the different modules. Many of the suggested methods and tools are appropriate for several of the modules and it was therefore considered advisable to reduce the number of modules or provide a clearer distinction between them. For example, it is at times not clear where to differentiate between KM Organisation and Human and Social KM. The same is true for the KM Strategies and Leadership modules which could be integrated into at least two other modules (KM Organisation and Human and Social KM Issues). The need for a separate module for KM Business Cases and Implementation was questioned, although the decision by the consortium to use this module to provide a set of guidelines for KM projects was considered useful and appropriate.

On the whole, the framework eventually adopted by the Project team emphasises the fact that companies should avoid trying to optimise knowledge activities in individual areas without considering the wider effects and that KM performs a bridging function among individuals, groups, and organisational structures.

2.7 Summary

The main objective of this chapter was to clarify the meaning of terms used in this study. Even though the reader might not agree with certain definitions I have chosen, she or he will know what is referred to when concepts such as eLearning or KM are mentioned. In the course of this study, agreeing on a joint terminology will emerge as one of the most important prerequisites for the successful introduction of computer-mediated knowledge exchange and transfer.

The brief introduction to the field of KM highlights the issues that play a role in the research at large, namely community and collaboration, the importance of human, social and cultural issues or the conceptual links between KM and eLearning. Many of the issues raised will resurface in subsequent chapters under different headings, such as the distinction between tacit and explicit knowledge: the transformation between the two types of knowledge is similar to the internalisation/externalisation process in activity theory by which mental models are influenced by external activity, artefacts or tools and, in turn, affect how a new technology will be used.

The KM Framework described above has many points that intersect with the activity theory framework, especially the modules Strategies, Human and Social Issues and Organisational Aspects. Cultural factors may not be mentioned explicitly in the KM Framework of the Project, a lacuna which has been filled with Holden's approach that regards culture as an object of KM. (Holden's approach will be discussed in detail in the following chapter.)

Furthermore, the systemic and dynamic approach reflected in the guidelines, methods and tools suggested for the actual implementation of the KM Framework, has much in common with activity theory's emphasis on the interrelatedness and thus interdependence of all the elements of a particular activity system.

But however useful the KM Framework can be for the introduction of KM, it cannot provide the concepts, models and methodological tools for investigating and analysing the use of technology in cross- and/or intercultural training contexts.

3 The Problem of Defining Culture

As already pointed out in the Introduction, the problem of defining culture has bedevilled many attempts to identify and analyse the impact of cultural factors on computer-mediated activities. Increasingly, product and application designers, however, are called upon to take into account the greater cultural diversity of their user groups, which is why methods of capturing cultural influences on application usage or interactions between trainers and students are required when drawing up requirements for and implementing computer-based systems.

3.1 Introduction

I start out by giving a very brief introduction to the different psychological approaches to the concept of culture and the various attempts that have been made to define culture. I then present some of the related models and concepts, such as Hofstede's cultural dimensions, which have been proposed for the identification and analysis of cultural factors. The majority of authors writing on the impact of culture on computer-mediated activities, including learning and instruction, make reference to Hofstede's model. Other authors, including Hall, Victor and Trompenaars, have developed their own models, which, while different to Hofstede's model, are equally based on a depiction of enduring national cultures or cultural differences and thus on a culture-as-essence and culture-as-difference approach.

Despite – or because of - its almost ubiquitous presence in the literature, the cultural dimension approach has recently come under attack from various sides. It has been criticised among other things for its focus on cognition and the fact that, when applied to concrete situations, many studies appear to succumb to the danger of reification. Alternative approaches have now emerged, such as the notion of cultural standards developed by Thomas. He suggests focusing on 'critical incidents' in intercultural interactions as a method for determining cultural standards in a particular domain or application. A further approach is represented by the cultural mental models and schemas suggested by Shore. He links the concept of 'culture' with cognitive concepts such as mental models and schemas.

A very cogent critique of Hofstede and his followers has been put forward by Holden in his work on cross-cultural management. The present study has been profoundly influenced by his KM approach to cross-cultural activities. It provides a new conceptual framework for dealing with culture in a world with instantaneous communications, global networks and multicultural work teams. By developing the notion of culture as an object of KM, he shows how culture can be understood as an organisational resource rather than presented as colliding zones of adversarial opposition.

From an anthropological point of view the whole debate about what culture "really is" is unlikely to yield any fruitful results. For some purposes, it is useful to view a people's cultural knowledge as if it were a single coherent system; for other purposes, it is necessary to take into account its distribution within a community.

3.1.1 Psychological approaches to the concept of culture

Different psychological theories have been applied to capturing the concept of culture and they often serve as theoretical underpinnings for the concepts and models described later in this chapter. They are associated with a particular outlook on cultural phenomena and tend to be accompanied by different methods.

Cross-cultural psychology is rooted in a positivist-empirical tradition and regards culture as an external variable which influences people's behaviour in different countries. Cross-cultural psychologists are concerned with more global aspects of human functioning, such as attitudes, values or personality, and generally take it for granted that their object of study is the outcome of cultural influences, although it should also be noted that the nature of such influences is rarely specified.

Cross-cultural psychology is based on the assumption that there are universal laws of human perception, thought, understanding and behaviour which can be identified scientifically. Cultural differences are therefore attributed to different stages of development of those universals or measurement errors incurred by psychological methods. Therefore, the problem of culturally adequate or 'culture-fair' methods of measurement is frequently discussed.

In contrast, **cultural psychology**, has a sort of pantheistic vision: no line is drawn between culture and the individual, since culture and mind are seen as being intricately interwoven. Therefore all behaviour is 'cultural' and cannot be taken out of its context. Human beings without culture are unthinkable (e.g. Jahoda (1996). Cultural psychology does not presume that the fundamentals of mental life are by nature fixed, universal, abstract or interior. It presumes instead that the life of the psyche is the life of intentional persons, responding and directing their action, their own mental objects or representations and undergoing transformation through participation in an evolving world that is the product of the mental representations that make it up.

While **intercultural psychology** is based on the concepts of cross-cultural psychology, it focuses on a particular field of application, namely the 'critical incidents' which occur when people from different cultural backgrounds meet or interact with each other. According to Thomas (1996), intercultural psychology analyses not only processes of perception, information processing, evaluation and assessment, but also the emotions that can direct people's behaviour in such interpersonal encounters.

As a result of increasing globalisation in both the technological and the economic fields, this approach is of particular practical relevance. People see themselves confronted with situations where traditional value systems or behaviour guidelines no longer apply. One of the aims of intercultural psychology consists in developing useful systems of orientation for intercultural encounters and interactions that include elements of both cultures. This approach has given rise to a series of methods, models and concepts, such as the cultural standards discussed below.

3.1.2 Attempts at defining culture

The anthropological concept of culture has been one of the most important and influential ideas in 20th century thought. Usage of the term 'culture' adopted by anthropologists in the 19th century has since spread to other fields of thought; it is now commonplace for humanists and other social scientists to speak of 'Japanese culture', for instance. However, anthropologists have not been very consistent in their usage. There are almost as many definitions of culture given in the publications surveyed as there are authors. Culture in anthropological usage usually refers to learned, accumulated experience, i.e. to socially transmitted patterns for and of behaviour.

Definitions of culture are subject to change over time, for example, since the mid-70s, there has been a stronger emphasis on function. The various attempts at defining this crucial concept reveal different facets of culture, for example:

- That complex whole which includes knowledge, belief, art, morals, law, custom, and any other capabilities and habits acquired by man as a member of society. (Tylor 1958)
- The man-made part of the human environment. (Herskovits 1965)
- A system of meaning that underlies routine and behaviour in everyday working life. (Bødker and Pedersen 1991)

The 'integrative' definition of culture according to Kroeber and Kluckhohn (1952), who collected more than 160 different definitions, is as follows:

> Culture exists of patterns, explicit and implicit, of and for behaviour acquired and transmitted by symbols, constituting the distinctive achievements of human groups, including their embodiments of artifacts; the essential core of culture exists of traditional (i.e., historically derived and selected) ideas and especially their attached values; culture systems may, on the one hand, be considered as products of actions, on the other as conditioning elements of further action. (p. 357)

Despite the plethora of definitions and the considerable differences among them, definitions of culture can be attributed to six categories:[7]

---

[7] The list of categories is based on Soudijn (1990), who in turn derived them from the analysis provided by Kroeber and Kluckhohn (1952).

1. Descriptive definitions
2. Historical definitions
3. Normative definitions
4. Psychological definitions
5. Structural definitions that emphasise the structure or organisation of culture
6. Genetic definitions that focus on the origin of culture.

In 1990, Soudijn et al carried out a revision of Kroeber and Kluckhohn's study complemented by a series of other more recent definitions of culture. By means of factor analysis, they were able to distinguish five factors or elements with which to describe the multidimensional concept of culture: localisation, function, Gestalt, composition and dynamics. These factors sketch out a space which can be used for classifying existing concepts of culture.

Soudijn et al argue that culture conceptualisations are instruments with a heuristic value. It makes more sense to define what culture means for a particular research domain than to try to find a universally valid definition. The above-cited 'meta-definition' by Kroeber and Kluckhohn is useful because it highlights in a very compressed form many important aspects of the concept of culture. Depending on the concrete research endeavour or empirical study, the aspects relevant to the issues involved can then be selected.

3.2 Concepts and models for identifying cultural differences

3.2.1 Culture as mental software

A widely used definition of culture in the literature on computer-mediated activities such as eLearning is derived from Hofstede (1991:4): "Every person carries within him or herself patterns of thinking, feeling and potential acting which were learned throughout their lifetime." Using the analogy of the way in which computers are programmed, Hofstede calls such patterns mental programs or "software of the mind". Mental programs vary according to the social environment in which they were acquired.

As we shall see in subsequent chapters, many authors refer to the cultural dimensions as propagated by Hofstede (1981), Hall (1959), Victor (1992) and Trompenaars (1993) to explain the cultural differences user interface designers or developers of eLearning program need to be aware of. The cultural model developed by Hofstede is the best known and most widely used cognitive model and has achieved almost canonical status. His classic work *Culture's Consequences: Comparing Values, Behaviors, Institutions and Organizations Across Nations*, first published in 1981, was released in a revised and updated edition in 2001. As in the previous edition and other books, he argues that people carry 'mental programs' which are developed in the family in early childhood and reinforced in schools and organisations, and that these programs contain components of national culture. They are expressed most clearly in the different values that predominate among people from different countries.

Hofstede founded, and for several years managed, the Personnel Research Department at IBM Europe. During that time, he developed a multinational survey to explore employees' personal values related to their work situation. The results of this survey, carried out in about 50 countries between 1967 and 1973, have greatly influenced the development of his model of culture. The four basic dimensions to which Hofstede assigned an index value for each country – Power Distance, Uncertainty Avoidance, Individualism *versus* Collectivism, Masculinity *versus* Femininity – remain the benchmark for discussions of national cultures or values. In his later studies, which had a stronger focus on countries influenced by Confucianism, Hofstede (1993) added the dimension of long- *versus* short-term Time Orientation to his original four dimensions.

His cultural model therefore comprises five cultural dimensions which are commonly used when researching the international variables of a target audience:

- **Power Distance** – refers to the extent to which less powerful members expect and accept unequal power distribution within a culture.
- **Uncertainty Avoidance** – relates to the way in which people cope with uncertainty and risk.
- **Masculinity *versus* Femininity** – refers to gender roles as opposed to physical characteristics and is commonly characterised by the levels of assertiveness or tenderness in the user.
- **Individualism *versus* Collectivism** – refers to the role of individuals and groups and is characterised by the level of ties between individual in a society.
- **Time Orientation** – refers to people's concerns with the past, present and future.

Cultural dimensions can focus on objective aspects such as political and economic contexts or differences in the day, date and number formats. They can also focus on subjective aspects such as values, beliefs, patterns of thinking and behaviour. However, given the extensive literature on Hofstede, this is not the place for yet another description of his ideas. Hoft (1995), Marcus (2000) and Simon (2001), to name but a few of the many authors, have all written on Hofstede's approach.

Hall's studies (1959/1973) are based on interviews and field research and focus on interpersonal communication. He distinguishes between high context communication (HCC) and low context communication (LCC). Whereas in LCC cultures communication tends to be very explicit and direct, communication in HCC cultures presumes a shared contextual knowledge and therefore tends to be implicit and not very straightforward. In addition to that, Hall distinguishes between polychronous and monochronous time orientation. The latter implies that people organise their actions in a linear and sequential way. In a society dominated by polychronous orientation, however, actions often tend to be carried out in parallel. Furthermore, they might be oriented towards the past, the present or the future.

Hall's writings are taken further in Victor's LESCANT model. The acronym stands for Language, Environment and technology, Social organisation, Contexting, Authority conception, Non-verbal behaviour and Temporal conception. It identifies the international variables in which cultural differences and similarities are said to manifest themselves. The chapter on 'Environment and technology' is of particular interest, since it is where Victor discusses how issues like geography, population, concepts of physical space and perceptions of technology affect business communication.

According to Victor cultural differences and similarities are essential to and inseparable from effective international business communication. Hoft (1995) has superimposed Victor's diagram of high- and low-context cultures on Hall's context square, which consists of context, information, and meaning to illustrate communication, which results in a continuum ranging from cultures such as the Japanese culture where information is implicitly stated, to others like the Swiss-German culture, in which information must be stated explicitly.

Trompenaars (1993) has a different set of dimensions for collecting cultural information of users. They include:

- Universalism *versus* particularism
- Individualism *versus* collectivism
- Neutral or emotional
- Specific *versus* diffuse
- Achievement *versus* ascription
- Attitudes to time
- Attitudes to the environment.

Trompenaars uses these seven international variables to describe how a group of people solves problems, which is his way of defining culture. According to Hoft, infusing an information product with cultural information derived from studying Trompenaars or Hofstede's variables would inevitably lead to radical localisation.

3.2.2 Critique of Hofstede's approach

Increasingly, Hofstede's depiction of enduring national culture or cultural differences is being challenged. One of the most sustained and thorough critiques is put forward by Holden (2002) in his work on cross-cultural management. He likens Hofstede's method of cataloguing culture to the periodic tables of chemistry and considers the sweeping acceptance of his cultural dimension model as "intellectually numbing" (p. 34). Also, he deplores the fact that it seems to be generally ignored that the data were gathered over 30 years ago and therefore apply to a world which no longer exists. Apart from changes in the political environment (e.g. the end of the Cold War and the decline of communism), values in the work place have seen many changes as well. Organisations worldwide, he argues, now emphasise cooperation and knowledge-sharing, encourage empowerment and localisation. Above all, however, he criticises Hofstede's essentialist concept of culture which has long been abandoned by the field of anthropology where it originated. What sets him apart from most other critics, is that Holden develops his own, alternative concept of culture (see 3.2.4.)

McSweeney (2002), who also has a management background, delivers an uncompromising critique, claiming that Hofstede's work relies on fundamentally flawed assumptions, such as 'every micro-location is typical of the national'. Mc Sweeney argues that the generalisations about national level culture from an analysis of small sub-national populations necessarily rely on the unproven, and unprovable, supposition that within each nation there is a uniform national culture and on the mere assertion that micro-local data from a section of IBM employees was representative of that supposed national uniformity. McSweeney also criticises Hofstede's notion of uniform worldwide occupational cultures and a uniform worldwide IBM organisational culture. She, like others (e.g. Limaye and Victor 1995), questions whether dimensions of national culture can really be identified by a questionnaire, and in particular by one which was originally not even designed for that purpose. Researchers such as Schwartz (1994) who asked different questions have come up with quite different descriptions of specific national cultures. Even if we assume, McSweeney argues, that the answers to a narrow set of questions administered in and mostly about the workplace are 'manifestations' of a determining national culture, it requires a leap of faith to believe that Hofstede actually successfully identified those cultures.

Myers and Tan (2002) criticise Hofstede's approach from an information systems angle. Although they agree that an understanding of cultural differences is important for the successful deployment of information technology, they consider the concept of 'national culture' too simplistic. Instead, they propose that information system researchers should adopt a more dynamic view of culture, one that sees it as contested, temporal and emergent.

Others object to Hofstede's focus on cognition. Even though he includes human actions (which he calls "practices"), behaviour is basically motivated by values and cognitive processes. Ratner (1997) puts forward his own approach based on activity theory.

> Culture is neither a vague, abstract 'social context', nor is it merely shared semiotic or symbolic processes. Culture includes social concepts but also concrete social institutions which are arranged in a division of labor and governed by definite principles of behavior, forms of control and power, allocation of opportunities, reward and punishments. (p.18)

A stronger focus on action can also be found in the work of Boesch (1991). He regards culture as a field of action, whose contents range from objects made and used by human beings to institutions, ideas and myths. Being an action field, culture offers possibilities but, by the same token, also stipulates conditions for action; it circumscribes goals which can be reached by certain means, but also establishes limits for correct, possible and also deviant action.

According to Boesch, the relationship between the different material as well as the ideational contents of the cultural field of action is a symmetric one; i.e. transformation in one part of the system can have an impact on another part. As an action field, culture not only induces and controls action, it is also continuously transformed by it. Culture is therefore as much a process as a structure.

3.2.3 Critique from an anthropological point of view

From an anthropological point of view, it is above all the danger of reification that is worth stressing. When describing 'a culture', anthropologists are trying to capture what is shared, the code of shared rules and common meanings. 'A culture' is always a composite, an abstraction created as an analytical simplification. In the real world, the knowledge described as cultural is always distributed among individuals in communities.

There is a danger of taking this abstraction as having a concreteness, an existence as an entity and a causal agent 'it' cannot have. Although both specialists and non-specialists alike are prone to talk about 'a culture' as if it could be a conscious being (e.g. "American culture values individuality") or to talk as if 'a culture' were like a group, i.e. something one could 'belong to' (e.g. "a member of another culture"), we need to guard against the temptation to reify and falsely concretise culture as a 'thing' and remember that 'it' is a strategically useful abstraction from the distributed knowledge of individuals in communities.

Hofstede's cultural dimensions lend themselves to the drawing of comparisons between different countries and/or cultures and categorising them accordingly. Unfortunately, they are often seen as a reason for intercultural behavioural differences and even have come to be applied as independent variables. A knowledge of cultural dimensions can create the illusion of 'knowing' a culture, without providing any deeper understanding of that culture or a system of orientation for concrete action. In Jahoda's (1990:123) words, "...it is apt to engender the illusion that a phenomenon is explained when one attributes it to either of these dimensions."

Most anthropologists have come to espouse what can be described as a "social constructionist approach". They tend to regard culture as based on shared or partly shared patterns of meaning and interpretation as opposed to sharing broadly consistent, yet complex, patterns of behaviour and modes of existence. Thus, people's identifications with, and affiliation to, a multiplicity of different cultures, e.g. national, organisational, professional, gender and generational cultures, are subject to change, and boundaries between cultural communities become fluid and contingent (e.g. Hannerz 1996). This implies that national, corporate or professional cultures are seen as symbolic practices that only come into existence in relation to, and in contrast with, other cultural communities. People's cultural identity constructions and their social organisations of meaning, are, in other words, contextual. This relational approach to culture suggests that every individual embodies a unique combination of personal, cultural and social experiences, and thus any communication and negotiation is ultimately intercultural.

Another issue in anthropology relevant in this context is that of culture as a system of public meanings *versus* private codes in the minds of individual members. Advocates of the former, such as Geertz (1966), point to the way 'Japanese culture' exists prior to (and irrespective of) the of the birth of any individual Japanese. They state that – like the Japanese language – it consists of rules and meanings that transcend individual minds. The counter-arguments in favour of what can be called a 'distributive model of culture' are equally compelling. Such a view takes as fundamental the distribution of partial versions of a cultural tradition among members of a society. Thus, it can take into account the different perspectives on a way of life held by men or women, specialists or non-specialists. 'A culture' is seen as a pool of knowledge to which individuals contribute in different ways and degrees. This attitude is very much in line with Holden's approach to the concept of culture discussed below.

In any case, a debate about what culture 'really is' is not likely to be fruitful. For some purposes, it is useful to view a peoples' cultural knowledge as if it were a single coherent system; for other purposes, it is necessary to take into account its distribution within a community.

3.2.4 Culture as an object of knowledge management

The starting point for Holden's (2002) reformulation of cross-cultural management as a form of KM was a dissatisfaction with the Hofstedian grip and the stubborn adherence to out-of-date ideas and assumptions that still permeates so much of the writing on issues of culture with specific reference to international dimensions. He felt that the new economy, with its global reach, instantaneous communications and complex multinational and multicultural involvements, required a new way of looking at things. This he tries to achieve by developing the notion of culture as an object of KM to illustrate how culture can be understood as an organisational resource instead of being presented as colliding zones of adversarial oppositions.

Culture is defined as "varieties of common knowledge; infinitely overlapping and perpetually redistributable habitats of common knowledge and shared meanings." Common knowledge, in turn, is described as

> Knowledge which is available in one location in an internationally distributed organization and which through interactive translation can be diffused to other locations within the organization in an appropriately intelligible form. Common knowledge is useful because there are different kinds of it, but it is dispersed messily both through organizations and the wider networks which encompass their stakeholders. (p. 315)

The new conceptual framework for cultures conceived in this way is provided by KM, but Holden does not exclude other possibilities. However, as far as cross-cultural management is concerned, it makes it much easier to write about networks, learning and KM as organisational processes. The transfer and sharing of knowledge and experience is conceived primarily in terms of collaborative learning where participants can draw from pools of common knowledge.

Furthermore, atmosphere is considered a major influence on these processes, both as a precondition for, and valuable product of, cross-cultural interactions.

> Atmosphere is the balm which allows cultures to intersect smoothly, and allows pools of knowledge to overlap freely. (p. 285)

His analysis of the case studies has generated two new concepts: **interactive translation** and **participative competence**. The former is seen as a form of cross-cultural work in which participants engage in (multicultural) groups to negotiate common meanings and common understandings. Interactive translation calls for participative competence, i.e. adeptness in cross-cultural communication, for facilitating and modulating the intra- and inter-organisational transfer of knowledge, values and experience.

Holden stresses that his new approach to cross-cultural management is basically derived from empirical research. Rather than test hypotheses, he has tried to answer questions which emerged in the course of his investigations and observations in global companies. His work offers new concepts and models, as well as valuable insights, which have implications not only for the management domain, but for other fields as well.

3.2.5 Cultural standards

Another alternative approach for identifying the influence of culture is presented by the model of cultural standards developed by Thomas, which owes a great deal to intercultural psychology.

Thomas (1991, 1996) emphasises the function of culture as a system of orientation which organises a specific field of action of individuals belonging to a particular society or community. He argues that culture is constituted by cultural standards or norms which can be identified by investigating so-called 'critical incidents' that (may) occur in intercultural interaction. This is where cultural differences surface and become effective, and by studying such incidents we can identify cultural models the parties involved might not even be aware of. Cultural standards therefore describe a 'typical' system of orientation or values in one culture as seen by another and are closely attached to concrete situations. Thanks to their strong empirical bias, cultural standards are particularly useful for the study of specific spheres of action.

Thomas emphasises the interdependency of cultural standards, i.e. a particular culture can only be understood in relation to another, which enables a comprehensive understanding of cultural context. They not only serve to describe observations, but also help us to try to discern the motivations behind a particular action in a particular context.

One of the main advantages of cultural standards is their strong empirical link to concrete situations. Thus, it is possible to identify them for a very specific domain or application area. Defining cultural standards for a specific use scenario should enable us to understand the structure of a specific 'culture'.

3.2.6 Cultural mental models and schemas

Shore's (1996) idea that abstract cultural models have an impact on concrete actions and in remembering has much in common with the concept of cultural standards, since it also deals with the interrelations between cultural orientation or value systems and the behaviour of individuals.

Shore tries to explain the interaction between individuals and a cultural community by way of a three-stage model in which he distinguishes between personal experience in a concrete situation (specific cases), instituted models and foundational schemas. The latter go beyond the experience and behaviour of an individual and thus constitute a specific culture. According to Shore, these three stages interact with each other through assimilation and accommodation, thus emphasising the dynamic aspect of culture.

Instituted models are social institutions – conventional, patterned public forms such as greetings, calendars, cockfights, discourse genres, houses, public spaces etc.

> [...] Instituted models always lead a double life, as part of an external society world and as products of intentional behaviour. They are models in two different senses. First, instituted models are human inventions, the product of the continual social production of publicly available forms. Instituted models are the externalisation in the social world of particular models of experience. Second, to the extent to which these instituted models govern concept formation of newly socialised individuals, they are also models from which individuals construct more or less conventional mental models. (Shore 1996:51)

Since it is always an active construction by an intentional, sentient, and creative mind, analogical schematisation introduces a gap, a crucial life-giving contingency, between the conventional forms of cultural life and their inner representations in consciousness. This gap guarantees the ongoing regeneration of conventions through practice in the same way that it makes possible inter-subjective meaning.

> Thus, to recognise the importance of cultural models and schemes in cognition does not entail viewing cultural cognition as either monolithic or ahistorical. For the dual creation – the two births – of cultural signs guarantees their double character as at once conventional and idiosyncratic constructs. (Shore 1996:372)

Shore's terminology and models provide a link between the concept of 'culture' and cognitive concepts such as mental models and schemas.

3.3 Summary

This study is based on the assumption that the planning, development and design of computer-based systems or applications is informed by culturally influenced expectations and assumptions about future user groups and use contexts. Defining the concept of culture is, however, notoriously difficult, as has been shown in the course of this chapter. It is suggested to look for the aspects that are relevant to the issues involved in a particular empirical study or theoretical investigation of a particular domain rather than look for a universally valid definition.

For the purposes of this study, i.e. investigating the influence of cultural factors on the development of eLearning programs or user interfaces, it is important to note that the cultural system of orientation is reflected both in artefacts (such as user interfaces) and institutions (i.e. economic organisations). Therefore, it can be assumed that not only does such a system have technical features, it has also been developed on the basis of mental models that are implicit carriers of specific systems of values shaped by culture.

This chapter provides the basis for any discussion of culture or cultural factors as well as the conceptual tools for identifying, capturing and analysing them. If, and indeed to what extent, they play a role in user interface design or the development of eLearning programs will be investigated in the following chapters.

4 Literature Survey and Recent Developments

4.1 Introduction

Because of the interdisciplinary nature of the topic, the literature is dispersed across a number of disciplines ranging from social anthropology, cognitive psychology, knowledge organisation, intercultural or cross-cultural communication and translation studies to information science and technology, human-computer interaction (HCI), computer-supported collaborative work and usability engineering. Furthermore, since the Project deals with computer-mediated learning and teaching, the vast amount of literature on educational, didactic and pedagogic issues is also relevant, at least when it concerns the virtual environment.

For the purposes of this study, however, I have restricted myself to the publications of immediate relevance to my topic, i.e. the implications of cultural aspects on the usability and accessibility of computer interfaces and on learning and teaching performance in a virtual environment. I have excluded publications such as manuals, guidelines or case studies, which are solely aimed at the practitioner even though these proved very useful for developing the pilot application and for planning and carrying out the user trials. Nonetheless, in many cases the genres of scientific research and its practical application merge. Furthermore, my research shows that literature which combines all the disparate strands of this study is very sparse indeed and therefore this selection criterion must not be too rigorously applied.

The structure of this chapter in many ways reflects the course of investigation I followed when preparing myself for the research tasks in connection with the EU Project. I start out by giving a brief introduction into recent developments in the fields of usability engineering and testing, whereby the focus lies on Web usability and the influence of cultural factors. It is surprising that despite the inherently global nature of the web, there seems to be little research that explicitly examines cultural differences as they relate to Web usability. The dearth of publications becomes particularly acute when looking for theoretical works or research publications about how cultural factors affect learning performance in connection with Web-based training modules.

Since interactive features play a major role in Web-based training, I have included publications on computer-supported collaborative working and communities of practice as these two areas are faced with similar challenges and questions. Furthermore, collaborative efforts are considered a major premise for effective learning to occur in a virtual environment (Kearsley and Shneiderman 1999).

4.2 Cultural factors in the realm of usability

It is above all in the HCI literature on topics such as internationalisation and localisation of products that cultural issues are investigated and analysed. Apart from a few books, e.g. Fernandes (1995), Hoft (1995) or del Galdo and Nielsen (1996), the greater part of relevant literature takes the form of journal articles (e.g. Russo and Boor 1993; Luong, Lok, Lok and Driscoll 1995; Yeo 1996; Onibere et al. 2001). In most cases they concern the accommodation of cultural differences in the design of software or other products.

4.2.1 Brief overview of the literature on internationalisation and localisation

Honold (2000) has analysed more than 100 publications on internationalisation and localisation. In the introduction, she states that the literature is very heterogeneous and widely scattered. Reports and writings linking cross-cultural and national considerations to problems requiring resolution in a broadly conceived ergonomics and its ancillary domains exist in widely disparate sources. As a result, a lack of common terminology, methods and/or theoretical models can be observed.

According to Honold, the publications fall into three distinct phases, each dominated by a particularly influential author:

- Human Factors Engineering at the beginning of the 1970s (e.g. Chapanis 1975)
- Internationalisation of software at the beginning of the 1990s (e.g. del Galdo and Nielsen 1996)
- Heterogeneity and the search for cultural models in the period from 1996-98 (e.g. Day 1998)

The first phase is marked by the year 1972 when the first international conference on national and cultural factors in Human Factors Engineering took place. It hailed the beginning of the cosmopolitan era and the introduction of modern technologies in underdeveloped countries, especially India.

Little was published between 1975 and 1990 and most of the actual publications dealt with classic ergonomics topics such as population stereotypes with regard to writing direction, colour allocation and other screen elements or ergonomic design for developing countries. Preferred methods were field research, work place analyses and experiments.

In the second phase, interest in internationalisation was largely motivated by economic interests. Since computers were now reaching out to people all over the world, American software engineers and usability experts felt the need to adapt their applications to the needs of an international user community.

Hoft (1995) is one of the first authors to refer to the 'interculturalists' Hofstede, Hall, Victor and Trompenaars and to direct attention to existing cultural models dimensions and use them as tools for optimising internationalisation.

The search for cultural models dominates in the years between 1996-1998, which see a tremendous surge in the amount of literature on international usability engineering. There is increasing use of approaches and methods derived from Participatory Design and growing attention to the context of usage. A shift can be observed away from guidelines about internationalisation/localisation, in which most problems seem to have been solved, to the management of the process of internationalisation.

Nevertheless, we still find a considerable number of publications on theoretical issues regarding internationalisation supplemented by practical case studies. They tend to fall into two categories: design solutions for international user groups *versus* design for specific cultural groups (e.g. Chinese software for the Chinese).

New topics include the explicit use of ethnological methods and interactive systems and groupware as objects of study. In 1998 a strong endeavour to develop cultural models can be discerned, but rather than adopt existing models from the fields of cultural psychology or anthropology, researchers tend to base themselves on HCI approaches. Gobbin (1998) introduces the term 'cultural fitness' to describe the acceptance of new technical products in different countries. Waldegg-Bourges and Scrivener (1998) emphasise the contextual aspects of meaning which have to be continually regenerated and negotiated for specific cultural contexts.

Based on this overview, Honold divides the heterogeneous field of intercultural usability engineering into four research areas:
1. Identifying culture-specific requirements of use
2. Culture-specific design of user interfaces
3. Culture-specific evaluation of user interfaces
4. Management of intercultural usability engineering.

In her opinion, the structuring of the field should facilitate modelling and contribute to the development of a theoretical framework for intercultural usability engineering. This, she argues, would allow us to better compare different studies and better communicate their results, factors which would ultimately also result in better practical implementation.

4.2.2 Current trends and key issues in intercultural usability engineering

Most current writing is based on the premise that it is the objective cultural aspects that are important in intercultural user interface design. Designers therefore should ensure that apart from language, time and date formats, the intended meaning of user interface representations such as symbols and icons are translated into the target cultures so that they are understood correctly. On the whole, current methods for internationalising products including Websites have been inspired by this approach.

In the article "Creating global software" Carey provides a useful overview on the development of international software (1998) by reviewing ten books in this field. She starts out with a series of definitions of the main concepts, compares the different approaches and methods, deals with organisational prerequisites for successful internationalisation (e.g. education, excellent communication levels, guides for programmers and writers, etc.) and examines cultural issues including the impact of culture on learning differences in software user training. Carey contends that we have to distinguish between comprehension and acceptance. It is not enough, she argues, to translate the representations, it is also equally important that users should feel comfortable with other cultural conventions. She then summarises best practice suggestions for designing international interfaces. These include guidelines for accessibility, documentation, testing or quality assurance and localisation procedures for Apple and Windows software.

As early as 1993, Russo and Boor suggested that interfaces should reflect the values, ethics and morals of target users in order to increase user acceptance. Del Galdo and Nielsen (1996) also support this view by presenting three levels of internationalisation, namely:

- Displaying the native language, character set and notations
- Translating the user interface and documentation so that it is understandable and usable
- Matching the user's cultural characteristics.

The last level goes well beyond avoiding offensive icons and should, for example, accommodate the way business is conducted or the way people communicate. Essentially, the taking into account of subjective cultural aspects is based on the premise that culture is about the way individuals behave and respond as well as their beliefs and values (Dunckley and Smith 2000).

Overall, we can observe an increasing awareness of the fact that developing truly effective interfaces for an international audience requires more than just translating text, it also involves a cultural transfer (see, for example, del Galdo and Nielsen 1996; Luong, Lok, Lok and Driscoll 1995; Russo and Boor 1993).

The above-mentioned authors tend to agree that interface elements affected by culture, such as images, icons or symbols, must be adjusted for cultural differences. Both images and words can raise problems because they can be understood differently by culturally diverse users who do not share knowledge of the context in which they are rooted. A well-known example is the Macintosh 'trash' icon, which British users tend to confuse with a postal box. Another example is the image of the owl, which Americans and Europeans tend to associate with wisdom whereas Latin American users relate it to magic and witchcraft. Social norms determine image acceptability in a culture and therefore great care must be taken when using images, symbols and icons depicting religious symbols (e.g. crosses, stars), the human body, women and hand gestures.

The same applies to colour, which can influence a user's expectations on navigation, links and content, and the interpretation of which varies between cultures. Examples frequently mentioned include the association of the colour red with danger in Europe and the United States, yet with happiness in China.

Furthermore, most internationalisation experts agree that number, date and time formats have to be converted and flow and layout must be designed around locale-specific user modules. Text and graphical elements of an interface are usually arranged to result in a logical flow of information as defined by the order in which words are read. Whereas speakers of Indo-European languages will feel familiar with a left-to-right, top-to-bottom layout, speakers of Arabic, Hebrew or Chinese speakers might feel lost.

Functionality, too, can be affected by cultural factors. Certain features, e.g. for encouraging interaction, might be taken for granted in one society, but be met with disapproval in another. One example cited in the literature on this subject refers to a poetry teaching tool developed for use in France. It was designed in such a way to accept the teacher's comments but not those of students. This was acceptable in France, but not well received in Scandinavia, where students are encouraged to contribute and interact with teachers (Russo and Boor 1993).

All the above-mentioned issues are well explored and documented in the HCI and software engineering literature on internationalisation and localisation.

4.2.2.1 Web usability

More recently, efforts have been made to apply the methods and guidelines developed in the field of software engineering to the usability of Websites. An article, or rather a selection of articles, which deals with Web-specific requirements of interface design, can be found in a special issue of the journal *Technical Communication* (Spyridakis and van der Geest 2000). They clearly distinguish between software interface usability research and Website usability research because even though knowledge about interfaces might be applicable to Websites, there is little proof of the benefit and effectiveness of guidelines originally developed for software engineering. Is it valid to assume, they ask, that the same usability principles or heuristics[8] , even if well-proven, apply to Web pages simply because Web pages are presented on screen? By extension, of course, this leads to the question of whether they also apply to Web-based training materials, just because they happen to be presented on a screen in a similar way to Web pages.

In my search for information and guidance on Web communication, the contributions contained in that special issue proved among the most valuable, well-grounded and empirically tested usability studies. The findings are based on research collaboration between two technical universities, one in the US, the other in the Netherlands, involving both faculty and students. The research also included summer workshops attended by participants from all over the world. The reviews were carried out by students as well as by experienced practitioners from major companies such as IBM, Unisys, Microsoft, etc.

---

[8] The term "heuristics" is derived from the Greek word for "discovering". Heuristics are procedures or principles that help their users work systematically toward a discovery, a decision or a solution. They are typically used in situations where there is more than one good answer, more than one solution.

According to the editors (Spyridakis and van der Geest 2000:301), the aim was to "develop instruments –i.e. five sets of heuristics – that will help designers and developers of Web pages or sites to consider crucial communicative aspects of Website design." These would increase the chance that a Website is not only technically sound but also effective in terms of communicative effect, intended as well as perceived, for particular target groups in particular contexts of use.

After defining essential concepts such as heuristics, heuristic evaluation, expert *versus* user-focused testing, process or product-oriented heuristics, the editors describe the role, function and scope of heuristics, how they were developed and conclude with an invitation for further discussion. For example, they point to the need for heuristics on information quality, good use of search engines, audience-function relationships and globalisation/localisation.

Their focus on informational Websites where descriptive and explanatory information dominates - as opposed to sites with a predominance of persuasive (e.g. for sales or ideological purposes) or entertaining (e.g. games) elements – coincides with the main objective of Web-based training modules, whose primary aim is to instruct. However, they exclude site elements primarily set up for person-to-person interaction (e.g. a chat room) which also play a role in eLearning tools and which pose different questions to designers and evaluators.

When preparing the user trials for the Project applications usability guidelines that originate in university libraries were found to be particularly useful because they tend to focus on instructional content and aim to support students in their search for and use of information for research papers. Heuristics are therefore primarily concerned with assessing the quality of information garnered from the Web. For the Web-based training applications in our Project the 'traditional' criteria of reliability and accuracy proved to be of utmost importance. Alexander and Tate (1999) have translated these into checklists on content and page features such as author information, update frequency or contact information.

In the same year, a special issue of *International Journal of Human-Computer Interaction* (2000) appeared, which was also devoted to Web usability. It proved even more relevant since it also included the influence of cultural factors. The articles aim to provide insights into navigation, internationalisation and other issues affecting usability on the Web but also to highlight the variety of research methodologies that can be employed (Sears 2000).

Among the contributions is a study by Dubach, Jacko and Sears based on research funded by Microsoft Corporation. They focus on information presentation and retrieval from Websites under the heading "International Aspects of World Wide Web Usability and the Role of High-End Graphical Enhancements". The authors focus on the effect of graphical enhancements such as animated graphics as they relate to the perceived usability of the Web. The study is based on comparing the responses of Swiss and US users to a large subset of the Microsoft Website and its simplified version (only simple, small-size graphics, no graphical buttons, but HTML hyperlinks). It explores the relation between cultural background, the media used and the users' perception of the site. The factors that influence the perceived usability of the sites include age, gender, computer literacy, Internet experience and command of English. Like the trainees at the site of the French Project partner, the Swiss users – employees of a major bank - were fluent in English and used to working in a multilingual environment.

The results show that basic demographics (i.e. age, gender, country) have a strong impact on Website usability, more so than computer and Internet experience. Swiss participants tended to be less positive about the Websites than US users, an observation the authors attribute to the fact that the site was developed primarily for a US audience. Overall, they basically confirm what most people, especially frequent users of the Internet, have felt all along, i.e. that graphical elements do not really enhance a Website. Only some enhancements such as the graphic buttons for navigational purposes might justify the additional time and expense.

The authors recognise that despite considerable overlap with internationalisation in the area of traditional software engineering, the Web poses its own set of challenges without actually delving into these issues any further. Instead they propose three solutions for international Web design:

1. Internationally aware Websites
2. Translated Websites
3. Fully internationalised Websites.

The first solution is the most economical approach. It does not rule out the possibility of fully internationalised versions at a later stage if this should prove desirable or if new markets open up where a command of the original language, usually English, cannot be taken for granted.

It is difficult to draw a clear line between 'internationally aware' and 'global' products since both are expected to be used in multicultural and multilingual environments without modification. The difference might be more a question of intention or attitude, i.e. whether customisation at a later stage is envisaged or ruled out right from the start. To ensure the highest possible acceptance around the world, the authors recommend using simple English, restricting oneself to graphics that assist during navigation and indicating the flow of information by means of arrows or other directional indicators.

Apart from designing culturally or internationally aware Websites, i.e. sites designed to work for readers from all cultures, the next option is to translate them into various languages and customise their design to address the needs of users in other countries and language communities. This is sometimes done by first creating a culturally-neutral site and then having it translated for different cultures.

Some companies go even further and completely redesign their Websites for different cultures, changing content, organisation, graphics, colours and so on. It goes without saying that the third option is the most costly and time-consuming and tends to be only espoused by big companies with a strong presence in foreign markets.

On the whole, the suggestions found in the literature on Web usability reiterate those found in the HCI literature about internationalisation supplemented by a few Web-specific considerations concerning deployment. In contrast with the deployment of software, so the argument goes, where the scheduling of releases is staggered for different countries and coordinated with marketing efforts, users around the world can all access a Website immediately. Therefore a company has to decide whether it wants to release the internationalised parts of a Website either in one go or on a staggered schedule, a decision that will largely be influenced by marketing considerations.

4.2.2.2 Web usability related to eLearning

Najjar (1998) in his review of the literature on research-based principles related to learning, lists the following characteristics of Websites that can significantly affect learning:

- Supportive multimedia – The information presented in one medium needs to support and extend the information presented in the other medium, e.g. adding closely related, supportive graphics to textual or auditory verbal information.
- Elaborative Processing – The extra cognitive processing of information helps to better integrate the material with prior knowledge.
- Interactive interfaces – Providing more interactivity in user interfaces that allow learners to control, manipulate and explore material, appears to have a substantial positive effect on learning.
- Directing attention – Multimedia can help direct the learner's attention to the most relevant information. The major considerations include motion, size, images, colour, text style and element location on a page.

According to Najjar, the strongest evidence is found for presentingof information in a multimedia and interactive form and for creating tasks that encourage learners to actively process or elaborate the information presented to them. This means that allowing learners to control, manipulate and explore material and have the learning software periodically ask learners to answer questions that help them integrate the material presented can improve a person's ability to learn and remember the contents of a Website.

4.2.3 Relevant publications in internationalisation, localisation and globalisation

The following section discusses a series of publications that illustrate how internationalisation in usability engineering in the fields of software design, Websites and information transfer in general has been investigated and/or implemented in practice. The discussion, however, is restricted to those studies that make an attempt at a theoretical grounding of the processes involved.

An interesting case study of the process involved in internationalising Websites is reported by Alvarez, Kasday and Todd (1998). They describe how considerations for internationalisation and accessibility were included at all stages (needs analysis, content selection, organisation, scheduling, coding, graphics design and testing and evaluation) in their construction of an international conference site. They regard these as basic tenets of good design and development in the modern marketplace.

A case study that illustrates the pitfalls of internationalisation efforts has been reported by Onibere and his co-authors (Onibere et al. 2001). They conducted a study with 324 end-users located in Botswana, a multicultural and multilingual country where English is the second language of most users. Although the authors encountered an "overwhelming desire" for a localised interface, the users showed little interest in localised icons (e.g. the image of a hut to indicate the start page) and could not agree as to which native language to use for text-based interfaces.
The authors attribute the poor response to the localised interface to the fact that the localised icons represent village culture and therefore seem out of place in a work environment. English is used for business purposes and therefore seems more appropriate in a work context, which is where computers tend to be used. The study also showed that the preferred style of interaction was menu-driven rather than by buttons or hot keys.

Barber and Badre (1998) have coined the term 'culturability', which they define as the capability of "capturing the cultural nuances of a targeted audience to enhance usability" (p. 4). The article attempts to ascertain whether there are interface design elements and features (e.g. icons, specific colours, grouping, font, links, shapes, orientation, flag, language etc.) which can be identified as culturally specific and/or genre specific. If certain elements prove to be prevalent, and possibly preferred, within a particular cultural group, they could be considered as so-called 'cultural markers'. Cultural markers may be indicators of belief systems, institutions, religion, customs, preferences, biases and the like and can be chosen both deliberately and subconsciously. Genres may include government, travel, news or advertising. They also investigate if any relationship exists between culture and genre as reflected in Web design.

To identify localisation elements and generalise them to cultural markers, the authors studied several hundred Websites in different countries and languages, limiting their study to sites provided in the native language of the host country. They then combined their observations with data from their own user survey and published studies of situated learning. They wanted to demonstrate that the presence or absence of cultural markers in international Websites can affect learning and performance in an electronic environment.

In their study, patterns emerged that reflected cultural practice and preferences, influenced both by country of origin and genre. The flag, for instance, serves as a symbol of immediate national recognition and is therefore often used to denote alternative language choices. Some cultural markers may be related to particular languages or scripts, e.g. both Arabic and Hebrew speakers are used to right-to-left oriented text and will therefore first focus on the right side of a Website. Some markers, however, seem to be particular to a given country and employed across genres. For example, in Brazil even government sites– despite their generally dry and official content - show a preference for multiple colours.

Barber and Badre do not intend to develop a generic global interface to be accepted by all cultures, but hope to develop a tool that can help automate design processes for particular cultural target groups.

A similar intention is professed by Yeo (1996), who proposes an internationalisation strategy that consists in separating the functional from the interface components. He suggests developing a single application with different cultural user interfaces (CUIs), which are "intuitive to a particular culture" and reflect "shared or common knowledge of a culture which could be defined by country boundaries, language, cultural conventions, race, shared activities or workplace" (p. 1). Yeo is one of the few authors to regard cultural diversity as an asset rather than an obstacle to be overcome and to explicitly extol the benefits of cultural diversity.

In a more recent publication, Yeo (2001) explores the efficacy of the development lifecycle for producing international software[9], which comprises three phases: design, implementation and usability evaluation. He concludes that techniques commonly used for assessing usability such as 'thinking aloud' or interviews may have serious shortcomings when applied in a non-Western context such as Malaysia. Among the characteristics that appear to influence the efficacy of these techniques, he mentions experience of users with similar software as well as cultural values such as the preservation of face. Referring to Hofstede, Yeo argues that preserving face is typical for a collectivist culture such as Malaysia and makes people reluctant to express criticism. He cites an example from Singapore where a subject actually broke down and cried during a software evaluation session, but was very positive about the software in the post-test interview.

Whereas many software products and international Websites are translated into various languages and their designs customised to address the needs of users in other countries and language communities, catering for a culturally heterogeneous user group as was the case in our Project requires a different approach. Rather than selecting the user groups on the basis of cultural background and customising the KM and eLearning system to suit their specific needs, the design has to both integrate cultural diversity and aim for cultural neutrality, respectively. This type of user sample is actually far from rare, and can be encountered in many international settings such as multinational companies, consultancy firms, banks or even non-governmental organisations which operate on a worldwide basis and/or have subsidiaries all around the globe.

---

[9] Yeo actually uses the term 'global software', which for the sake of consistency, has been replaced here by 'international software' in line with the use of terminology in the rest of the chapter.

A study dealing with a comparable user sample has been conducted by Bourges-Waldegg and Scrivener (2000). Like the trainees of our French Project partner, their users had a good command of English, but nevertheless misunderstandings occurred when users were asked to evaluate two English Websites aimed at an international audience. Most misunderstandings could be attributed to a lack of shared context, which made it difficult for some users to grasp the meaning of certain icons or expressions. The authors argue that the cultural differences affecting usability and design are mainly representational and that a culturally determined usability problem can be characterised as the user's difficulty in understanding the meaning of a representation in a particular context. The meaning of a representation, the authors argue, is determined by its context of use. In their study, they therefore emphasise the importance of using unambiguous, concise and even simplified English rather than the idiomatic, jargon-rich language usually cherished by Website designers.

4.3 Current trends and key issues in eLearning

In the introduction, eLearning has been defined as "the use of various technological tools that are either Web-based, Web-distributed or Web-capable for the purposes of education" (Nichols 2003:3). The term 'online learning', which is described as the use of eLearning tools in a distance education mode using the Web as the only medium for all student learning and contact, has been considered unsuitable for the purposes of this study because the Project never aimed to replace or abolish face-to-face instruction.

Before the term 'eLearning' became a household word, terms such as

- open distance learning
- Web-based training
- computer-based training
- technology-based learning and
- online learning

were used and are indeed still in use today. As stated in the chapter on Terminological Issues, Í have adopted the terms 'computer-mediated learning/instruction' or 'eLearning' to describe the use of new information and communication technologies to improve the quality of learning by facilitating both access to resources and services as well as remote exchanges and collaboration.

There appears to be an increasing awareness that for technical innovation to be effective, the use of information and communication technologies has to be adapted to the educational environment and the needs and requirements of users. In addition, there is a call for standards to be agreed and adhered to, support measures such as training of teachers to be undertaken and learning structures reorganised. This view is also reflected in the recent eLearning Action Plan published by the

European Commission.[10] The future of education is seen in making learning happen within activity and culturally rich collaborative social environments that never existed previously but are now made possible through the intelligent use of technology and new learning paradigms.

At recent conferences such as Learntec in Karlsruhe or Learning 2.0 in Vasteras, Portugal, experts deplored the fact that up to now far too much focus had been placed on the 'e', i.e. the electronic media, in eLearning, and not enough on didactic and pedagogic methods.[11] By concentrating on content and delivery, the argument goes, context and community have been neglected. By ignoring aspects such as acceptance by users or efficacy of methods, many eLearning initiatives fall short of the networked learning environments and constructivist learning models made possible through the intelligent use of new communication technologies and learning paradigms.

Instead of replicating conventional didactic models and viewing information and communication technologies as little more than an 'add-on' to traditional forms of training and learning, learning scientists advocate new models of content development characterised by collaborative working, adaptiveness and intercultural communication. At the same time, they call for the exploration of problem-solving strategies using authentic scenarios and learning situations or simulations (e.g. Brown, Collins and Duguid 1989). The eLearning applications, it is argued, must make an effort to capture the context of artefacts included in a learning management system such as documents, graphics, charts, videos etc. They should aim to develop and exploit more flexible forms of content (learning objects, multimedia assets) in training and learning that are sensitive to contexts of use and to the cultural values and background of users.

4.3.1 Learning management systems and learning objects

The terms 'electronic learning environments' or 'learning management systems' as well as 'learning objects' have become the new buzzwords in the usage of information and communication technologies for education and training. These learning environments often take the form of shells in which a multitude of tools and functionalities are integrated and offer a common space where content in any form can be placed. They normally include e-mail facilities and synchronous communication services in the form of chats or multimedia-sessions as well as shared calendars and other tools for scheduling and collaborative working.

Koper (2000:11) defines a learning environment as "a social system focused on the permanent development and certification of human knowledge and competencies in a particular domain." When this definition is applied to an electronic learning environment, it includes subsystems that can occur distributed in time and place and information and communication technologies which ensure integration, representation, personalisation, cooperation and process management. Content

---

[10] The eLearning Action Plan - designing tomorrow's education. Communication from the Commission to the Council and the European Parliament (2001).
[11] For example Wolfgang Kraemer, IMC Saarbrücken, one of the leading eLearning solution providers in Germany; cited in *iX* 5/2002, p. 121.

can be represented in a variety of forms ranging from documents, presentations, spreadsheets, audio and video files, Web pages including external links and any other digital resource that might be of use for learning and training. The instructional designer provides both the content to be studied as well as the assignments students have to complete and submit for evaluation.

The concept of 'learning objects', i.e. breaking down content into manageable, reusable entities that can be delivered across multiple platforms is now widely recognised as the most appropriate way of developing and delivering learning content. Such objects should not, however, be regarded as simply content, assets or resources, but contain some element of pedagogy that is intended to determine how they are to be used by learners and their teachers (McCormick 2003).

In practice, most eLearning providers and publishers still focus on creating learning content as large 'packaged' or fully integrated courses with limited reusability for other purposes. Some may produce innovative interactive activities and in some cases simulations of experiments or activities (such as flying a helicopter) that allow students to control or manipulate aspects of the activity. At its heart, however, this is still a *presentation* of material and thus rooted in a world of individual instruction using information processing views of learning, where knowledge is to be consumed and reproduced by learners. Assessment is carried out mainly by assigning numerical grades and allowing only few opportunities for adapting to individual learning processes. The pedagogic elements called for by educational scientists such as Koper (2000) are virtually absent.

However, there appears to be a conflict between the emphasis on context as seen by contemporary views of learning (which argue that what is learned is closely tied to the context within which the learning takes place) and the need to decontextualise learning objects to make them re-usable and thus maximise the possibility of learning objects being interoperable in compliant virtual learning environments (see Wiley et al 2003).

McCormick (2003) argues that the prospects of a development of learning objects based on social-constructivist or constructivist principles are poor and that efforts to build a definite pedagogy into learning objects are doomed to failure. Instead, he advocates putting the pedagogy into the learning environment constructed by the instructor. He proposes an approach that advocates the development of learning assets with sophisticated, high-quality media representations of content, around which instructors build learning activities and assessment methods. He suggests using pedagogic templates that give guidance on typical pedagogies, such as problem-based or inquiry-based learning.

4.3.2 Recent publications in eLearning

A very useful introduction to the world of eLearning is provided by the *Theory Into Practice* (TIP) database which is maintained by Kearsley, one of the leading figures in the field. It gives an overview of current theories, themes, experts and important publications in this field and contains descriptions of over 50 theories relevant to human learning and instruction including Social Development Theory (Vygotsky), Social Learning Theory (Bandura) and Situated Learning (Lave).

Each description includes an overview, scope/application, examples, principles and references. Relationships between theories are identified by highlighted text within articles. These can be connections between specific theories or links to concepts that underlie a number of theories. Theories are selected for inclusion in the database based upon their relevance to some aspect of human learning and instruction. Although they are all derived from published literature in English, the TIP Database also serves as a useful point of reference for experts outside the Anglo-Saxon orbit.

The literature available abounds in debates about the respective merits of these diverse theories and their implications for the design of learning materials or environments. But increasingly, a more pragmatic view which advocates a blending of the different learning theories appears to be asserting itself. Margules (1996), for example, suggests that education professionals use their collective expertise and knowledge of behaviourist, cognitive and constructivist learning theories and combine these with that of experts in communication, environmental design and engineering to design and deliver the most appropriate solutions for a variety of learners and learning situations.

It is not surprising that a great deal of the writing on eLearning should deal with the technologies and tools used in various educational settings. Many publications discuss the use of synchronous and asynchronous communications, videotapes, teleconferencing, business TV, collaboration tools, avatars and tools such as streaming audio and video, which usually require equipment more commonly found in highly industrialised countries. Settings might range from academia to in-house company training, virtual classrooms with no on-site students to online courses for use in primary schools. Even though the technocentric view of eLearning has come under attack, we still find recent publications, such as Porter's review of the field (2001), which are almost devoid of any concerns about pedagogic issues and see most of the relevant issues as being technical.

Apart from the vast amount of literature on the use of information and communication technologies, many publications also deal with the benefits of information and communication technologies for education and training, mostly citing cost savings, and the advantage of being able to learn anytime, anywhere and thus enjoy greater control over the pace of learning and delivery style. The pedagogic rationale normally given for the use of information and communication technologies for education and training processes is that these add value to traditional learning and teaching processes.

The literature also includes many articles on specifications and standards in the eLearning field with regard to metadata, learning objects and learning architecture as well as the exchange, transfer, use and reuse of digital materials between computer-based learning systems. And as is the case with usability, there are also innumerable case studies, guidelines and reports addressed primarily at practitioners and of interest mainly to those who are considering the implementation of an eLearning platform or designing digital content for instruction.

4.3.3 Cultural factors in the eLearning literature – a topic of benign neglect?

In the overview of current eLearning themes provided by Kearsley in the above-mentioned TIP-Database, cultural factors are not mentioned, at least not explicitly, although they could be expected to play a role in some of the themes discussed, including in particular collaboration, student-centredness, community and, above all, authenticity. This last principle implies that to achieve 'real-world' relevance, the information conveyed has to reflect the environment and the social and cultural settings in which students or trainees live and work.

Even though Kearsley mentions "the exciting aspects of global networking" which allow people from all nations to interact easily and participate in courses, he is only concerned about language. The fact that people speak different languages is considered an obstacle to communication. As a 'solution' to the problem, he proposes automatic translation programmes that will convert text from one language to another.

On the whole, educational scientists writing on eLearning do not discuss the possible impact of cultural factors – at least not in explicit terms – even though they might call for context- and user-centred approaches and emphasise collabora-tion. McCormick (2003), for example, considers intercultural communication a key skill required by the Information Society, but fails to elaborate on it.

However, the issue is addressed at length by the editors of *Learning for Life in the 21st Century – Sociocultural Perspectives on the Future of Education* (2002). In their introduction to this collection of essays, Wells and Claxton (2002: 9) argue in favour of recognising cultural diversity in the classroom:

> [...] there are different identities and values that have their origins in cultural, linguistic, class and gender differences, as well as in individual trajectories of experience and current levels of performance...

and they ask the question:

> How can such diversity be made a resource in education activities rather than a problem to be overcome or a basis for divisive practices? To put it another way, how can the situated and variegated nature of learning-and-teaching activities be reconciled with the (understandable) administrative concern for mastery of a standardized, prespecified curriculum and for common outcomes?

They regard all learning situations as social and cultural, even if they involve no face-to-face interaction. In their opinion the recent proliferation of electronic forms of communication actually have re-emphasised the extent to which thinking in the cultural-historical tradition is fundamentally 'cultural'. They believe that these new media open up new opportunities and demand the development of new mental competencies and attitudes. They may also require forms of support which differ from those exercised or afforded by traditional education. Since students tend to study eLearning materials in a solitary mode, they lack many of the forms of social and emotional support – ideally – available in face-to-face learning communities.

Another publication which deals with cultural issues and distance education has appeared in the International Journal of Medical Informatics (McPhee and Nøhr 2000). The authors recognise that in today's society, the changing roles of both the teacher and the learner and the use of new communication technologies call for the development of new pedagogic approaches that are sensitive to cultural diversity. Culture is defined as the "acquired preference in problem solving" (cp. Trompenaars 1993). Unfortunately, the study lacks concrete detail, abounds in sweeping statements such as "Differences in language can lead to participation barriers" (p. 293) and finally, reveals the fact that the results are based on the observations and feedback of one (!) Australian student who participated in a long-distance Masters programme at a Danish University.

4.4 Computer-supported collaborative work and communities of practice

A link between the two main facets of the present study, i.e. usability and computer-mediated learning and teaching, can be established by the interactive and collaborative features present in both areas. In the discussions leading up to the development of the eLearning platform, we soon recognised that these were the areas where cultural factors might have a significant impact on the usability and thus acceptance of the application. Wherever interaction occurs, e.g. in online exams aimed at testing students' progress, and including the way in which results are communicated, cultural traditions might influence participants' expectations.

Cultural differences might also play a role in collaborative or community features, e.g. discussion fora used for exchange between trainer and students as well as among students. In a study of interdisciplinary collaboration (physicians and social workers), Abramson and Mizrahi (1996) have found that while organisations and teams have boundaries, some of the most difficult obstacles to overcome are those defined by ingrained professional opinions and power structures. Their observations have been largely confirmed by our own Project where the results of the usability tests show that mechanics and pilots have different learning styles, interaction patterns and information retrieval and processing behaviour.

Furthermore, whereas older models of computer-based learning focused on individualised instruction and the student's interaction with the computer, more recent approaches such as the engagement theory proposed by Kearsley and Shneiderman (1999) emphasise human interaction in the context of group activities, not individual interaction with an instructional program. In addition, collaborative efforts are considered a major premise for effective learning to occur, also in a virtual environment.

The intimate connection between group work and learning is explored by Vick (1998) in "Perspectives on and Problems with Computer-Mediated Teamwork: Current Groupware Issues and

Assumptions". Her article begins by asking why in many companies there has been resistance to the adoption of seemingly very useful technologies designed to support the work of distributed teams. She contends that, apart from the increasing pace of change and the high degree of complexity of solutions based on new technologies, lack of acceptance might be due to the fact that the design of technology reflects its culture of origin, which is, of course, not shared by all users in cross-cultural teams.

According to Vick, "future group performance depends on meaningful results occurring during each cycle as well as on technological support for team memory" (p. 12). This is in line with the focus of engagement theory on meaningful and real-world learning activities (Kearsley and Shneiderman 1999). As far as technological support is concerned, it has been found that group members who are also members of informal affinity groups or communities of practice tend to adopt new technologies faster than those who do not engage in informal communication (Stewart 1996).

After reviewing the variables or factors considered by researchers studying work groups and computer-mediated support of teamwork, Vick draws up an inventory of measures and conditions gathered from numerous studies and subsequently clusters them into a set of categories such as contextual factors, team attributes, process, performance (output), task attributes, team member attributes and individual difference variables. Various combinations of these factors constitute individual work group situations.

Vick observes that what is noticeably missing in the studies she has reviewed is any reference to empirical testing of variables specific to cross-cultural research. Indeed, this is confirmed by my own search for relevant literature, which has yielded only a few studies on computer-supported group work in cross-cultural teams. An interesting experiment has been reported by Mejias, Vogel and Shepherd (1997) about the use of a groupware application with groups in the United States and Mexico in which Hofstede's cultural model served as a framework to determine the impact of cultural differences on group consensus and individual satisfaction in parallel testing sessions.

It turned out that the possibility of anonymous input offered by the technology had more impact on participants whose culture was characterised by collectivism, high power distance and femininity (e.g. Mexico) than on representatives from an individualistic, low power-distance, masculine culture such as the United States. The latter seemed to take the idea of equal participation for granted. The authors conclude that firstly, culture does affect both group outcomes and the adoption of information technology, secondly, the design and implementation of group support systems needs to be sensitive to cultural norms and, thirdly, the exchange of information is common to problem-solving regardless of culture.

Other studies have focused on using group support systems to reduce the effects of power distance (e.g. Tan, Wei and Watson 1995), the influence of individualism and power distance on consensus and equity in meetings that are facilitated by group support systems as well as on the effectiveness of virtual teams using electronic mail to collaborate on unstructured tasks (Knoll and Jarvenpaa 1995).

In "Perspectives on Groupware for Cross-Cultural Teams" Nordbotten (1998) criticises his colleagues for having neglected cross-cultural teams. In his opinion, the impact of cross-cultural characteristics on international, distributed teamwork is an increasingly important concern and there is an urgent need to remedy the lack of knowledge about how the use of groupware tools affects international team member participation.

Nordbotten seems to regard cross-cultural aspects of teamwork primarily as a potential source of problems, whereas Vick – though not denying the problems arising from different languages, cultures or attitudes – also sees them as a source of competitive advantage.

> Despite the difficulties of global/cross-cultural teamwork, the opportunity to obtain expertise from a variety of individuals who can supply more accurate international perspectives for decision-making is invaluable and working to leverage this expertise can help create the synergy needed to work effectively across cultures... The cross-cultural knowledge gained through cross-pollination by moving people among the branches of an organisation creates the opportunity for team members to learn from and teach one another. (Vick 1998:17)

Effective collaboration, however, requires that team members come to regard values not as universal principles, but as norms particular to their society. Even though Nordbotten's criticism may be justified to some extent, it does not alter the fact that Vick's paper is a valuable attempt at investigating the implications of cultural factors in the design and use of groupware systems.

4.5 Summary

It is interesting to note that we can observe similar trends in the recent writing on usability and on eLearning issues. In both fields, increasing attention is attributed to context and the situations in which computer-mediated activity occurs and to the participation of users.

In the usability arena, the participatory and iterative design approach has come to be widely recognised as the best way to increase performance and acceptance of systems. This involves developing computer-based systems by means of a process taking into account user feedback right from the outset.

Similarly, in eLearning, educational scientists and practitioners advocate new models of content development characterised by user engagement, user-centredness, adaptiveness and attention to contextual factors. They also tend to advocate problem-solving using 'real-life' authentic scenarios.

At the same time, a shift from individual to collaborative perspectives can be discerned. Whereas traditional approaches focused on the individual learner or user sitting at a computer and receiving instruction or retrieving information, the weight of opinion now seems to regard such an individualised approach as being too limiting. Thus, in HCI studies, the domination of the field by cognitive ergonomics is now increasingly giving way to approaches such as situated action and distributed cognition, approaches that emphasise both context and community or collaboration. In the eLearning field, situated Learning and social learning theories have replaced individual instruction as the predominant credo.

Furthermore, we can observe a growing eclecticism when it comes to the selection of methods for designing either learning environments or user interfaces. An eLearning platform might therefore include elements that correspond to the 'traditional' instructivist approach and are more suited to imparting basic information to novices, yet, at the same time, also include elements or tools that encourage the construction of new knowledge as well as exchange and/or collaboration with peers. Also notable is a tendency to view users and learners as experts rather than passive absorbers or consumers of information.

Even the methodological implications of this shift in paradigm are similar: McCormick (2003) suggests using pedagogic templates that give guidance on typical pedagogies, supported by tools that instructors can use particularly when working in particular domains of knowledge. Marcus (2000), in turn, advocates the creation of templates or versioning tools for developing multiple versions of Websites for different cultures.

Another aspect of convergence is the fact that a growing number of recent publications see activity theory as a possible approach or meta-approach. In eLearning, we can observe a move towards sociocultural theories inspired by Vygotsky, Leontiev and Kaptelinin, and usability experts increasingly consider activity theory as a means of structuring and guiding field studies into HCI.

Above all, the activity theory approach provides a response to the search for a common nomenclature and thus fills a lacuna pointed out by many experts, e.g. Honold (2000) for usability engineering and Nichols (2003) for eLearning. They both see the lack of a consistent terminology and common framework as a serious impediment to the comparison and communication of findings.

Although theoretical issues are mentioned in this survey, they will be discussed in more detail in the following chapters. In the course of this chapter it will have become obvious that most publications exhibit a lack of theoretical foundation.

5 Theories and Models in Human-Computer-Interaction

The first part of this chapter provides a brief outline of some of the major approaches in human-computer interaction (HCI) and includes details on their main characteristics, their shortcomings and the extent to which they take into account cultural factors. Based on the literature survey conducted for this study, four approaches have been selected which dominate current discussion in the field of HCI, namely:

- cognitive ergonomics, the most influential and predominant approach at the moment,
- situated action, which emphasises the situational context surrounding the use of a product,
- distributed cognition, which moves the unit of analysis to the system, whereas in traditional views of cognition the boundaries are those of individuals, and, finally,
- activity theory as a meta-approach.

Cognitive ergonomics serves as the theoretical underpinning for many models and methods prevalent in the HCI field. It rarely addresses the concept of culture and, by and large, studies based on this approach tend to ignore the context in which HCI occurs.

This shortcoming has been largely remedied by the situated action approach with its focus on real activities in real situations. It takes into account both context and community and favours ethnographic methods for studying and describing in minute detail the situations in which interaction occurs.

Distributed cognition also recognises the need to look at real activity – to study cognition 'in the wild' as its advocates like to call it – in order to understand interactions between people and technologies. Unlike cognitive ergonomics, it extends its reach beyond the individual to focus on whole environments.

More recently, activity theory has emerged as an approach that can help overcome the shortcomings of the information processing models of cognitive science and the lack of abstraction and modelling capacities of the situated action approach.

5.1 Introduction

HCI deals with usability engineering from a scientific and research point of view and brings together a wide range of disciplines including artificial intelligence, information technology, linguistics, physiology, cognitive psychology, social and organisational psychology, sociology, anthropology and philosophy.

Usability engineering can be considered as a process-oriented part of ergonomics, human factors engineering or HCI and can be defined as the optimisation of matching between user and product or application. The process of usability engineering can be seen either as linear or iterative. The linear approach is correctness-driven, but not very flexible and fault-tolerant. In our Project, we applied an iterative approach, which implied conducting reviews at several stages and feeding the results back into the design process. Furthermore, it was participatory, which meant that user requirements with regard to user interface design and functionality were integrated in the design process at an early stage.

The concepts or terms used in the various HCI publications tend to reveal more about the scientific background of the author than the actual content. Because of the abundance of theories derived from a variety of disciplines such as those mentioned above as well as from other approaches like task analysis and scenario-based design, there is a lack of a unifying theoretical perspective. According to many usability engineering experts (e.g. Honold 2000) fragmentation in the field undermines not only the conceptual integrity of HCI but also its impact on the practice of design, evaluation and use of computer systems.

In the following sections, I consider the basic tenets of the four approaches, discuss their shortcomings and evaluate the extent to which they take cultural factors into account.

5.2 Cognitive ergonomics

Cognitive ergonomics, sometimes also referred to as 'human factors engineering' or just 'human factors', is oriented towards the psychological aspects of work, both in the way work affects the mind and the way the mind affects work. It has gained wide acceptance in the usability engineering community.

> Classical ergonomics made considerable advances in understanding the nature of man-machine interaction and the principles have in many ways become the psychological 'common sense' knowledge of the engineering domain. (Hollnagel 1995:304)

Apart from what can be observed from outside and measured, cognitive ergonomics also examines the objectives, intentions, expectations and mental models or constructions of users. The methodology is influenced by the (quantifiable) laboratory experiments prevalent in cognitive psychology. 'Thinking aloud' is frequently used as a method for examining the interaction between a user and a technical application.

5.2.1 Role of culture

Cognitive ergonomics aims to provide universally valid statements about the perception and processing of information in the realm of HCI. As far as cultural factors are concerned, these tend to be either ignored or relegated to the individual mind. Most cognitive psychologists see culture as a system of values that resides in the brain of an individual and thus as a characteristic of the user such as age, gender or level of education. This means that culture is considered an attribute of the user rather than of the interaction between the user and the context of usage or the computer-mediated activity.

In addition, the scientific community associated with this approach seems to find it difficult to reconcile the grouping or categorising of users in terms of cultural criteria with their idea of political correctness, as is noted by Singleton:

> This is a sensitive topic on which to conduct research or establish principles that, in spite of the extensive effort, [...] there is not great deal of knowledge beyond argument. (1989:92)

Only in the discussions about technology transfer to developing countries do scientists deal with differences among members from different cultures. These discussions, however, tend to be limited to the 'classic' ergonomic themes such as anthropometry, population stereotypes, etc.

5.2.2 Critique

Cognitive ergonomics, with its focus on the computer-user or computer-programmer dyad, has tended to neglect the context and the environment in which human-computer-interaction occurs and has largely ignored the real activities users are engaged in. Its research methods have been based mostly upon experimental models borrowed from the natural sciences and focus on measuring.

This often results in a lack of consideration of other aspects of human behaviour, interaction with other people and with the environment and the influence of the history of the users (including their cultural and/or professional backgrounds). Many studies influenced by this approach are characterised by a focus on models rather than human beings and the products themselves. Context is often neglected in favour of measurability. According to Suchman (1987), the terminology reflects the fundamental equality assumed between man and machine:

> Insofar as the machine is somewhat predictable, in sum, and yet both internally opaque and liable to unpredicted behaviour, we are more likely to view ourselves as engaged in interaction with it than just performing operations upon it, or using it as a tool to perform operations upon the world. (p. 16)

Man is seen mainly as an information processing machine and plans rather than the environment are seen as crucial in shaping behaviour. Many HCI studies informed by cognitive ergonomics concentrate on representations in the head such as plans or 'rational problem solving' as the object of study.

5.3 Situated action

The situated action approach draws on disciplines such as anthropology and sociology and focuses on human activities in particular situations and settings. The situational context surrounding the use of a product is the main unit of analysis or in Lave's (1988) words: "the activity of persons-acting in setting. The unit of analysis is thus not the individual, not the environment, but a relation between the two."

A central tenet of the situated action approach is that the structuring of activity is not something that precedes a situation, but something that can only grow directly out of the immediacy of the situation. Suchman (1987), for example, states that every course of action depends in essential ways upon its material and social circumstances. The extent to which the user is embedded in a specific (cultural) context and a framework of reference is therefore recognised.

> The term underscores the view that every course of action depends in essential ways upon its material and social circumstances. Rather than attempting to abstract action away from circumstances and represent it as a rational plan, the approach is to study how people use their circumstances to achieve intelligent actions. (Suchman 1987:50)

When developing an (interactive) application, advocates of this approach suggest basing one's design on a very detailed observation and description of the situations of use. For this, ethnographic methods such as field research and participant observation are favoured.

The situated action approach has also been applied to computer-mediated work and computer-supported collaborative work, for example, by Mantovani (1996). Mantovani expanded the approach to include not only the interpretation of situations and the local interaction with the environment as in Suchman's work, but also to regard the symbolic order or structure as an integral part of the social context.

5.3.1 Role of culture

Since Suchman's excellent critique of the prevailing cognitive science model of purposeful action owes a great deal to insights from anthropology, the importance attributed to culture does not come as a surprise. In the preface to her book *Plans and Situated Actions* (1987), Suchman describes her endeavour as follows:

> I am not just examining the cognitive science model with the dispassion of the uncommitted anthropologist of science, I am examining it in light of an alternative account of human action to which I am committed... (1987:x)

The embeddedness of the user in a specific (cultural) context and a framework of reference is recognised and, thus, the role of culture in users' interactions with the machine or computer.

Mantovani further expanded the approach to include not only the interpretation of situations and the local interaction with the environment, but also regard the symbolic order or structure as an integral part of the social context, which is in line with the view argued for in ethnomethodology that the social order is constructed from within (e.g. Garfinkel 1967).

As mentioned above, the problem of the situated action approach lies mainly in the lack of conceptual tools with which to identify, elicit or analyse the impact of cultural factors on human action and on human-machine communication.

5.3.2 Critique

For many, situated action represents a welcome corrective to the dominant cognitive credo because it takes into account the specific context surrounding the situations of use. However, this consideration relies almost exclusively on the observation of specific situations described in meticulous detail, yet tends to ignore the users' view of the situation, for example their explanations and thoughts as expressed in interviews.

> Situated action models have a slightly behaviourist undercurrent in that it is the subject's reaction to the environment (the 'situation') that finally determines action. (Nardi 1996:81)

The situated action approach has also been criticised for its lack of reference to overall motives, intentions and objectives. This point of criticism, however, has to be qualified. Although it is true that Suchman and other advocates do not regard intentions and objectives as a determining factor in people's actions, they would certainly not deny their existence or negate their influence on behaviour.

A more serious shortcoming is the fact that the approach does not provide tools or models with which to describe motives or goals, especially if these go beyond the immediate situation.

> One finds oneself in a claustrophobic thicket of descriptive detail, lacking concepts with which to compare and generalise. The lack of conceptual vocabulary, the appeal to the situation in its moment-by-moment details, do not lead themselves to higher-order scientific tasks where some abstraction is necessary.
> (Nardi 1996:92)

The focus on concrete situations can result in a loss of sight of enduring structures. Nevertheless, because of its strong empirical commitment, the situated action approach can serve as the basis for empirical investigations and guide the analysis when trying to come to grips with the often perplexing flux of training activities.

5.4 Distributed cognition

The distributed cognition approach is a new branch of cognitive science devoted to the study of interactions between people and technologies. Its advocates propose it as a new foundation for HCI and an integrated framework for research that combines ethnographic observation and controlled experimentation as a basis for theoretically informed design of digital work materials and collaborative workplaces (Hollan, Hutchins and Kirsh 2000). These authors also suggest focusing on:

> [...] distributions of cognitive processes across members of social groups, coordination between internal and external structure, and how products of earlier events can transform the nature of later events. (2000:193)

Thus, it goes far beyond the traditional information processing approach of cognitive ergonomics, which focuses almost exclusively on single individuals interacting with applications derived from decompositions of work activities into individual tasks.

Hollan and his colleagues feel that for HCI to advance in the new millennium a better understanding is called for of the emerging dynamic of interaction, which is now no longer confined to the desktop but instead reaches into a complex world of information networks. Therefore, the unit of analysis is moved to the system, for example, to small socio-technical systems such as an airline cockpit, whereas in traditional views of cognition the boundaries are those of individuals.

The cockpit can be understood only when we understand the contributions made by the individual agents in the system (e.g. the pilots) and the coordination necessary among them to achieve their goal, that is, to successfully complete a flight. Another instance of coordination has been described by Flor and Hutchins (1991), who studied the way in which two programmers performing a software maintenance task coordinated their activity between themselves.

Distributed cognition is also concerned with structure – representations inside and outside the head – and in the transformations these structures undergo. Contrary to traditional cognitive science, the focus of interest is on cooperating people and artefacts, not just individual cognition. According to Nardi (1996), this emphasis on representations and their transformations brings persistent structures to centre stage.

Distributed cognition has produced analyses of work practices that span specific situational contexts. A series of studies on end-user computing, for instance, have found a strong pattern of cooperative work among users of a variety of software systems in different arenas, including users of word processing programs, spreadsheet software and computer-aided design systems. Unlike the situated action approach, distributed cognition allows generalisations to be made and broader patterns sought for.

As already mentioned, ethnographic ethnography, including interviewing, surveys, participant observation and video and audio recordings, is the favourite method for capturing the constituents of interactions among people and between people and artefacts. These require the establishing of a rapport with the members of a community, which in turn requires domain-specific knowledge.

5.4.1 Role of Culture

One of the central tenets of distributed cognition is that the study of cognition is inseparable from the study of culture, because agents live in complex cultural environments (Hollan, Hutchins and Kirsh 2000). In the words of one of distributed cognition's main proponents:

> This means, on the one hand, that culture emerges out of the activity of human agents in their historical contexts, as mental, material and social structures interact, and on the other hand, that culture in the form of a history of material artifacts and social practices, shapes cognitive processes... (Hutchins 1994)

Culture is also seen as a provider of intellectual tools and as a reservoir of resources for learning, problem-solving and reasoning.

5.4.2 Critique

Distributed cognition returns culture, context and history to the picture of cognition and thus offers an integrative framework for HCI studies – at least in its more recent form proposed by Hollan, Hutchins and Kirsh (2000). Thus, it is very close in spirit to activity theory as confirmed by Nardi (1996), who believes that the two approaches will merge over time. In her opinion, however, activity theory will continue to probe questions of consciousness outside the scope of distributed cognition – at least as formulated at the time of her writing, prior to the article by Hollan, Hutchins and Kirsh (2000).

The main problem – which is also conceded by Hollan, Hutchins and Kirsh – is that the integrated research programme described in their article does not yet exist. They realise that it is ambitious in scope, requires research skills not normally included in graduate training programmes and addresses issues that are highly complex.

The authors have embarked on a research enterprise coordinated by the integrated framework they have sketched out and now await the results. Like advocates of activity theory, they insist on the urgent need for a theory that views HCI within a larger context to ensure that the design of people's intellectual workplaces will meet human needs.

5.5 Activity theory

Activity theory is a set of basic principles that constitute a general conceptual system rather than a highly predictive theory and, since it is a dynamic and systemic approach, it can cope with a rapidly changing environment. People are seen as embedded in a sociocultural context with which they actively interact. The complex interaction of individuals with their environment is called activity and is regarded theoretically as the fundamental unit of analysis.

Activity theory traces its roots back to psychological perspectives in the Soviet Union in the 1920s. Its basic foundations were laid by psychologists such as Vygotsy, Luria and Leontiev. It was only with the collapse of the Soviet Union at the end of the 1980s that activity theory became known to HCI researchers in the West. It was above all Bødker's works (1989, 1991) that stimulated interest in activity theory and its potential benefits to the HCI community. Her ideas have been taken up and developed further by researchers such as Kuutti (1992), Bannon and Bødker (1991), Engeström (1996) and, above all, in the compilation of articles edited by Nardi (1996).

Although activity theory now supports studies in other fields, especially in developmental psychology and educational technology (which will be discussed in the following chapter), it also provides a broad framework for describing the structure, development and context of computer-supported activities and a foundation on which HCI researchers might base common discourse and from which they can derive tools for design and evaluation (see e.g. Kaptelinin and Nardi 1999).

Tool mediation is one of the most important concepts of activity theory. Tools or artefacts refer to culturally produced means for changing the environment and achieving goals. Humans are seen as continually changing tools or artefacts or creating new ones. From an activity theory perspective, computer technologies and the Internet, for example, are considered tools.

At the same time, activity theory shifts the focus from interaction between users and computers or computer-based systems to the wider context of interaction between human beings and their environment. According to Kaptelinin (1996), understanding the use of computers in a particular case requires an analysis of the computer's history and its potential developmental transformations. Furthermore, the author states that the term 'user' encompasses not only individuals, but also groups and organisations. The HCI field, therefore, needs to be recognised as an open system consisting of the meaningful context of the user's goals, environment, available tools and interactions with other people. The inclusion of both communicative and collaborative aspects makes activity theory also an appropriate basis for addressing important aspects of HCI, including computer-supported cooperative work and cross-cultural aspects of computer use.

The value of activity theory for contextual studies of HCI has been convincingly described, for example in Nardi's book *Context and Consciousness* (1996). According to Nardi, the greatest contribution of activity theory might lie in its ability to provide disparate approaches to HCI with a common vocabulary for emergent issues in the study of technology usage. Its basic concepts and principles can be applied to the analysis of problems of HCI and problems of design and evaluation and help to understand how computers are used in the context of real activity.

5.5.1 Role of Culture

Culture and its historical roots enjoy a prominent place in activity theory. People are seen as embedded in a sociocultural context with which they actively interact. Whereas for Vygotsky (1978) the unit of analysis was still the mediated action of an individual, Leontiev (1975) extended it to include the collective activity, something done by a community with a motive.

Kaptelinin (1996) is also very explicit about the role of cultural factors in activity theory and considers it to provide a wider theoretical basis for HCI studies than cognitive psychology. He also argues that although cognitive psychology can be successfully applied to a number of HCI problems, such as the user's perceptions, mental models, control of the system and user interface *versus* functionality of the system, one of its serious limitations is what he terms 'ecological validity' (1996:106). Since the information processing loop is closed, it is difficult to take into consideration the phenomena that exist outside it, i.e. the social, organisational and cultural context in relation to the goals, plans and values of the user.

From an activity theory perspective, the computer, or an eLearning system, is considered as a mediating tool that needs to be seen in the context of the entire environment within which it will be used (e.g. the classroom setting, the presence or lack of presence of an instructor and his/her role, the role of other students etc.). Tools are regarded as carriers of cultural knowledge and social experience.

5.5.2 Critique

Despite the many benefits of activity theory for HCI studies, its advocates do not promote it as the panacea for HCI studies, but instead argue in favour of an eclectic approach that combines models and concepts from distributed cognition, situated work theories and activity theory. Kaptelinin (1996), in particular, in his outline of the potential impact of activity theory on the study and design of computer use in real-life settings also mentions some of the limitations and shortcomings of activity theory. These include:

- Activity theory's original focus on understanding individual activity, not that of a group or organisation
- Activity theory's narrow view of culture
- Its perspective on tool mediation has not anticipated the representation problems of virtual reality.
- Its lack of operationalisation.

The last point has also been taken up by Honold (2000), who deplores the comparative lack of concrete applications of activity theory. She notes that its very comprehensiveness implies great freedom for researchers when it comes to applying its basic principles, but at the same time harbours the danger of arbitrariness and theoretical aloofness. Thus, she echoes Ratner (1996), who criticises the fact that certain studies might use the terminology connected with activity theory, yet in fact do not comply with its demand for contextual embeddedness.

However, the shortcomings enumerated by Kaptelinin are currently in the process of being remedied. Chapter 7 discusses recent studies that have applied concepts and models from activity theory to collaboration in groups and to virtual reality.

5.6 The use of cultural models in human-computer interaction

Few authors in the HCI field have tried to define the concept of culture or establish links between existing concepts in cultural psychology with HCI theories. Hoft (1995) was one of the first to direct attention to existing cultural models and encourage her readers to use them as tools for optimising internationalisation.

In her book *International Technical Communication* Hoft provides a complete guide to the planning, writing and designing of documentation for distribution to an international audience. She discusses each individual phase in creating more effective international technical communication, whether it be verbal, graphic, printed or electronic, and carefully describes the intricacies of page layout, colour, example choices, graphics, worksheets, help screens and other features. Given the very practical slant, Hoft also describes the whole document cycle for international product distribution and provides strategies, techniques and practical tips on how to communicate internationally quickly, cheaply and well. She illustrates her arguments by citing a host of case studies from Canada, Germany, Japan and the United States.

To explain the cultural differences publication teams must be aware of when producing documentation, she refers her readers to the cultural dimensions as propagated by Hofstede (1991), Hall (1959), Victor (1992) and Trompenaars (1993). According to Hoft, cultural dimensions can focus on objective aspects such as political and economic contexts or differences in day, date and number formats. They can also focus on subjective aspects such as values, beliefs, patterns of thinking and behaviour.

An author who has not only applied cultural models to usability engineering, but also conducted an in-depth scientific investigation into the relevant theoretical issues is Honold (2000). In her doctoral thesis on the impact of cultural factors on the design and use of technical products, she compares concepts and models for gathering cultural information during requirements analysis, attempts to define the notion of culture and examines the role of cultural factors in usability engineering. She then proceeds to describe the methods – focus group discussions and interviews – for determining culture-specific requirements and the problems associated with their use in a non-Western environment.

Honold's research is based on and has accompanied two concrete applications: the first concerned the adapting of German washing machines to an Indian context, while the second involved assessing and comparing usage patterns of mobile phones in Germany, Italy, India and China. She concludes with a series of recommendations on intercultural usability engineering.

An article Honold published with colleagues at Siemens proved very relevant to the Project work because of the similarities in organisational environment and methodology (Beu, Honold and Yuan 2000). Like our French partner, Siemens sells its products in many countries around the world. Whereas the internationalisation process used to come right at the end of the development schedule, country-specific requirements for the major markets are now assessed and interpreted as early as possible so that appropriate design objectives can be defined.

They have realised that true adaptation goes beyond translating operating instructions and changing formats and must instead take into account different requirements in terms of functionality, which can change over time. They have also looked into differences in the infrastructure, key qualifications in international cooperation and the development of appropriate test methods.

When defining culture, Beu, Honold and Yuan take into account the professional environment as the specific context in which activities are performed, even though they assume – referring to Hofstede (1980) – that the national cultural orientation systems acquired early in life have a strong influence. However, they consider the information content of the culture-related concepts such as Hofstede's individualism/collectivism as insufficient for the actual design of products. They argue that in addition to these concepts a precise understanding of work objectives and work contexts is needed. To illustrate their point they cite a recent study by Dong and Salvendy (1999), which found that Chinese users only preferred a vertical menu structure if the user interface was in Chinese. Linguistic tradition was thus overridden by contextual factors.

A very interesting example, which shows how relevant factors can change over time, is reported in two earlier studies by Honold (1995 and 1999) concerning the use of mobile phones. Whereas Chinese who had bought mobile phones at the beginning of the mobile boom hesitated to ask questions, so as not to reveal their lack of knowledge and avoid losing face, asking for assistance from sales staff or friends later became an accepted learning strategy and one which also tied in with China's collectivist culture.

In their study, Beu, Honold and Yuan stress the importance of documenting the procedures, responsibilities and communication channels for handling usability projects. They see this as a fundamental prerequisite for cooperation in a multicultural, geographically distributed team. Extra commitment and mutual understanding, however, are required to surmount some hurdles, such as the differences in communication behaviour between usability experts from the United States or

Germany and their Asian colleagues. They found, for example, that while the former felt quite at ease communicating by e-mail and telephone, the latter tended to prefer personal contact.

They have also found that usability questionnaires are only really valid and can only be administered in a specific language area. Qualitative procedures such as focus group discussions also have to be adapted to culture-specific communication behaviour. In China, in particular, culturally related barriers to the effectiveness of this method can be observed. Due to the cultural tendency to avoid direct criticism, exert caution and treat others with respect, the authors had to find different ways of gathering feedback on the usability of products.

More recently, the term 'cultural usability' has cropped up, especially in the writings of Sun. According to Sun (2003), the term refers to a new model which distinguishes itself from other explorations on cultural dimensions of product design in that:

> [Cultural usability] defines culture as a dynamic process and attends to both general and ethnic cultural factors. It is a developing response to the contextual problems in usability studies, which integrates methods and key concepts from activity theory, genre theory, and British cultural studies. (2003:670)

Sun intends to apply the model to investigate the success of mobile text messaging, a phenomenon which is hard to explain with traditional usability theories given the inherent constraints of mobile phones such as the small display, poor input methods, moving environments and noisy surroundings. According to Sun, two major trends have emerged in response to the surprising success of short message systems (SMS): one focuses on the 'text aspect' of this technology to explore how messaging technologies affect people (especially teenagers) by studying the process of social shaping and its implications for future design (e.g. Brown, Green and Harper 2001), while the other is interested in how ad-hoc chats can support collaborative projects and work conversations as a business tool (e.g. Nardi, Whittaker and Bradner 2000).

The author proposes to combine the two in a localisation case study of use patterns and mediation practices of mobile text messaging between American and Chinese users to examine the dynamic relationships between cultural contexts and usability and shed light on the way cultural factors affect product design and use. The use of SMS will be explored by conducting a use pattern survey, diary study and contextual interviews supplemented with desk research. So far no results seem to have been published.

Although Sun's approach emphasises both the cultural dimensions and the context of use of artefacts, it seems unnecessary to refer to cultural studies to study messaging technology in its sociocultural context since – as will be demonstrated later – activity theory can accommodate this dimension easily within its framework. Similarly, connecting design with use, which the author intends to achieve by applying the concept of genre, can also be achieved within the framework of activity theory as has been shown by Gould, Verenikina and Hasan (2000), who have applied it to the design of interactive Web-based information systems.

One of the most relevant papers for the purposes of this study has been written by two South African researchers, Gabrielle Ford and Helene Gelderblom. In their study, they examine "The Effects of Culture on Performance Achieved through the Use of Human Computer Interaction" (2003). Using Hofstede's cultural dimensions, i.e. uncertainty avoidance, power distance, femininity/masculinity and individualism/collectivism, they first identify the characteristics of the various cultural dimensions, select the test subjects (students) and then test the interfaces (Websites) that display the appropriate cultural dimensions. Finally, they assess how the cultural dimensions affect performance in terms of speed, accuracy and satisfaction levels.

They start out by arguing that designers have to take into consideration the cultural diversity of users to enable global distribution of products and services through Websites. Like Carey (1998), whose contribution to internationalisation has already been discussed above, they distinguish between objective (language, date and time formats etc.) and subjective (values, ethics) cultural aspects, which they believe can be described through cultural dimensions as proposed by Hofstede, Trompenaars, Victor and others. They argue that it is necessary to determine which cultural dimensions affect human performance, so that these can then be integrated into the design of user interfaces in the future.

According to Ford and Gelderblom, performance is based on a cognitive process that consists of four stages: attention, identification or recognition, analysis and response. They give the following examples to illustrate the influence of cultural dimensions on the various stages:

> In the first stage, i.e. attracting the attention of users and helping them identify the stimulus, objective cultural elements such as language or metaphors play a role. These should be pertinent to the cultural dimension of the user. High Power Distant users, for instance, are expected to be more attracted to metaphors suggesting expertise, authority, official stamps, etc., whereas Low Power Distant users would prefer images of equality, such as playgrounds and public places. Similarly, Feminine users would identify better with family oriented metaphors.

At the analysis stage, the authors assume that the concreteness of data may alleviate complexity and thus facilitate understanding in general. However, whereas High Uncertainty Avoidant users might prefer detailed explanations, Low Uncertainty Avoidant users would prefer summarised data. Furthermore, High Uncertainty Avoidant users are generally assumed to be more emotional and more anxious about how to navigate through a site than they are on concentrating on the problem itself. Masculine and Short-Term Oriented users are expected to be naturally impatient and want to complete tasks quickly, which is why slow response times might cause a loss in concentration and therefore reduce the accuracy of performance. High Power Distant users might be worried about disappointing their superiors, which can cause anxiety and equally affect performance.

During the final phase of the cognitive process, namely the response stage, the authors assume that Collectivist users would be uncomfortable with having to express personal opinions, while Individualist users would find it unacceptable not to be able to give their opinion. This might affect functionality as was illustrated in the poetry example cited in Russo and Boor (1993) mentioned above. The fact that this particular poetry tool did not allow students to add their comments made it unacceptable in societies with an egalitarian and/or individualist tradition, such as in Scandinavian countries.

The results strongly indicate that the sites that displayed the characteristics of users of high Power Distance, high Uncertainty Avoidance, Masculinity or Collectivism were found to be the better sites and had higher measures of performance. The design of high Uncertainty Avoidance sites was characterised by clear and familiar metaphors, simple and precise articulation and limited menu options and navigation controls and included precise, detailed feedback on status to reduce uncertainty. Masculinity sites provided limited navigation choices, high-level executive views, were goal-oriented and delivered quick results for limited tasks. High Power Distance sites also offered wizards or guides to assist with navigation.

The authors therefore conclude that "there is insufficient evidence to support the hypotheses that any of the four cultural dimensions tested significantly affect human performance" (p. 228). Furthermore, they suggest that "... differences in scores could have been attributable to variables in the sites or users other than the cultural dimension being tested" *(ibid)*.

Actually, all the above-mentioned features correspond to the principles and guide-lines of good user-centred design as proposed by numerous experts (see Table 3: General usability guidelines by Nielsen) because they help to increase user speed, accuracy and satisfaction levels regardless of cultural background. The authors concede that the theoretical foundations for cultural influences on interface design are still lacking. Despite the lack of evidence, the authors refrain from questioning their basic research premises and continue applying the essentialist approach espoused by Hofstede and others, suggesting instead making changes to the design of the experiment and rephrasing or rather refining the research questions.

Another author who has adapted Hofstede's dimensions is Simon (2001). In his article "The Impact of Culture and Gender on Websites: An Empirical Study", he emphasises that his is an exploratory study and therefore the four sites used as a basis for comparison did not conform to the characteristics of cultural and global communication as would be required for controlled experiments. Also, the indi-viduals in the sample, i.e. 160 college students in the United States, might not be representative of the mainstream population. On the other hand, they were probably more in line with the demographic characteristics and the socio-economic profile typical for the Internet user community, at least as it stood a couple of years ago.

Simon uses an adapted version of Hofstede's cultural dimensions as a means of differentiation. He is primarily interested in clustering the subjects by means of Power Distance and Individualism, while the Masculinity-Femininity dimension serves as the basis for gender differentiation. The results suggest that differences exist between the cultural clusters and gender groups within the following cultures: Asia, Europe, Latin and South America and North America. The perception of the Asian and Latin/South American users were found to be similar, as were those of their European and North American counterparts. A qualitative analysis indicates that women's preferences differ strongly from those of the males within certain cultures. Men tend to be more tolerant of risks and have a selective information strategy. Women, in turn, tend to apply a comprehensive strategy and attempt to assimilate all available cues, whereas the male information processing strategy is to use efficiency-striving heuristics determined by the nature of the task.

The paper by Kamentz and Womser-Hacker (2003) deals with culture as a determining factor in the development and graphical design of learning systems. They compare German and American computer-based/web-based training courses in terms of usability, presentation of content and didactic approach. This is supplemented by examining the cultural aspects of computer usage. They argue that, in addition to technical and subject-specific issues and guidelines or style sheets for interface design and information organisation, the development of Web-based training courses also has to take into account didactic aspects. If Web-based training is addressed to an international audience, the issue of the cultural adequacy of learning environments is raised.

Since the focus of their paper is on cultural differences in learning behaviour, the design of interactive learning systems and scientific discourse, it will be discussed more in detail in the following chapter on Theories and Models in eLearning.

The article by Terri Griffith on "Cross-cultural and cognitive issues in the implementation of new technology: focus on group support systems and Bulgaria" (1998) has been included in this survey because it explicitly makes use of Hofstede's cultural dimensions to predict and possibly explain difficulties in technology transfer and implementation across cultural boundaries. Griffith focuses on user satisfaction as a form of proxy measure for implementation success. Her cognitive implementation model is based on the concept of 'frames', the dynamic, thematic perceptual dispositions that increase or decrease the salience of the information people perceive. She espouses the so-called 'limited-information approach', which has been successfully employed in the United States and assumes that users learn by experience rather than by being told. Therefore they have to be given the opportunity to take responsibility for their own learning, which might also include challenging the assumptions of experts in their efforts to learn more. However, in societies with high Power Distance, i.e. the least equal superior/subordinate relationships, people are expected to be less likely to challenge authority or experts and therefore less successful in adapting to new technology.

Based on Hofstede's study and the assumption that conformity and lack of initiative had been a survival technique in Bulgaria until the recent political changes, the author expected Bulgarian users to be reluctant to disagree with their superiors.

Her hypothesis, however, is not born out by the empirical study, i.e. Bulgarian users were equally or even more ready to challenge the experts than American users. But although the original assumptions based on Hofstede's cognitive model are not confirmed, the author does not question the underlying approach to culture but attributes this 'deviation' to factors such as the special circumstances of a society in transition.

5.7 Summary

As has already been shown in the literature survey in Chapter 4, publications in the field of HCI rarely deal with cultural differences beyond interface design. Authors, on the whole, make little effort to define the concept of culture or to establish links between existing concepts in cultural psychology with HCI theories.

Traditional cognitive theories such as cognitive ergonomics, for example, largely ignore cultural differences or view culture as a body of content on which the cognitive processes of individuals operate. The more recent approach of distributed cognition, however, moves the boundary of the unit of analysis beyond the individual and thus situates the individual as an element in a complex cultural environment. Cognition is therefore no longer isolated or separate from culture.

Distributed cognition favours ethnographic methods for capturing the interactions between people and artefacts and supplements them with experiments. The loop from observation to theory to design and back to new ethnographic observations is an important cycle of activity in the distributed cognition framework and very much in line with the emphasis of recent usability studies on participatory and iterative design.

The more empirically grounded situated action approach, which takes into account cultural and contextual factors, provides a welcome corrective to the rationalistic accounts of human behaviour found in traditional cognitive theories. It has been criticised, however, for being too global to provide guidance to applied studies and, on the other hand, too concerned with microscopic and detailed analysis.

Activity theory brings about a change in perspective: man and computer are no longer at the same level. Computers return to being tools which mediate between subjects or agents and their goals within a particular socio-historical context. Contrary to the situated action approach, activity theory aims to discern and identify structures which go beyond a particular situation.

Activity theory is not exclusive of other approaches, but is seen by leading advocates such as Kaptelinin and Nardi (1996) as a backbone for analysis which can be enriched by distributed cognition's focus on representations and the commitment to grappling with the complex flux of everyday activity of the situated action perspective.

6 Theories and Models in eLearning

There is a plethora of views, theories and schools related to eLearning, and most electronic learning environments and eLearning programmes are based on the principles of one or a combination of learning theories. But even among the adepts of a particular theory, viewpoints may differ considerably.

After outlining the characteristics of the three main approaches that have dominated educational research in the last few decades – behaviourism, cognitivism and constructivism – I discuss various models and concepts of learning which can, in turn, be subsumed under three metaphors which overlay or intersect with the major learning theories, namely the metaphors of acquisition, participation and knowledge creation.

Subsequently, I investigate the implications of learning theories and concepts for eLearning on the instructional technology community where several divisions or 'camps' can be discerned, such as modellers *versus* non-modellers, advocates of instructivist *versus* constructivist theories and individualist *versus* communicative or sociocultural theories.

I then present four pedagogical models that are particularly relevant to the development of eLearning materials and systems and thus to the research issues of the present study. The models comprise: authentic learning context, collaborative learning, problem-based learning and progressive inquiry learning. The last model appears to be the most comprehensive and also the most appropriate for the empirical setting.

Finally, the (potential) impact of cultural factors on eLearning materials and/or environments is discussed. I conclude by presenting activity theory as an integrative framework for investigating cultural issues in the realm of learning and teaching, whether this takes place face-to-face or at a distance.

6.1 Introduction

The structure of this chapter differs from the previous chapter on Theories and Models in HCI, where each presentation of a theoretical approach was followed by a critique and remarks on the role a particular approach assigns to cultural factors. In the following chapter, I have decided to discuss the role of culture across the whole range of theoretical approaches, concepts and models. The reasons for this decision are twofold: on the one hand it is difficult to make any general statements about any individual theory as they tend to cover such a wide spectrum of attitudes (e.g. from cognitive to social constructivism) and, on the other hand, because there are very few explicit references to cultural factors to be found in the literature unless it has been influenced by the sociocultural approaches.

Implicitly, however, culture does play a role, mostly in the realm of metaphors and certain camps in the eLearning field where issues such as the role of social communities, interaction, cultural practices and the like are discussed. As already pointed out, it is above all in the so-called sociocultural approaches to learning and teaching, including situated learning, cognitive apprenticeship, learning by expanding or guided participation, that cultural factors are considered. Studies based on these approaches usually not only address the instructional use of information and communication technologies, but also emphasise the influence of cultural factors, a fact that is to be expected given their roots in the cultural-historical approach of Vygotsky, Leontiev and their followers.

As is the case with usability studies, most researchers refer to Hofstede for identifying and analysing cultural factors. Apart from Hofstede, the discourse on culture in the domain of learning and teaching is also influenced by the work of Clyne and Galtung, who have investigated cultural differences in the structure and culture of intellectual discourse and academic writing style.

Authors who have used cultural models for determining the impact or implications of cultural factors in this area and/or used them for differentiating user groups tend to argue that cultural differences affect the conceptual structure of learning software, but also the design of user interfaces of multimedia learning systems. Thus a link between eLearning and HCI is established.

The sociocultural approaches in educational research and practice whose origins lie in the work of Vygotsky and Leontiev can accommodate (inter-)cultural factors, cope with computer-mediated collaboration processes and take into account the environment in which learning and teaching activities occur.

6.2 Brief historical outline of learning theories with reference to computer-based instruction

The design of the earliest computer-based instructional technology was founded on a behaviourist theory of learning with an emphasis on observable and measurable behaviour and its modification. In the late 1970's and 1980's behaviourist views were replaced with cognitive theories of learning that focus on the 'hidden' mental processes that must take place for learning to occur. Cognitive theories tend to regard learning as an active, constructive, cumulative, self-regulated and goal-oriented process where the learner plays a central role (Shuell 1992). In addition, they can also see learning as diagnostic and reflective.

More recently, constructivism and sociocultural approaches to learning have emerged as the popular trends that are influencing the design of computer-based instructional technology. The constructivist paradigm regards learning as an active process in which learners construct knowledge on the basis of prior knowledge. Approaches based on the constructivist paradigm emphasise that the construction of knowledge is mediated by the social and cultural circumstances in which it is experienced. This is normally associated with a situated approach to learning, where the development of knowledge and its transfer are assisted by the authenticity of the tasks or activities.

Sociocultural theories of learning and teaching inspired by Vygotsky have also addressed the instructional use of information and communication technologies. Kaptelinin (1996) lists several such theories, among them situated learning (Lave 1988), cognitive apprenticeship (Collins et al 1989) and learning by expanding (Engeström 1987). His list could be expanded by adding the more recent concept of 'scaffolding' or 'guided participation' described by Wells and Claxton (2002).

In behaviourism, the learner is expected to adapt to his or her environment while being exposed to certain stimuli. Desirable behaviour can be reinforced by immediate and positive feedback (Schulmeister 1998:93). The method of 'programmed instruction', in which the subject-matter is divided up into segments and where the progress of learners is checked after each step by the system giving adequate feedback, is based on the behaviourist approach.

Cognitivism emphasises the internal processes that take place during learning and classes them as information processing, including information input, processing and storage. Successful learning depends on the way in which information is presented and on the cognitive activities of the learner. This is achieved by constructing mental models or schemata and integrating them into existing knowledge. The main objective is to impart information or knowledge about problem-solving which allows the use of different methods to form a correct answer. During the process of problem-solving, the learners might be assisted by a tutorial system. Both the behaviourist and the cognitive approaches stress the importance of instruction, whereby constructivism focuses on instruction from the learner's perspective.

Constructivism regards learning as an internal process that occurs on the basis of the learner's experience and respective context. It assumes humans construct knowledge actively and individually build on their existing knowledge. Consequently, learning processes are difficult to predict, and learning is influenced more by the context of the learning process than by the presentation of information.

Apart from the authors whose writing is informed by the sociocultural approaches (e.g. Wells and Claxton 2002, Ratner 1991, Wertsch 1994), few educational scientists make any explicit reference to cultural factors. Nevertheless, it can be assumed that the constructivist approach, and especially its social variant, is most likely to accommodate the impact of cultural factors given its emphasis on context and the learner's perspective. 'Social constructivism' is concerned with the social processes associated with knowledge construction, whereas 'cognitive constructivism' sees learning primarily as individuals constructing knowledge.

Each theory stresses different aspects of learning and has its own benefits and shortcomings. Behaviourism supports the presentation and memorisation of basic knowledge or skills (Baumgartner and Payr 1997). Learning systems built in line with behaviourist principles are often considered tedious and repetitive by learners who have used them for some time. The cognitivist theory is mainly suitable for problem-solving, but it is difficult to gain knowledge about the internal processes that occur during learning in real situations. This, however, would be required if information is to be presented in a way that will help learners to construct the correct mental model. The constructivist view focuses on learning how to deal with complex situations and makes the learner responsible for the organisation of the learning process.

An increasing number of experts in the eLearning field are concerned with basing the development of virtual learning materials and the associated electronic learning environments on contemporary views of learning (e.g. Koper 2003; Orrill 2002). Most of them call for the development of eLearning materials or learning objects that are based upon constructivist principles. However, just what is meant by these principles is less clear.

Like with the concept of culture, terms such as 'virtuality' and 'reality' are also often used without clarifying their meaning. Welsch (1998) therefore demands that defining the concept of reality is a prerequisite for any discussion of virtual reality. For this purpose, he examines the concept in different contexts of use and in the works of various philosophers including Plato, Aristotle, Kant, Leibniz and others. Welsch argues that we cannot draw a sharp line between virtual and real experience because the latter has already been shaped by fiction, the arts or rituals. In his opinion the two aspects are closely interwoven with each other and their relationship is in constant flux.

6.3 Metaphors of learning

The three basic learning theories outlined above are overlaid or intersected by models and concepts of learning which have been subsumed under two metaphors by Sfard (1998), namely the acquisition and participation metaphors. Paavola et al (2003) later added the metaphor of knowledge creation.

The acquisition metaphor regards learning as a process of transmitting knowledge to an individual learner. This may either be a more traditional receptive process or, as emphasised by Sfard (1998), an active and 'constructive' process. Learning tends to be examined in terms of knowledge structures or mental models or schemas residing within an individual mind. Knowledge is thus understood as a property or capacity of an individual mind. Many constructivist learning theories are also related to this metaphor, particularly if they concentrate on individual learning processes.

An alternative approach is represented by the participation metaphor with its emphasis on the role of social communities. Learning is seen as an interactive process of participating in various cultural practices and shared learning activities and becoming a member of a community by gradually transferring from peripheral to full participation (Lave and Wenger 1996). The focus is on activities, on 'knowing', and not so much on outcomes or products of learning, i.e. on 'knowledge'. In this framework, terms such as acquisition or accumulation are supplemented or even replaced with concepts such as discourse, interaction, activity and participation.

The distinction between the acquisition and participation metaphor of learning is closely linked to the cognitive *versus* situated perspectives of human cognition and expertise and knowledge. Whereas the acquisition view is rooted in traditional cognitive theories, in which the concept of expertise refers to a well-organised body of domain-specific knowledge to be used for solving complex problems, the participation view is embedded in a situated perspective of cognition where learning is seen as embedded in a web of relations and networks of distributed and shared activities. According to this approach, expertise develops dynamically through participating in an expert culture or community of practice that 'owns' cultural knowledge of the domain and provides access to cultural tools and practices (e.g. Lave and Wenger 1996; Wenger 2000). The assumption is that knowledge and knowing cannot be separated from the situations in which they are used or take place.

Thus, the acquisition metaphor presupposes certain structures of knowledge that learners are guided to assimilate. The emphasis of the participation metaphor is on increased mastery of a community's knowledge without any deliberate effort for transformation or conceptual change. The third metaphor, that of knowledge creation, however, focuses on deliberately creating and developing new knowledge. According to this metaphor, learning is tantamount to innovative processes of inquiry where new ideas, tools and practices are created collaboratively and the initial knowledge is either substantially enriched or significantly transformed during the process. Models of learning based on this metaphor, such as Engeström's model of expansive learning (Engeström 1987) as well as a number of collaborative learning or inquiry learning models explicitly emphasise processes, practices and social structures that are likely to encourage the formation of new knowledge, artefacts and innovations.

The knowledge-creation metaphor implies progressive problem-solving, i.e. the urge to move beyond what is already known and embrace new challenges (Bereiter and Scardamalia 1993). It also tends to be connected with collaborative activities that are aimed at creating new knowledge, which in turn leads to an increase in individual cognitive competencies on the one hand and collective knowledge advancement on the other. The focus lies on the process, i.e. how various forms of knowledge become transformed through knowledge creation, how experience or tacit knowledge can be made explicit and how concepts and theories can guide practices.

6.4 Approaches in the field of eLearning

Whereas the approaches and metaphors discussed above apply to learning and teaching in general, the following categories apply primarily to learning and teaching in virtual environments. According to Jones and Mercer (1993) several divisions or 'camps' can be discerned in the eLearning or instructional technology community:

- modellers *versus* non-modellers,
- advocates of instructivist *versus* constructivist theories and

- advocates of individualist *versus* communicative/sociocultural theories.

6.4.1 Modellers *versus* non-modellers

The roots of this dichotomy lie in the book *Computers as Cognitive Tools* by Derry and Lajoie (1993), in which the authors see the members of these two imaginary camps as theoretically opposed on how advanced educational technology can be used to facilitate learning. They present modellers as advocates of the traditional approach that supports tutorial control, diagnostic feedback and is based on student models. This may result in intelligent tutor systems that model learners, the knowledge domain and learning strategies. Non-modellers are seen as promoters of the constructivist view of the learner as a social tool user. Current trends, such as cognitive apprenticeship or situated cognition, are also associated with this camp (Brown, Collins and Duguid 1989).

Derry and Lajoie, however, argue that the general principles that can be gleaned from these current trends apply equally well to both perspectives. They propose a middle camp where the two can merge and argue that the presence of an intelligent modelling capability within a system does not necessarily imply that any particular instructional strategy or philosophy be built upon it.

6.4.2 Instructivists *versus* constructivists

Rieber (1994) distinguishes two divergent interpretations of instructional technology: the cognitive and behaviourist approaches to learning and instructional design, which he calls 'instructivism', and constructivism. Much of the development work in these fields to date has been associated with direct instruction (also known as instructional systems design or objectivism), that is, instruction based largely on the application of behavioural principles.

In contrast, constructivism is characterised by discovery and experiential learning. The major goal of constructivist education consists in developing rich sets of cognitive tools to help learners explore their environment and encourage them to create knowledge that reflects their comprehension and conception of information rather than focusing on the presentation of objective knowledge. The educators or developers favouring the constructivist approach have therefore sought to tap the potential of modern information and communication technologies to create an environment in which learners can experience and develop sophisticated ideas from a variety of domains.

Increasingly, however, educational experts such as Jonassen (1991), Rieber (1992, 1994) or Margules (1996) see the different perspectives not as being in opposition to one another but as being at opposite ends of a continuum, with the most realistic model of learning lying somewhere in between. Jonassen, for example, argues that instructional designers should recognise that cognitivism holds important lessons on how to interpret the results of learning and how to design environments to support that learning. Both branches of educational psychology offer tools that, taken eclectically, can strengthen the effectiveness of lessons and encourage understanding of the learning process.

6.4.3 Individualistic *versus* communicative or sociocultural theories

A further distinction that permeates much of recent writing on computer-mediated learning and instruction is that between individualistic theories of learning and communicative learning approaches within the sociocultural perspective. According to Jones and Mercer (1993), individualistic conceptions of learning are to be found with both behaviouristic and constructivist views. In their opinion, the individual approaches fail to take into account the social quality of most learning. Instead they propose the cultural-historical theory of human activity developed by Leontiev (1975), Vygotsky (1978) and further expanded by Kaptelinin (1996). Whereas for Vygotsky the unit of analysis was still the mediated action of an individual, Leontiev extended it to include the collective activity.

Davydov (1988) applied Leontiev's activity-theoretical approach to the learning process and developed a psychological theory of learning activity which focuses on the goal-oriented, joint activity of adult and child within the social context of development. From this perspective, the computer is considered as a mediating tool that needs to be seen in the context of the entire learning environment in which it will be used (e.g. the classroom setting, the presence or not of a teacher (and his or her role), the role of other learners, the curriculum, etc.).

Much of the contemporary research (e.g. Collins et al. 1989) that falls under the umbrella term 'sociocultural theory', has been inspired by Vygotsky and his followers. Educational research based on this theory tends to address learning and instruction from a communicative and collaborative perspective and often focuses on Vygotsky's concept of the zone of proximal development, i.e. the difference between a child's real level of development and its potential level of development. The instructor is seen as an active, communicative participant, not just as a provider of a rich learning environment or reinforcer of positive behaviour.

6.5 Towards a theory of eLearning

Recently, Nichols (2003) formulated ten hypotheses, or rather statements, about seeking to implement eLearning on a firm theoretical foundation. He justifies this move by arguing that although many practitioners of eLearning seem to manage quite well without reference to any theoretical concepts or models, an eLearning theory could at least point them to education principles and make them aware of the considerable body of education theory directly relevant to their endeavour.

Nichols' statements are included here because they reflect and summarise current thinking on eLearning:

- eLearning is a means of implementing education that can be applied within varying education models (for example, face to face or distance education) and educational philosophies (for example behaviourism and constructivism).
- eLearning enables unique forms of education that fit within the existing paradigms of face to face and distance education.
- Whenever possible the choice of eLearning tools should reflect rather than determine the pedagogy of a course however as a general rule how technology is used is more important than which technology is used.
- eLearning advances primarily through the successful implementation of pedagogical innovation.
- eLearning can be used in two major ways; the presentation of education content, and the facilitation of education processes.
- eLearning tools are best made to operate within a carefully selected and optimally integrated course design model.
- eLearning tools and techniques should be used only after consideration has been given to online *versus* offline trade-offs.
- Effective eLearning practice considers the ways in which end-users will engage with the learning opportunities provided to them.
- The essential process of education, that is, enabling the learner to achieve planned learning outcomes, does not change when eLearning is applied.
- Only pedagogical and access advantages will provide a lasting rationale for implementing eLearning approaches.

According to Nichols, these statements were by and large validated by other experts.[12] He summarises his position as follows:

> We must research to establish theory not evaluation, principles not practices, pedagogies not applications. Only then will a literature base be developed that can be applied across multiple institutions and education settings. (2003:8)

Technology is pedagogically neutral and can therefore be applied quite merrily to all the pedagogies listed further below. It follows then that the poor implementation of technology must reflect poorly implemented pedagogy, or an over-estimation of technology's potential (or a blend of the two).

---

[12] See his post-discussion summary in Nichols, M. (2003). A theory for eLearning. *Educational Technology & Society*, 6(2), 1-10, available at http://ifets.ieee.org/periodical/6-2/1.html, checked 19 June 2004.

Most experts agree with Nichols that the selection of an educational approach or philosophy is more important than the selection of the technology itself.

On the other hand, effective pedagogical decisions can make simple technologies extremely useful. There are multiple examples to illustrate this point, such as the many communities of practice around the globe who collaborate and communicate effectively through simple text-only listservers. Nichols argues that, as a general rule, it will be breakthroughs in teaching practice that will make eLearning more useful and not breakthroughs in technology, though the latter could provide opportunities for the former. From this follows that eLearning should be driven by instructional designers not technologists. It will be the innovative educators who will maximise eLearning and ensure its further development.

6.5.1 Engagement Theory

An earlier attempt to create a conceptual framework for technology-based learning and teaching was undertaken by Kearsley and Shneiderman (1999). They developed the so-called 'Engagement Theory', which emerged from their own experiences with teaching in electronic and distance education environments. The fundamental idea underlying the framework is that students must be meaningfully engaged in learning activities through interaction with others and worthwhile authentic tasks. While in principle, such engagement could occur without the use of technology, Kearsley and Shneiderman believe that technology can facilitate engagement in ways that are otherwise difficult to achieve.

Although not directly derived from other theoretical frameworks for learning, engagement theory has much in common with several of them. For example, its emphasis on meaningful learning is very consistent with constructivist approaches. Its emphasis on collaboration among peers and a community of learners, can be aligned with situated learning theories.

Engagement theory is presented as a model for learning in technology-based environments which brings together many elements from past theories of learning. The major premise is that students must be engaged in their training activity in order for effective learning to occur. The theory posits three primary means to accomplish engagement:

4. an emphasis on collaborative efforts
5. project-based assignments, and
6. non-academic focus.

It is suggested that these three methods result in learning that is creative, meaningful, and authentic. The role of technology in the theory is to facilitate all aspects of engagement. The authors feel that the use of e-mail, online conferencing, Web databases, groupware, and audio/videoconferencing significantly increases the extent and ease of interaction amongst all participants, as well as their access to information. The vast array of software tools available for analysis, design, planning, problem-solving and making presentations enable students to do sophisticated and complex tasks.

Kearsley and Shneiderman believe that engagement theory represents a new paradigm for learning and teaching in the information age, which emphasises the positive role that technology can play in human interaction and evolution. Many aspects of their theoretical approach can be found in the pedagogical models introduced below, which provide input for much of the writing and thinking on how to implement successful eLearning initiatives.

6.5.2 Pedagogical models

In recent discussions, various pedagogical models have emerged in the attempt to put the 'learning' back into eLearning and thus overcome the technocentric approach that has long dominated eLearning discourse. As noted in the Literature Survey, the emphasis on technologies has gradually given way to a focus on users, context and community. There is an increasing awareness that the use of new multimedia technologies and the Internet will only improve the quality of learning if it is accompanied and supported by sound pedagogical arrangements, scenarios and methods. The choice of eLearning tools should therefore reflect rather than determine the pedagogy of a course; how technology is used is more important than which technology is used (cp. Nichols 2003).

If eLearning is a means to education, then it can be applied in accordance with varying pedagogies. In the following, four pedagogical models will be presented in more detail, namely:

- Authentic learning context
- Collaborative learning
- Progressive inquiry learning
- Problem-based learning

The selection is based on two factors: firstly, their relevance to the training objectives and environment in the Project and, secondly, the fact that they are closely connected to some of the issues that have been found to affect user interface design for eLearning materials, namely:[13]

- Motivation problems
- Relating learning simulations to real-world experiences
- Device independence and usage contexts
- Meeting the needs of diverse user groups
- Up-front information
- Feedback.

---

[13] See Quinn "Why people can't use eLearning. What the eLearning sector needs to learn about usability." Published in *Frontend* on 5th June, 2001. Available at
http://infocentre.frontend.com/downloads/Why_people_can't_use_eLearning.pdf, visited on 30.6.04

6.5.2.1 Authentic learning context

According to this model an authentic task, activity, or goal provides learning experiences that are as realistic as possible, taking into consideration both the age and competence level of the students as well as environmental constraints such as safety and resource availability. Educators utilising this idea attempt to replicate the intellectual dilemmas of those working within and across disciplines, requiring students to acquire and apply knowledge for problem-solving in similar ways to experts in a particular field. They consider preparing students for a world in which knowing how to locate and use appropriate information to solve real problems infinitely more important than merely committing content facts to memory.

Complexity is part of authenticity. Simplified situations often provide naïve or erroneous understandings that inhibit future learning and refinements. Advocates of this approach argue that students exposed to a situation in its natural complexity create richer knowledge structures that are more useful for future application and learning. The knowledge is more likely to be used in new situations when acquired in a problem-solving student-centred mode rather than in a factual-knowledge teacher-directed mode. The complex learning contexts require students to solve interconnected sub-problems. Because students are usually encouraged to work together to solve these complex problems, they are exposed to multiple perspectives in an environment that gives them an opportunity to test out their ideas, solutions and processes.

The model recognises that authenticity is a relative concept. For example, learning a language during an internship in a country by living with native speakers might be the most authentic context but it is not a realistic learning context for all people. But learning a language by using the language supported by authentic documents (radio, video, news, ...) in classroom conversation is more authentic than reciting sentences from a text. The concept of authenticity exists on a continuum.

6.5.2.2 Collaborative learning

The importance of collaborative interactions in the learning process has been underlined by many researchers in reference to a socio-constructivist approach. Group and interpersonal interactions involve the use of language in the re-organisation and modification of one's personal understandings and knowledge structures, so learning is simultaneously a private and a social phenomenon.

There is a positive correlation between the occurrence of collaborative interactions and learning performances for complex tasks which demand high level cognitive operations (decision, argumentation...). In contrast, for tasks which require low level cognitive operations (procedure, algorithm...) individual learning might even be more efficient.

Learning in groups does not automatically imply collaborative learning. For collaborative learning to effectively exist, certain components are required. These include, for example the existence of positive interdependence, when students perceive that they are linked with fellow students in such a

Theories and Models in eLearning

way that they cannot succeed unless the others do (and vice versa), or that they must co-ordinate their efforts with the efforts of their colleagues or crew members to complete a task.

6.5.2.3 Progressive inquiry model

The origins of this model are to be found primarily in the research into primary and secondary level education. The aim is often to model and facilitate inquiry in natural sciences, e.g., scientific visualisation technologies to support inquiry-based learning in the geosciences or project-based science and laboratory work. Many of the general ideas behind discovery learning can also be considered to belong to this background. But it may be argued that in more vaguely defined domains, the process of inquiry takes different emphases than in well-defined scientific fields. In the latter, problem-setting, hypothesis testing, systematic data collection and analysis demand more attention, whereas in more vaguely defined domains – such as the social sciences or philosophy – efforts at theory building, conceptual clarification, argumentation and critical evaluation are more often the focus of activity – although the overall structure of the inquiry cycle is rather similar.

In progressive inquiry, students' own, genuine questions and their previous knowledge of the phenomena in question form a starting point for the process, and attention is drawn to the main concepts and principles of the domain. Although students are learning existing knowledge, they may be engaged in the same kind of extended knowledge-seeking processes as scientists and scholars. From a cognitive point of view, inquiry can be characterised as a question-driven process of understanding. The aim is to explain the phenomena in a deepening question-answer process, in which students and teachers share their expertise and build new knowledge collaboratively with the support of information sources and technology.

6.5.2.4 Problem-based learning

Koschmann (1996), a leading proponent of problem-based learning, defines it as "a collaborative, case-centered, and learner-directed method of instruction" (p. 96). Collaborative instruction is seen as a method by which teachers and students abandon their traditional classroom roles in favour of more collegial roles as collaborating learners; case-centred instruction is described as the class of methods in which teaching is devoted primarily to the study of authentic problems or cases.

If this definition is adopted, problem-based learning can in fact be considered the most comprehensive model and the one most suited to the adult learners in our Project. As will be shown in the empirical case study, the relationship between instructor and trainees often bore far more resemblance to a peer-based relationship than to traditional roles and the process of learning had more in common with an exchange of knowledge and experience based on a discussion of particular cases or emergencies than a transfer of knowledge to individual learners.

Another feature which makes this model particularly relevant to this study is the importance attributed to the concept of breakdown, which corresponds to the concept of contradiction in activity theory, where it is seen as the driving force behind development. Koschmann refers to the

American educational philosopher Dewey, who in his work "Logic: The Theory of Inquiry" (1938/1991) states, "Inquiry begins with an indeterminate situation", that is a situation that is experienced as problematic or a psychological state of puzzlement. According to Koschmann, Dewey's description of inquiry is based on an orientation to the way meaning is constructed within a socially and materially defined situation. The meanings of words, actions and observations are therefore not fixed, but instead continuously re-negotiated within the contexture of active inquiry. In Koschmann's view, Dewey's notion of inquiry can be helpful in developing a clearer specification of problem-based practice.

6.6 Theoretical approaches, concepts and models and the role of culture

As mentioned in the Introduction, explicit references to cultural factors are rare in the literature on learning and teaching, whether it be face-to-face or distance learning. On the whole, educational scientists appear to regard cross-cultural learning situations as fundamentally problematic. Kearsley, for example, one of the leading figures in the eLearning field, regards linguistic diversity as an obstacle to communication to be overcome with automatic translation programs.

It is only in the sociocultural approaches derived from Vygotsky and Leontiev that culture plays an important role. Wells and Claxton (2002), the editors of *Learning for Life in the 21st Century*, see culture as shaping the development of individual minds.

> As people work, play and solve problems together, so their spontaneous ways of thinking, talking and acting – the ideas that come to mind, the words they choose and the tools they make use of – embody an accumulated set of cultural values and beliefs that have been constructed and refined over previous generations. (2002:3)

According to them, all interactions between people involve using, adapting and mastering cultural tools. It is above all through language, the most eminent semiotic tool, that shared meaning is made and experience structured and organised as knowledge.

> Human development depends on the appropriation and reconstruction by each individual of the resources that have been developed within their culture. (Wells and Claxton 2002:7)

The use of the term 'reconstruction' implies that people not only absorb their cultural heritage, but they may also transform it. This view, they argue, encourages teachers to see students as modifying and improving valued resources from the past rather than simply equipping them with these resources.

Sociocultural theories also recognise the diversity among learners, juxtaposed with an increasing convergence of political and economic organisational structures and homogenisation in global educational provision. However, this diversity, regardless of whether it is due to differences in age, cultural background, gender, language or class, is not seen as a problem to overcome, but as a resource for educational activity. The challenge consists in reconciling being responsive to students' ideas and needs whilst ensuring that they acquire the skills that are culturally valued or part of a standard curriculum.

Recently, those educational scientists whose work is rooted in the sociocultural approach have turned to adult and even distance learning, instead of focusing above all on early childhood and elementary school years as they had done in the past. They emphasise that all learning situations are indelibly social and cultural, including the learning that takes place in a virtual environment.

> The recent proliferation of electronic forms of communication, and the opportunities for solitary and distance learning to which these technologies have given rise, have re-emphasized the extent to which CHAT [cultural historical activity theory] thinking is fundamentally 'cultural' rather than necessarily 'social'. (Wells and Claxton 2002:10)

But for distance learning, new forms of social and emotional support are required to support students in their learning endeavours. Northedge from the British Open University (2002) sees students not as absorbers of bodies of knowledge, but as self-selected apprentices to a scholarly discourse community or community of practice. To become a member of a particular community of practice, they have to be able to connect their own pre-existing knowledge to the discourse and worldview associated with it. He also argues that the empathy with which the writers of eLearning materials offer the student bridges, and thus facilitate their making such connections, is of critical importance for success.

6.7 Cultural models and their application to learning and teaching

Hofstede, the doyen of intercultural studies, whose cultural dimension model has influenced much of the writing on internationalisation, localisation and globalisation in HCI studies, is also one of the most influential and frequently cited authors in the field of eLearning. He is one of the few authors to have paid particular attention to cultural differences in teaching and learning. In his article "Cultural Differences in Teaching and Learning" (Hofstede 1986), he draws on three sources of information:

- his earlier research on differences in work-related values in over 50 countries which led to his famous 4-Dimension Model of Cultural Differences,

- his and others' personal experiences in teaching and learning in different cross-cultural situations and
- his experiences as a parent of children attending local schools abroad.

His investigations and experiences lead him to identify four main problem areas:

- differences in the social positions of teachers and students,
- differences in the relevance of the training content,
- differences in cognitive ability profiles between the populations from which teacher and student are drawn and
- differences in expected patterns of teacher-student interaction

Differences in student-teacher interaction are listed with reference to the four dimensions of Individualism *versus* Collectivism, large *versus* small Power Distance, strong *versus* weak Uncertainty Avoidance, and Masculinity *versus* Femininity.[14]

Hofstede concludes that the burden of adaptation in cross-cultural learning situations should be placed primarily on the trainer and advocates increasing awareness and sustained effort on both sides to cope with the perplexities which can arise as a result of cultural differences.

The author does not discuss online learning and teaching, which at the time of writing was non-existent or at least still in its infancy. Indirectly, however, Hofstede's ideas do have implications for computer-mediated learning and instruction, especially 'problem areas' 3 and 4, i.e. cognitive ability profiles and differences in mutual role expectations between teacher and student. These address the training process and issues of interaction rather than the content of training. Some of the studies discussed below have tried to translate the differences identified by Hofstede into the design and evaluation of eLearning programmes and environments.

Apart from Hofstede's cultural dimension model, the work of Galtung and Clyne also has had an impact on investigations of cultural factors in learning and teaching. Based on his experience of working with scholars from different cultural backgrounds, Galtung (1981) distinguishes four approaches when comparing the structure, culture and intellectual style prevailing in different societies: saxonic, teutonic, gallic and nipponic. By intellectual style he understands basic culturally-bound models of thought and behaviour shown mainly by intellectuals. Despite the clear allusions of these designations, Galtung stresses that these styles are not to be identified directly and exclusively with patterns of behaviour and thought in specific countries. According to him, teutonic style is not only found in Germany, it is also prevalent in Eastern Europe and Russia. Similarly, gallic style is said to prevail not just in France, but also in Italy, Spain, Portugal and Latin America.

---

[14] The cultural dimension of "Time Orientation" was added at a later stage (Hofstede 1991).

The saxonic style – characterised by its focus on the production of hypotheses – can be found among both British and American scholars as well as those from former Commonwealth countries. Finally, nipponic style, with its non-linear, circular thought pattern and argumentation structure, is said to dominate academia in Japan and other East Asian countries.

The features of the different styles are analysed according to four dimensions, i.e. paradigm analysis, generation of hypotheses, theory construction and peer review. Despite its strength in producing hypotheses, the saxonic style is said to be weak on theory formation and paradigm analysis. In contrast, the teutonic and gallic styles are considered strong on theory formation and paradigm analysis, but weak on formulating hypotheses, with the gallic style attributing great significance to the elegance of expression.

Clyne (1991), in his analysis of student essays, has identified several categories with regard to cultural discourse and scientific writing styles. He argues that different conventions exist in different cultures when it comes to the composition of written discourse. When comparing English and German essay writing, he found several areas of cultural difference, namely:

- linearity *versus* digressivity,
- focus on form *versus* content,
- textual symmetry,
- abstractness *versus* concreteness of content,
- content structure,
- continuity in argumentation,
- integration of data,
- use of advance organisers and
- writer responsibility *versus* reader responsibility.

According to Clyne, these conventions need to be observed when composing teaching materials and developing learning software. In addition to those of Hofstede, Galtung and Clyne, the cultural models of Trompenaars and Hall also play a role in some studies investigating the influence of cultural factors on learning and teaching.

Hofstede's dimensions and the categories proposed by Galtung and Clyne can certainly provide useful signposts for observing student behaviour in the classroom, but they are unlikely to prove adequate to account for the complex web of interactions which are characteristic of training situations. As already pointed out in the chapter on Defining Culture, Hofstede's concept of culture as essence and difference has limited explanatory value for this study or for current research in general. In the world of international computer networks and multinational teams notions such as language, nationality and ethnicity no longer play the kind of role they used to. Even though cultural orientation systems acquired early in life – Hofstede calls them the 'collective programming of the mind' – have a strong influence on human beings, they are insufficient when it comes to accounting for behaviour differences in training situations where factors such as occupation, status or corporate culture also play a major role. Furthermore, when it comes to the actual design of products like Web-based training modules, a precise understanding of work objectives and work contexts is required.

6.7.1 Applying cultural models to eLearning studies

One of the few papers dealing with the impact of cultural factors on computer-mediated learning has been written by Chase and his co-authors (Chase et al 2002). In their article "Intercultural Challenges in Networked Learning", they describe phase one of a longitudinal, large-scale analysis of intercultural communication factors in the information and communication technologies elements of international, networked learning courses. The authors identify differing communication patterns and instances of miscommunication in online exchanges between culturally diverse learners and online facilitators. Subsequently, using ethnographic methods and informal discourse analysis, they proceed to cluster these instances and try to develop a taxonomy of intercultural communication problems.

The relevant cultural dimensions which are expected to vary among participants and therefore to be examined include: task *versus* relationship focus, attitudes toward authority, masculinity *versus* femininity, group *versus* individual focus, attitudes towards time, high *versus* low context communication patterns (Hall 1990) and universalism *versus* particularism (Trompenaars 1993).

This has resulted in a list of relevant topics such as online culture, face-to-face *versus* online issues, identity creating, technical issues, participant expectations, academic discourse *versus* 'stories' and time. The authors emphasise that their results are preliminary and more detailed investigations and analyses are still to be conducted. They have identified the major themes, but eventually aim to develop a framework for analysing the use of information and communication technologies in eLearning contexts across cultural boundaries.

A highly relevant recent publication, which has already been mentioned under 5.6 The use of cultural models in human-computer interaction, is by Kamentz and Womser-Hacker (2003). It deals with the impact of culture on the development and graphical design of eLearning systems. The authors compare existing German and American Web-based training courses in terms of usability, presentation of content and didactic approach, whilst at the same time also examining cultural aspects of computer usage.

They assume that the development of teaching aids and learning processes in different cultural contexts can be described and analysed using the cultural categories proposed by Galtung, Clyne and Hofstede, but for the purposes of their analysis of the differences in cultural and scientific discourse, elected to base themselves on Hofstede's cultural dimensions, in particular:

- individualism *versus* collectivism
- uncertainty avoidance and
- power distance

and examine their implications for the design of learning settings and the interaction between teachers and students. To this end, they evaluated a total of eight existing learning modules and tutorials and conducted interviews with 74 students from different countries about their learning approaches and computer usage.

They conclude that given the considerable differences that have emerged in the course of their study, user-oriented design of interactive learning environments definitely requires cultural adaptation and that their study should contribute to defining culture-specific requirements for the design of Web-based training courses.

Interestingly enough, it is primarily in the literature on intercultural or international user interface design that suggestions can be found on the influence cultural factors might exert on the design of instructional materials or learning environments.

Marcus (2000), for instance, believes that Hofstede's dimension of individualism *versus* collectivism may affect the aspect of motivation, which plays a major role in eLearning. Another point relevant for the design of eLearning materials is rhetorical style: whereas users from individualist cultures might prefer controversial or argumentative speech and tolerate or even encourage extreme claims, those from collectivist cultures will abhor such usage and be in favour of official slogans and subdued hyperbole and controversy. He also believes that countries with long-term time orientation would prefer content focused on practice and practical value rather than on truth and certainty of beliefs. Similarly, they would prefer relationships as a source of information and credibility rather than rules.

Marcus explicitly addresses the issue of educational Websites by asking whether the objectives of distance learning change what can be learned in individualist *versus* collectivist cultures and whether these sites should focus on tradition, skills, expertise or earning power. How should online teachers or trainers act – as friend or gurus? he asks (2000:25). As the Web continues to develop globally, answering and exploring these questions will become a necessity, not an option for successful theory and practice, he argues. It is an argument that so far does not seem to have found much echo in the eLearning scientific community.

6.8 Activity theory as an integrative framework

In their introduction to *Learning for Life in the 21st Century*, the editors Wells and Claxton (2002) note that a growing number of educators, among them the contributors to the volume they compiled, are finding inspiration in the work of Vygotsky, one of the originators of the Cultural Historical Activity Theory. They concede that what they prefer to call 'sociocultural theories' to education might at first sight appear complex, but their "fundamental insights are relatively simple, and they are of profound relevance to educational practitioners and policy-makers" (p. 2).

Advocates of activity theory in the educational realm tend to stress different aspects of theory than HCI researchers. Although they agree on the main tenets – such as the key role played by artefacts for mediating actions, the social, situated nature of all activity and the importance of collaboration and interaction – more emphasis is placed on semiotic or meaning-making tools such as language, the concept of 'zone of proximal development' (or ZPD) and on recognising diversity among learners. One of the most fundamental tenets, i.e. that all action must be understood in its situated complexity, is shared by both fields. When applied to learning and teaching, educational scientists influenced by sociocultural theories, therefore advocate that decision-making, e.g. on curricular aspects, has to be responsive to the needs and concerns of students and the communities to which they belong.

Wells and Claxton see activity theory primarily as a theory of human development that regards human societies and their individual members as mutually constitutive. It is impossible therefore to introduce a new learning method into a culturally and historically constituted situation – like a classroom – and expect a common outcome. They argue that this is even more true of a multicultural classroom or training environment, where both trainees and instructors have different identities and values whose origins lie in cultural, linguistic and status differences as well as in individual experience and background. Like Holden (2002), they regard such diversity as a potential resource to exploit rather than a problem to be overcome or a source for divisive practices.

They also stress the need to look beyond individual actors to the communities to which they belong and the environments in which people learn. The 'higher mental functions' do not develop simply as a result of individual learning or intellectual maturation. Rather, they argue, they depend on mastering the use of culturally created semiotic tools such as language or scientific methods or procedures which occur interactively. They warn that collaboration should not be equated with agreement and conformity, even though consensus might be the ultimate aim. Expressing and considering alternative ideas, experiences and opinions may be essential if genuine understanding is to be achieved. As in HCI, disagreement and contradiction can act as a source of development because learners are encouraged to move beyond ways of acting and thinking repeated from the past.

The concept of 'zone of proximal development' originally developed by Vygotsky is related to this as it implies transcending individual constraints and limitations. It is through the support of more experienced others that we expand the scope of what we can learn and achieve. The concept extends to eLearning, where it is generally referred to as 'scaffolding' or 'guided participation', i.e. assisting the learner through feedback, explicit explanations of procedures or detailed guidelines.

It has already been noted that an increasing eclecticism can be observed when it comes to selecting pedagogical models or didactic approaches for designing teaching aids or setting up learning environments. Depending on the objectives, target groups or training contexts, different elements are chosen from the different models or approaches. Activity theory looks like the ideal umbrella to cover all of them.

7 The Quest for a Theoretical Framework

In this chapter, I draw together the different threads of the various investigations, i.e. the attempts to define the concept of culture and identify cultural factors in both HCI studies and eLearning, the importance of context, as well as the role played by community in computer-mediated systems and activities and the different theoretical approaches, models and concepts that have been proposed to examine and analyse these issues.

The quest for a theoretical framework that has been underlying the discussion of the various theoretical approaches, models and concepts has led to the adoption of activity theory as an overarching framework. After briefly explaining why I consider the activity approach more appropriate than other approaches such as distributed cognition, which has also been proposed as an integrated research framework, I present the main tenets, concepts and principles of activity theory.

Finally, I discuss various studies that have applied activity theory in the field of HCI and eLearning as well as studies focusing on collaborative and community aspects. These publications testify to the flexibility and adaptiveness of the approach, whilst at the same showing how it can be combined with other approaches to tackle the complex issues involved in interdisciplinary research on computer-mediated activities.

7.1 Introduction

As pointed out in the introduction to this thesis, this study requires a theoretical framework that can supply concepts and models both for human-computer-interaction as well as for learning and teaching in a virtual environment. At the same time, the framework has to accommodate human, social and cultural factors, cope with computer-mediated collaboration processes and take into account the environment or context in which activities such as learning and teaching occur.

Identifying a theoretical framework that meets this challenge represents an original contribution to research in these fields and should also have important practical implications since this combination of requirements represents a scenario that will be increasingly common in the future.

Product and application designers increasingly have to take into account the greater cultural diversity of their user groups, which is why ways to investigate and assess cultural influences on application usage or interaction between trainers and students are required when drawing up requirements for computer-based systems. The research carried out for the Project was based on the assumption that the planning, development and design of computer-based systems or applications is always informed by culturally influenced expectations and assumptions about future user groups and use contexts.

I started out with the problem of defining culture and the different approaches for determining the influence of cultural factors and elected to opt for a pragmatic approach and look for the aspects that are relevant to the issues involved in this particular investigation rather than a universally valid definition. For investigating the influence of cultural factors on the development of eLearning programs or user interfaces, it can therefore be assumed that such a system not only has technical features, but has also been developed on the basis of mental models that are implicit carriers of specific systems of values shaped by culture. These mental models are acquired through interaction with the environment. They do not determine the behaviour of individuals but point to probable modes of perception, thought and action.

The discussion of the various theoretical models and concepts prevailing in HCI and eLearning studies in the previous chapters has shown that not all of these take cultural factors into account. When cultural factors are taken into account in HCI studies, they tend to be restricted to their impact on interface design. In the case of eLearning, it is only in the sociocultural approaches to education that cultural factors are given any explicit consideration.

Although the number of studies that apply activity theory to investigate and/or analyse the sort of complex interdisciplinary issues that were associated with the Project is still very small, the chances are very great that this will improve considerably in the years to come.

7.2 Reasons for choosing activity theory as a theoretical framework

Firstly, activity theory provides a response to the search for a common nomenclature and thus fills a lacuna that has been pointed out by many experts such as Honold (2000) for usability engineering and Nichols (2003) for eLearning. They both deplore the lack of a consistent terminology and common framework, which, in their opinion, can seriously impede the comparison and communication of findings. Similarly, Nardi (1996), a leading advocate of activity theory, believes that one of its greatest contributions is to provide disparate approaches to HCI with a common vocabulary for issues emerging in the study of technology usage.

At the same time, activity theory does not deny the usefulness of models or concepts derived from other approaches. Leading advocates of activity theory, such as Kaptelinin and Nardi (1996), for instance, regard it as a backbone for analysis which can be enriched by distributed cognition's focus on representations and the commitment to grappling with the complex flux of everyday activity found in the situated action perspective. Honold (2000), too, stresses that fertile concepts from cognitive psychology, such as the concept of mental models, should not be ignored, even when activity theory is selected as a meta-approach. After all, they do not contradict activity theory, but on the whole do not take sufficient account of the contextual framework.

Actually, distributed cognition also claims to provide an overarching research framework. Hollan, Hutchins and Kirsh (2000), for example, propose this approach as a new foundation for HCI which integrates the merging dynamic of interaction. Indeed, distributed cognition not only has a great deal in common with activity theory, it also shares many of its tenets, as is confirmed in Nardi's (1996) comparison of three approaches to HCI – situated action, distributed cognition and activity theory. Nardi sees activity theory and distributed cognition as very close in spirit and believes that the two approaches will "mutually inform, and even merge, over time" (1996:89).

In distributed cognition, digital objects can encode information about their history of use, which can be compared to the idea of 'crystallised knowledge' in activity theory. According to Bannon and Bødker (1991), artefacts embody their own historical and cultural development. To understand a phenomenon means to know how it developed into its existing form. In addition, distributed cognition, like activity theory, holds that cognitive activity is constructed from both internal and external resources and that the meanings of actions are grounded in the context of activity. It is not enough to know how the mind processes information, it is also necessary to know how the information to be processed is arranged in the material and social world.

In contrast to 'classical' cognitive theories, distributed cognition moves the boundary of the unit of analysis beyond the individual brain, thus situating the individual as an element in a complex cultural environment. The focus task is no longer confined to the desktop, but instead reaches into a complex networked world of information and computer-mediated activities. Cognition is therefore no longer isolated or separate from culture.

Unlike earlier versions of cognitive ethnography, which focused on the knowledge of individuals and largely ignored action, distributed cognition as proposed by Hollan, Hutchins and Kirsh (2000) focuses on events. Thus, both activity theory and distributed cognition help to overcome the shortcomings of the information processing models of cognitive science, which have long held sway in educational and HCI research.

As is true of both situated action and activity theory, distributed cognition favours ethnographic methods for capturing the interactions between people and artefacts and supplements them with experiments. But, unlike the situated action approach, it attempts to free research from the particulars of specific cases and to discern the important constituents of interactions among people and between people and material artefacts. Distributed cognition therefore allows generalisations and has actually begun to generate a body of comparative data on patterns of work practices in various domains such as aviation or navigation.

The problem with the distributed cognition approach is that although an outline exists as an integrated research framework, it has not yet been implemented. Hollan, Hutchins and Kirsh (2000) admit that the integrated research programme they have sketched out is ambitious in scope and in the skills demanded and describe the efforts they have embarked on in this respect. But they concede that they will need to await the results of their various ventures to better understand the consequences of putting into practice what they propose.

In contrast, activity theory's usefulness to HCI and eLearning studies has been demonstrated in a considerable body of literature as is illustrated below (7.5) by the studies that have applied activity theory to a variety of issues in both fields.

Another factor that has tipped the balance towards activity theory is the virtual absence of models or concepts derived from distributed cognition in the field of eLearning. In contrast, many recent publications in eLearning are permeated with activity theoretical concepts and models. It is in the sociocultural approaches to learning and teaching, in particular, that activity theory has shown it can provide the conceptual tools for addressing the difficult issues of consciousness, intentionality, culture and history.

But, most important of all, it is its extreme adaptiveness that makes activity theory applicable to virtually any human activity involving the use of tools, be they physical artefacts or mental constructs. For the purposes of this study, the fact that it is being and has already been applied to a wide variety of issues related to learning, teaching and to HCI, and that this has resulted in the production of a corresponding body of literature has also been a decisive factor.

Given the above-mentioned reasons, activity theory appears to be the most comprehensive framework available for tackling the issues connected with this research. Activity theory can be used to derive models and concepts for analysing social and cultural structures and processes in usability engineering as well as computer-mediated learning and teaching. It offers a unified framework for the study of computers as tools to achieve certain goals and for exploring issues connected with these activities. Furthermore, it is not restricted to activities performed by individuals, but includes those carried out by groups and organisations.

Activity theory can influence the methodology, analysis and evaluation used and thus help in obtaining valid and reliable data relevant to real-life contexts and organising field observations. Furthermore, it can make an important contribution to the development of design support tools. The design of any new interactive system, be it for learning, training or information management, involves the design of a new activity – either at an individual or an organisational level. Activity theory can be used to develop a representational framework that will help designers to capture current practice and build predictive models of activity dynamics. The availability of such conceptual tools could assist designers to achieve appropriate design solutions, particularly in the early phases of design.

In addition, activity theory appears capable of coping with subject matters that are subject to rapid change. When current methods, styles and standards in HCI or eLearning are applied, results are inevitably obsolete soon after they have been formulated. Activity theory puts results both in the context of basic, invariant principles underlying human activity and thus provides a better chance for creating a theoretical framework with predictive potential.

Advocates of activity theory in the educational realm tend to stress different aspects of the theory to HCI researchers. Although they subscribe to the same essential tenets, such as the key role played by artefacts for mediating actions, or the assumption that all action must be understood in its situated complexity, more emphasis is placed in educational circles on semiotic or meaning-making tools such as language.

7.3 The main tenets and principles of activity theory

Activity theory is a set of basic principles that constitute a general conceptual system rather than a highly predictive theory. It dates back to the 1920s, when its main ideas and premises were first developed by the Russian psychologists Vygotsky, Rubinshtein, Leontiev and others. However, it was not until the iron curtain came down in the late 1980s that this approach became more widely known and gained recognition in the West.

In the meantime, a thriving tradition of activity theory has developed in HCI studies in Scandinavia, with its main proponents including authors such as Kuutti (1992), Bannon and Bødker (1991) and Engeström (1996). Growing interest in activity theory and HCI can also be noted in other European countries, the United States (e.g. Nardi 1996), Canada and Australia (e.g. Gould, Verenikina and Hasan 2000). Increasingly, activity theory is seen as a foundation on which HCI researchers might base common discourse and from which they can derive tools for design and evaluation (see e.g. Kaptelinin and Nardi 1999).

In educational research, activity theory now supports studies in developmental psychology and educational technology around the world. As discussed in the chapter on learning and teaching theories, its concepts and models have been incorporated into the sociocultural approaches to education, in particular.

It can therefore be said that activity theory provides a broad framework for describing the structure, development and context of computer-supported activities and, as a dynamic and systemic approach, it can cope with rapidly changing environments. People are seen as embedded in a sociocultural context with which they actively interact. This complex interaction of individuals with their environment is called activity and is regarded theoretically as the fundamental unit of analysis.

Tool mediation is one of the most important concepts of activity theory. Tools or artefacts refer to culturally produced means for changing the environment and achieving goals. Humans are seen as continually changing tools or artefacts or creating new ones. From an activity theory perspective, computer technologies and the Internet, for example, are considered tools.

The following sections introduce the basic principles of activity theory, including the hierarchical structure of activity, object-orientedness, internalisation and externalisation, tool mediation and development.

7.3.1 Hierarchical structure of activity

As its name suggests, the principal unit of investigation and analysis in activity theory is the activity of human beings. An activity is determined by the particular motive or objective to be fulfilled by performing that activity, i.e. it is directed at an object which motivates activity and gives it a specific direction.

Each activity can be divided into individual actions that are carried out to achieve specified objectives. Actions are regarded as conscious, and different actions may be undertaken to meet the same goal. These actions are then implemented by operations that take account both of the objectives and the context, in other words the actual situation (e.g. Bedny and Meister 1997; Kaptelinin 1996).

Operations do not have their own goals; they instead provide for an adjustment of actions to current situations. The boundary between operations and actions is fluid. For example, when we first learn to drive a car, our use of the gear lever is most likely to be a conscious action. As time goes by, however, it becomes more and more automatic and therefore turns into an operation. This results in a hierarchical structuring of activities: the objective of an activity can be achieved in various situations by various actions and operations. Furthermore, activity theory holds that the constituents of activity are not fixed, but can change dynamically as conditions change.

7.3.2 Object-orientedness / Environment

The principle of object-orientedness states that human beings live in a reality that is objective in a broad sense: the elements that constitute this reality not only have properties that are considered by the natural sciences to be objective, they have socially and culturally defined properties as well. To understand an activity, one must understand how artefacts mediate the activity within the cultural context in which the activity is situated.

Human beings are seen as embedded in a physical, cultural and social context, which is taken to be a social construction of reality. The social construction is considered equally as 'real' and has a similar impact on people's actions as the physical environment.

The Quest for a Theoretical Framework

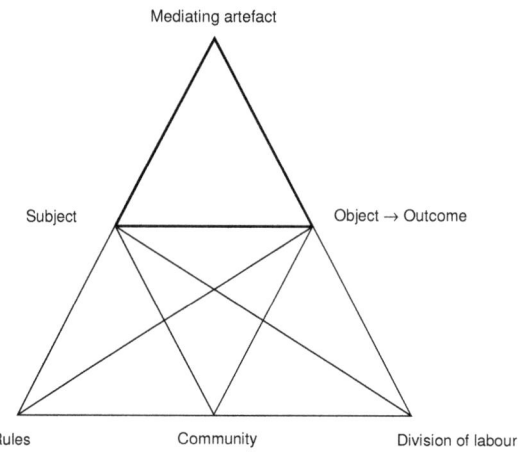

Figure 1: Extended Activity Triangle

The figure above illustrates the complex relationships between elements of an activity: Artefacts such as tools and symbol systems (e.g. language) mediate between the individual (the subject of the activity) and the individual's purpose (the object of the activity). Engeström (1987) has extended this basic 'triangle' consisting of Subject, Object and mediating Artefact to show that the individual is part of a Community and the activity is influenced by his or her participation within this community. In addition to that, the subject's relationship to the community is mediated by formal and informal Rules (also called 'praxis'). In turn, the community's relationship to the object of the activity is mediated by the Division of labour – how the activity is distributed among the members of the community.

7.3.3 Internalisation/externalisation

Activity theory emphasises the interdependence of (internal) cognitions and (external) activities. It is thus based on the premise of a unity of human activity and human consciousness. According to Kaptelinin (1996), mental processes arise from the internalisation of external actions. On the other hand, such processes manifest themselves when we perform external actions and check our conceptions against reality. From this follows the assumption that cognitions cannot be understood if they are analysed separately from external activities, because the two transform into each other.

Internalisation is the transformation of external activities into internal ones. Internalisation provides a means for people to try potential interactions in reality without performing any actual manipulation with real objects (mental simulations, imaginings, considering alternative plans, etc.).

Externalisation transforms internal activities into external ones. Externalisation is often necessary when an internalised action needs to be "repaired," or scaled. It is also important when a collaboration between several people requires their activities to be performed externally for reasons of coordination.

Meister and Bedny (1997) express this idea as follows and at the same time point out the difference to the cognitive approach:

> Here we should emphasise an important distinction between the theory of activity and the area of cognitive psychology called "human information processing". A basic principle in the Theory of Activity is the unity of cognition and external practical behaviour. Psychological processes are considered to be a system of mental actions or operations with ideal objects. Basic to the development of these objects are external material actions. Accordingly, internal mental actions cannot be correctly understood in isolation from external practical actions. (p. 2)

7.3.4 Mediation by tools

Activity theory postulates that human activity is mediated by tools or artefacts, i.e. human action is performed by way of a tool which acts as a mediator between humans and the environment. Tools can be external or physical such as knives, hammers or technical systems (e.g. computers), or internal or psychological such as language, heuristics, concepts or theories. Artefacts also include rules such as guidelines regarding usability, quality standards, industry-specific standards, document templates, e-mail protocols, hardware and software platforms. All qualify as artefacts, i.e. as things created by humans.

It is not always possible to make a clear distinction between humans, artefacts and the environment, - or in other words - between what belongs to humans and what belongs to the external system. Artefacts may even be considered to be functional organs, for example when a blind man uses a stick to find his way around. The extent to which a tool corresponds to a functional organ depends on its concrete use (Kaptelinin 1996).

Tools are created and transformed during the development of the activity itself and carry with them a particular culture. Consequently, the use of tools is an accumulation and transmission of social knowledge. Tool use influences the nature of external behaviour and also the mental functioning of individuals.

Artefacts can be characterised as 'crystallised knowledge', i.e. operations are developed in the use of one generation of technology are later incorporated into the artefact itself in the next generation. Thus, to learn something about the present shape and use of an artefact, any analysis of practices with that tool must also be supplemented by a historical analysis of the artefact.

Before we can produce the optimum design for these tools, we therefore need to investigate both how they are used and the context in which this use takes place. This fact is also stressed by Bannon and Bødker (1991), who consider the importance of a particular artefact to come from its practical social use.

7.3.5 Development

As previously pointed out, it is important to examine individual and historic lines of development beyond the situation at a given moment. "According to activity theory, to understand a phenomenon means to know how it developed into its existing form" (Kaptelinin 1996:109). The crystallised knowledge mentioned above may manifest itself in visible objects (tools, buildings etc.) and in institutions and rules that regulate the relationship between the individual and society.

Culture and its historical roots play a central role in activity theory. The cultural and social determinedness of activities and associated tools (such as the factors of production, but also semiotic tools such as language) and the reciprocal influence of cultural-historic structures and activities are constant themes in literature influenced by activity theory.

As explained in the previous chapters, this is why activity theory is a particularly useful instrument for conceptualising culture as a factor in both usability engineering and learning and teaching. It defines not only the interaction between humans, tools and the environment but also the interaction between individual activity and its sociocultural context.

Moreover, culture is not just a factor of an activity: the activity itself also influences the formation of sociocultural structures. This dynamic aspect goes well with the process-based nature of computer-based activities such as usability engineering and corresponds to the reality of technical and social developments. Activity theory provides models and concepts for recording and analysing cultural-historic structures and processes in both the HCI and eLearning fields.

In activity theory, development not only forms an object of study, it also acts as a general research methodology. The basic research method in activity theory does not involve traditional laboratory experiments, but instead focuses on the formative experiment, which combines active participation with the monitoring of developmental changes in the study participants. Ethnographic methods that track the history and development of a practice have come to be recognised as the most appropriate for this purpose.

As discussed above, contradiction is seen as a source of development. The concept refers to all insufficient or inadequate matches, e.g. between the different goals or elements required to achieve a goal. Contradictions can manifest themselves in problems or system faults and breakdowns. These, in turn, can motivate people to change existing practices.

These basic principles of activity theory should be considered as an integrated system, because they are all associated with various aspects of the whole activity. In a systematic application of any of these principles, it will eventually become necessary to engage all the others.

7.4 Unifying concepts

As already mentioned, the **concept of breakdown or contradiction** plays an important role in activity theory, where it is regarded as a source of development and a force for change. Whereas educational scientists tend to talk about differences and disagreements, HCI researchers prefer terms such as 'breakdown', 'critical incident' or simply 'contradiction'. In a similar vein, the American educational philosopher John Dewey (quoted by Koschmann 1996) states, "Inquiry begins with an indeterminate situation" or, in other words, a situation that is experienced as problematic or a psychological state of puzzlement, and thus encourages problem-based learning.

In both areas, i.e. HCI and learning and teaching, contradiction can act as a source of development as it encourages learners or system designers to go beyond accepted ways of acting and thinking repeated from the past. This concept has much in common with the idea of cultural standards developed by Thomas (1996), who suggests focusing on 'critical incidents' in intercultural interactions as a method for determining cultural standards in a particular domain or application.

Development is a central concept in activity theory and features in most studies that apply it. However, its meaning can vary considerably depending on its context of use. On the one hand, development refers to the sociohistorical and cultural roots of an artefact. On the other hand, it can also refer to the developmental context relevant, for instance, to both the individual level and the group or organisational level when analysing computer use. According to Kaptelinin (1996), an introduction of new technologies causes new tasks to emerge which can trigger unpredictable structural changes. One solution consists in supporting users in customising the system according to their current needs. However, users often require substantial assistance even in formulating their own needs. From this Kaptelinin (1996) concludes:

> Thus, a conceptual analysis of the basic factors and regularities or organizational development is needed to predict this development and to provide an efficient use of information technologies.
> (p. 111)

Another aspect of development that is discussed in literature on activity theory, yet is by and large neglected by the cognitive approaches is the development of individual expertise. It is difficult to account for the qualitative changes that cognitive skills undergo in the process of development by means of cognitive models of skill acquisition.

In educational research, scientists tend to talk about the 'zone of proximal development', which implies transcending individual constraints and limitations. It is through the support of more experienced others that we expand the range of what we can learn and achieve. The concept also extends to eLearning, where it is generally described as 'scaffolding' or 'guided participation', i.e. assisting the learner through feedback, explicit explanations of procedures or detailed guidelines on how to solve a problem.

Closely related to the ideas of development and guided participation is the concept of **community**, which can serve to cast light on collaborative processes in both HCI and eLearning. Community is an important part of activity theory and belongs to the basic structure of an activity. A mediated relationship exists between both subject and community and between community and object. In the case of the former, the relationship is mediated by rules, whereas in the latter, it is mediated by division of labour. These relationships are critical to the context of the activity and the development of tools and software to assist in mediating the relationships.

Bannon and Bødker (1991) describe this concept as 'praxis', which implies the shared collective ensemble of ways, methods and traditions of doing things, such as building houses, for instance. In general, several carpenters will in the process divide the work up between themselves, but each of the people who share a praxis may change it by developing new ways of doing things.

According to the participation metaphor discussed in the eLearning section, learning is seen as embedded in a web of relations and networks of distributed and shared activities. Expertise develops dynamically through participating in an expert culture or community of practice that 'owns' cultural knowledge of the domain and provides access to cultural tools and practices (e.g. Lave and Wenger 1996; Wenger 2000).

This means that the concept of community goes beyond individual skills and knowledge to also account for the development of new tools over time. The inclusion of community aspects makes activity theory an appropriate basis for addressing important aspects of HCI such as computer-supported cooperative work.

Finally, through the concept of community a bridge, can be established to current research on communities of practice. Although Etienne Wenger (1998), one of the leading figures in this field, does not explicitly refer to activity theoretical concepts or models, it is easy to detect common points.

Communicative ability is closely linked with meaning, which, according to Wenger, "exists neither in us, nor in the world, but in the dynamic relation of living in the world" (p. 54). "Participation" is defined as "to take part in or share in some process or activity", "reification" as "to treat [an abstraction] as substantially existing or as a concrete material object... the process of giving form to our experience by producing objects that congeal this experience into 'thingness'"(p. 58). Examples of this could include drafting a law, composing a memo with new rules or procedures or developing a tool. In other words, a community of practice engages in the negotiation of meaning through the processes of participation and reification and, at the same time, forms the environment in which these processes can occur.

The fact that meaning is to be found in the "dynamic of living in the world" evokes the activity theory concept of shared social meaning brought about by activity. Wenger's concept of doing or activity in a social and historical context is also quite consistent with activity theory's cultural historical roots.

Last but not least, Wenger's discussion of participation and negotiation of meaning has a great deal in common with Holden's concept of interactive translation, which is seen as a form of cross-cultural work in which groups negotiate common meanings and common understandings.

Another link to the conceptual world of KM is provided by the principle of **internalisation and externalisation** which has much in common with the knowledge spiral as described by Nonaka and Takeuchi (1995). This becomes especially clear when looking at the activity checklists developed by Kaptelinin and Nardi (1997) and the questions associated with the various principles of activity theory. In the checklists, they prefer to refer to 'Learning, cognition and articulation' in order to describe the internal (mental) and external components of activities which can transform into each other or in Nonaka and Takeuchi's terms: where tacit knowledge is transformed into explicit knowledge.

One of the questions in the Learning category addresses what could be termed as 'tacit knowledge':

> Knowledge about target technology that resides in the environment and the way this knowledge is distributed and accessed. (Kaptelinin and Nardi 1999:37)

In order to coordinate individual and group activities, this knowledge has to be externalised, which might need "support of problem articulation" (*ibid*).

According to Nonaka and Takeuchi, tacit knowledge is personal, context-specific and therefore hard to formalise and communicate. Explicit knowledge, on the other hand, is transmittable in formal and systematic language. The interaction between the two types of knowledge brings about what is referred to as the four modes of knowledge conversion, i.e. socialisation, externalisation, combination, and internalisation:

	To tacit knowledge	To explicit knowledge
From tacit knowledge	Socialisation	Externalisation
From explicit knowledge	Internalisation	Combination

Table 1: Spiral of knowledge creation

The process of knowledge creation is based on a double spiral movement between (a) tacit and explicit knowledge and (b) individual-group-divisional and corporate-wide levels.

7.5 Discussion of relevant publications

As is shown in the following discussion of studies that have applied activity theory, it proves to be the only theory which is not only relevant but has also been applied to both usability and eLearning, thus testifying to its great versatility and flexibility. In a few cases, publications straddle both fields, for example the contribution by Bellamy (1996).

In addition, I have included publications related to computer-supported collaborative work since communal and collaborative aspects now play an increasingly important role in both HCI and EL studies.

The discussion also shows that activity theory is not an exclusive theory, but can be combined with other approaches. Spagnolli, Luciano and Daniele (2002), for instance, complement activity theory with situated action, whereas Guribye and Wasson (1999) combine three approaches – activity theory, distributed cognition and situated action – in the evaluation of telelearning scenarios. Others, such as Honold (2000), recommend using activity theory as a meta-approach to serve as an umbrella for theoretical models derived from other theories.

7.5.1 Application of activity theory to HCI studies

Context and Consciousness (1996), a collection of articles edited by Nardi, provides an excellent introduction to activity theory as a theoretical alternative to the cognitive science approach that still dominates much of HCI research. In addition to discussing the basics of activity theory, Nardi compares three different approaches to studying human actions in context: activity theory, situated action and distributed cognition. She delineates their distinct characteristics and concludes with an argument for activity theory.

The second part of the book examines some practical applications of activity theory by giving research examples as well as providing clear suggestions for research methodology. Christiansen, for instance, uses ethnographic research methods to explore how computers become mediating tools for activities in the Danish National Police. The author argues that activity is both culturally and socially formed by the individuals in a community of practice and by their respective roles within that community.

Another highly relevant contribution comes from Nardi herself in which she reflects on how the use of activity theory would have been a better choice in analysing her data from a field study of slide makers. The aim of the study was to ascertain whether end-users prefer task-specific or generic application software. By comparing the analysis of data before and after the application of activity theory, the reader gains a good insight into the 'added value' of activity theory as an analytical tool.

Bødker introduces the concepts of 'breakdown' and 'focus shift'. As can be seen from the discussion of the article written by Spagnolli, Luciano and Daniele (2002) below, the concept of breakdown provides a link to Thomas' cultural standards approach in which critical incidents are used for capturing cultural differences in the use of technology. Studying breakdowns or critical incidents when designing or evaluating the use of applications enables us to identify usability problems.

As already mentioned, Spagnolli, Luciano and Daniele (2002), who share a background in psychology, have applied the concepts of activity theory to the analysis of breakdowns. In their study, they combine activity theory with the situated action approach to analyse breakdowns in a virtual library. They place action at the centre of the analysis of users' interaction with the technology to examine it from a structural and organisational level.

The authors argue that combining the two approaches allows us to concentrate on the breakdowns occurring during users' interaction with the virtual environment and study these episodes from a situated point of view. They proceed in two steps: identifying and collecting breakdown episodes, recording them on videotapes and then analysing their structure, circumstances and development including any possible actions taken to remedy the problem.

Gould, Verenikina and Hasan (2000) have applied activity theory to the design of interactive Web-based information systems. They base themselves largely on the principles outlined by Leontiev (1978), but adapt certain concepts to make them more suitable for usability. Instead of referring to internalisation/externalisation, they use the term "structure and dynamics of interaction", while "mediation and development" is referred to simply as "development" and object orientedness is replaced by "environment". Gould and his co-authors attribute the appeal of activity theory to its broad view of the human psyche and behaviour and its well-structured categories for analysis.

Another HCI researcher who recommends activity theory because of its adaptiveness to a wide range of domains is Honold (2000) in her work on intercultural usability engineering. She argues that activity theory can serve as the underlying approach for tackling the complex interdisciplinary issues that arise in the design of products for different cultures.

Also worth mentioning is yet another example of the wide applicability of activity theory, namely a study in which it is used for drawing up requirements for work situations. Turner, Turner and Horton (1999) show how activity theory concepts can be used to structure and organise ethnographically acquired data on work processes in a software house, or more specifically, a video record of a series of meetings held between a group of software designers. This work by Turner, Turner and Horton expands on the design checklist drawn up by Kaptelinin and Nardi (1999) and adapts it to their specific context and goal, i.e. requirements definition.

7.5.2 Application of activity theory to eLearning studies

Although Bellamy's article is published in Nardi's compilation of articles on activity theory and HCI (1996), his contribution is more relevant to the field of eLearning. Bellamy discusses the development of educational software, which in his eyes should act as a mediator between learning and change in an educational community.

He concludes by describing three principles for designing educational environments conducive to educational change, namely

- authentic activities
- constructive environments and
- collaborative environments.

These principles are very much in line with recent developments in the field of pedagogical and didactic research, where approaches emphasise the importance of authentic scenarios or cases and collaboration with peers for problem-solving.

In their paper, Guribye and Wasson (1999) apply activity theory to evaluate collaborative telelearning scenarios. They describe the conceptual framework used to identify patterns of collaboration and for their framework, draw on three different, yet interrelated approaches, namely activity theory, distributed cognition and situated action.

According to the authors, when taken together these approaches constitute a rich framework for describing, evaluating and analysing collaborative telelearning scenarios. They all underscore the need to look at real activities in real situations and include the context in studies of human activity. Furthermore, they can all be subsumed under the heading of a socio-cultural perspective, which regards learning and thinking as phenomena that cannot be studied in isolation, but as processes situated or distributed in an environment.

The different approaches, so it is argued, each emphasise slightly different elements of the framework: Situated action highlights the emergent, contingent nature of human activity and the way it grows directly out of the particularities of a given situation. Distributed cognition takes a cognitive system composed of individuals and the artefacts they use as a unit of analysis and emphasises the distributed nature of cognitive processes and the role played in them by different artefacts. Finally, activity theory, whilst emphasising the mediating role of artefacts, also takes into account their particular culture and history and focuses on the institutional and cultural elements involved in the learning activity.

The exploratory study was carried out within a project concerning the design and use of artefacts in collaborative telelearning scenarios aimed at teacher training programmes. The authors analyse four different scenarios:

1. The use of a software tool for collaborative working
2. the design of a textual artefact involving inter-cultural simulations (students from Norway, German, Spain and France develop a treaty)
3. the collaboration of Norwegian students with students from 13 other countries to contribute solutions to contemporary problems facing the EU
4. the design of a visual artefact to be used in teaching a subject of choice

The four collaborative telelearning scenarios vary with respect to:

- actor characteristics (e.g. within a common community vs. disparate and heterogeneous cultural backgrounds; similar vs. highly divergent levels of know-how and skills etc.)
- aspects of the learning activity (e.g. text-based vs. visually based; well-defined vs. ill-structured or vague learning tasks and goals etc.)
- the kinds of artefacts they have access to (e.g. the artefacts provided in the various internet environments), and
- the kinds of artefacts they are to design (e.g. textual or visual)

The findings of their study are expected to further our understanding of how instructors, students and other learning facilitators organise their learning and work.

7.5.3 Activity theory and collaborative and communal aspects

According to Engeström, Engeström and Suntio (2002), an activity theory framework can be used both as a tool for implementing new teaching-learning approaches and for analysing the processes of computer-supported collaboration in general. In their paper "From paralysing myths to expansive action: building computer-supported knowledge work into the curriculum from below", they analyse how the teaching staff at a school engaged in an attempt to change their instructional practices by means of incorporating information and communication technologies in pilot curriculum units. The technical tools, however, were subordinate to the pedagogical ends – or in activity-theoretical terms – the tools were not confused with the object.

In a very practically oriented study, Marlin Cluts (2003), describes and analyses the introduction of computer-supported cooperative work software in a bank combining the concepts of activity theory with the principles of communities of practice. In his opinion, together the two approaches provide a useful model for understanding the evolution of the meaning of artefacts (tools, rules, division of labour), the sharing of artefacts by communities and the role of conflicts and contradictions as a source for change and development.

According to Cluts, users need to experience results within the activity system and social structure of the community to establish meaning and credibility. Based on the tenet that "Meaning is in doing" (2003:150), usage is considered the main prerequisite for the credibility of artefacts and is therefore considered an indicator for success, especially the use of the software by key people within a firm. Cluts believes that the accomplishment of work depends more on a process of local negotiation than on written procedures. This is in agreement with the work carried out by Suchman (1987), who has demonstrated that the accomplishment of tasks is rarely a reflection of the structure imposed but rather a matter of negotiated meanings and the everyday practice of the people involved.

Cluts concludes by deriving a series of implications for software design. These correspond largely to standard practice, e.g. considering the context of use and integrating all artefacts within an activity system. Activity theory provides a unifying theory and embeds additional meaning into his guidelines. The case study is a good illustration of how concepts from activity theory can be applied to cooperative work and how contradictions can serve as a source for development.

> Using the activity theory framework, artefacts were created to mediate relationships between subject, object, and community in the form of tools, rules, and division of labor. They often evolved out of conflict in the activity system where a disruption forced the actors to create a new artefact. In this study, integration led to adoption of a new, more powerful tool (Transcend). ... In essence the evolution and adoption was a natural function of the activity system. (p. 148)

Furthermore, people use other people's visible activity to frame their own goals. If people see everyone else using a particular software application, they will feel they ought to do so as well.

7.6 Summary

Given the above-mentioned reasons, activity theory appears to be the most comprehensive framework for this study. From it, we can derive models and concepts for analysing social and cultural structures and processes in usability engineering as well as computer-mediated learning and teaching. It offers us a unified framework for looking at the use of computers as tools to achieve certain goals and for exploring issues connected with these activities. Furthermore, it is not restricted to activities performed by individuals, but also includes those carried out by groups and organisations.

As illustrated by the discussion of relevant publications, activity theory provides models and concepts for analysing cultural, social and historical structures and processes for a whole range of computer-mediated activities: from the design of user interfaces, the drafting of system requirements to the analysis of telelearning scenarios. Furthermore, it can accommodate both contextual and collaborative aspects and do justice to the rapid changes typical of fields characterised by dynamic development.

Despite its great adaptiveness and usefulness, concepts derived from other approaches must not be discarded, in particular in instances when they can cast light on specific issues or aspects involved in the research. As illustrated by some of the above studies, concepts such as that of mental models derived from cognitive psychology or the attention to contextual detail propagated by the situation action approach, are in any case not in contradiction with activity theory, but can serve as useful complements. The combination of activity theory and communities of practice, can also yield fruitful synergies. By defining the characteristics of a community of practice and their practical constellations, the concept of community in activity theory can be expanded to enable an exploration of additional dimensions.

As already pointed out in the Introduction, the inadequacy of existing models and the lack of a general framework to accommodate all the diverse aspects of my research, finally led me to 'discover' and explore activity theory as a possible alternative. In the following chapters I shall discuss its methodological implications and show how it can be used for analysing the empirical data that were gathered during the Project using a variety of methods such as participant observation, interviews and focus group discussions.

8 Methodology

Based on the discussion in the previous chapters, I will now discuss the methodological implications of using activity theory as a theoretical framework and explore the ways in which it can be combined with concepts and models from other theoretical approaches. In concrete terms, the following questions relating to methodology will be investigated:

- To what extent can activity theory serve as an analytical tool for the empirical data gathered?
- To what extent can activity theory integrate the role of cultural factors in the development of computer-based information or eLearning systems?
- To what extent can activity theory cope with contextual and collaborative aspects in such systems?
- How well can activity theory be combined with other methods to deal with these issues?

The chapter begins with a discussion of the various methodological approaches suggested for identifying and capturing cultural factors, especially with regard to their impact on usability. The next section deals with the checklists that have been developed to present the theoretical structure of activities in an operational form. They are practical tools to provide guidance and structure for empirical work and should be used in combination with other methods and techniques.

This is followed by an examination of ethnographic methods for research into computer-based systems in general, their benefits and their (supposed) limitations such as lack of generalisability or data formalisation.

After that, the different methods applied in usability engineering and testing are discussed, among them heuristic evaluation or expert reviews and end-user tests.

Grounded theory is explored as a method for data analysis that aims less at verifying existing hypotheses, but more at conceiving new models which can be derived from the available data. Finally, I summarise the methodological approach adopted for this study by taking the extended 'activity triangle' proposed by Engeström (1987) and adapting it to the research issues of this study.

8.1 Introduction

Since it was only in the course of my research associated with the Project that I 'discovered' and was subsequently able to explore activity theory as a potential tool for tackling the complex interdisciplinary issues connected with the objectives of the Project, activity theory has mainly been applied to make sense of and interpret the data gathered. It was not possible to apply its concepts and models in the earlier stages of the research, e.g. in the analysis of the requirements for the KM and eLearning systems or the preparation and conducting of the usability tests and expert reviews.

Nevertheless, it turned out that my own methodological procedure corresponded to a great extent to the methodological requirements that can be deduced from applying activity theory, which can be summarised as follows:

- Adequate duration of study
- Contextualisation
- Methodological mix

I was fortunate enough to be able to spend several months in the field, giving myself an opportunity to immerse myself in the environment where the KM and eLearning systems to be designed as part of the Project would be used. This allowed me to see what people were actually doing as opposed to what they said they were doing and gain an in-depth understanding of the instructors and trainees, as well as the organisation and the broader context within which they work.

As already indicated in the Introduction, the emphasis on context in both HCI and eLearning has encouraged the use and incorporation of techniques, methods and theories from anthropology, sociology and social psychology, to name but a few of the disciplines which deal with social, human and cultural factors. Ethnographic techniques such as participant observation and interviews have become widely recognised as a good way of gathering contextual information. They are best suited to capturing the social, cultural and historical environment in which computer-mediated activities such as information management and eLearning occur.

The ethnographic approach is also in line with the emphasis of activity theory on the embeddedness of any activity in a cultural-historical continuum and a wider social context. The trainees on the campus are just one set of participants in the activity of training, which also encompasses instructors, designers, interpreters, management representatives, colleagues from subsidiaries, etc. Therefore, it is necessary to address not just the classroom and training activities but all aspects of the training situation. Only by understanding and designing for the complete training situation is it possible for technology to produce the expected benefits.

8.2 Defining culture-specific usability requirements

Culture-specific requirements can be defined as requirements, which are due to culturally determined differences between user groups and usage situations. They are shared by a specific group rather than being the result of individual subjective idiosyncratic preferences. They can change over time and can be identified by observing critical incidents that occur in the use of a technical product or application.

Honold (2000), who recently conducted a study on Intercultural Usability Engineering, has noted the lack of guidance available for identifying culturally influenced usability requirements. She thus echoes the frustration already voiced by Cushman and Rosenberg (1991):

> Obtaining useful design information relating to foreign cultures is difficult. No comprehensive book on the subject has been written. Chapanis' (1975) *Ethnic Variables in Human Factors Engineering* provides a good discussion on several selected topics, however. Perhaps the best way to obtain information about foreign culture is to work with people who live in the countries where the product eventually will be marketed. (p. 30)

On the whole, guidelines are limited to the area of software engineering and their validity and usefulness are questionable because they tend to be both restricted to case studies and lacking in theoretical foundation. This state of affairs is not conducive to building up a repository of design knowledge that extends beyond specific cases in specific countries.

8.2.1 Adapting evaluation methods to different cultures

Research conducted by Helfrich and others (1993) has yielded the following criteria for assessing the quality of evaluation methods for different cultures:
1. Equivalence of constructs or conceptual equivalence
2. Equivalence of operators or operational equivalence
3. Equivalence of the assessment process or evaluation equivalence

Ad 1)
When designing and interpreting questionnaires as well as assessing interfaces, it is important to make sure that the concepts used have the same meaning. Attention also has to be given to the relative weighting of a concept. Visual attractiveness, for instance, might be rated more highly in a particular culture.

Ad 2)
According to the researchers, it is necessary to check not only the underlying concept, but also to what extent it is functionally equivalent in other cultures. The quality of a user-interface design cannot be judged by the number of negative or positive comments, for example, because criticism is expressed differently in different cultures. People from Asian countries are far more reluctant and cautious that their Western counterparts when it comes to expressing direct criticism.

Ad 3)
To ensure there are no systematic distortions between cultural groups, all participants in a study should be equally familiar with the contents of the user interface.

It appears to be generally accepted that questionnaires can only be applied in a specific language area and have to be adapted to different cultures. Adaptation goes far beyond simple translation, since quite often not even the rating scales can be transferred (e.g. in China people are not used to discrete rating scales).

8.2.2 Cultural factors in the research environment

The immersion into the field raised the question regarding the definition of culture and thus, the issue of culture-specific requirements. Whereas I set out by attempting to define criteria for dividing the trainees into culturally homogeneous user groups according to country of origin, my observations in the classroom and the many interviews conducted with both instructors and trainees challenged the conventional, anthropologically inspired bias towards equating culture with ethnic or national identities.

In the course of the interviews, as well as in the usability testing, it gradually emerged that organisational and professional cultures played a more important role than ethnic or national background. For instance, pilots' expectations and needs regarding the user-friendliness of computer interfaces differed from those of mechanics. Also, they had different learning styles, interaction patterns and information retrieval and processing behaviours. Thus, a different perspective on cultural factors emerged which had closer links with organisational culture (e.g. military *versus* civil background) and profession (mechanics *versus* pilots).

This perspective does not contradict Honold's view of culture as an organising principle according to which user groups are composed and which influences use situations. Culture is seen not as an 'additive', but as a system of orientation which forms the basis for the use of a product and thus has an impact on use requirements. The difference consists in the fact that in the context of the training campus, professional culture was more important as an organising principle than national identity or language.

Similar observations were made in a study of interdisciplinary collaboration (physicians and social workers), conducted by Abramson and Mizrahi (1996) who found that the most difficult obstacles to overcome were those defined by ingrained professional opinions and power structures.

After examining the various approaches to identifying and communicating the influence of cultural factors on usability and eLearning and the ways these could be taken into account in the design of computer-based systems, I finally reached the conclusion that – at least as far as the training objectives and target groups in our Project were concerned – the hypotheses derived from the various cultural models were not born out by the results.

The inadequacy and lack of explanatory value of most existing cultural models has been confirmed by other experts, such as Ford and Gelderblom (2003) or Griffith (1998), who have applied these models, especially the cultural dimension model developed by Hofstede. The results of the study carried out by Ford and Gelderblom showed that the usability of the interfaces increased for all users if features (purportedly) accommodating uncertainty avoidance, masculinity, collectivism and high power distance were incorporated into the design. The authors therefore conclude that "there is insufficient evidence to support the hypotheses that any of the four cultural dimensions tested significantly affect human performance...". (p. 228)

Similarly, Griffith, who makes use of Hofstede's cultural dimensions to predict and possibly explain difficulties in technology transfer and implementation across cultural boundaries, found that – contrary to her expectations based on Hofstede's cognitive model – Bulgarian users were equally or even more ready to challenge the experts than American users.

However, none of the authors seem prepared to question the underlying approach to culture, preferring instead to attribute the 'deviations' to factors such as the special circumstances of a society in transition (Griffith) or suggest making changes to the design of the experiment and refining the research questions (Ford and Gelderblom).

In the field of eLearning, the role of cultural factors is even more complex since little research has been carried out to date on how different learning and teaching traditions, cognitive styles or discourse models might translate to a virtual environment and how they might affect the usability of eLearning environments or materials.

Kaptelinin (1996) concedes that activity theory has adopted a narrower view of culture than the cultural-historical approach developed by Vygotsky (1978). In Kaptelinin's view, activity theory was influenced by the example of the natural sciences and therefore tended to interpret reality in formal schemes (see Zinchenko 1996). This tendency, however, does not apply to the sociocultural approaches discussed in the section on eLearning, since these are rooted in the Vygotskian tradition, which encompasses culture, values, motivation, emotions, human personality and personal meaning. Thus, the limitation of activity theory described by Kaptelinin can be offset by incorporating elements from the sociocultural approaches.

Another limitation of activity theory according to Kaptelinin is represented by virtual realities because here the tool mediation perspective – otherwise one of the most important advantages of activity theory – can in fact restrict the potential application of activity theory concepts. Kaptelinin argues that:

> [...in virtual realities] the border between a tool and reality is rather unclear; information technology can provide the user not only with representations of objects of reality but also with a sort of reality as such, which does not obviously represent anything else and is intended to be just one more environment with which the individual interacts. (p. 64)

To overcome the problem, he suggests enriching activity theory's basic principles with new ideas from the cultural-historical tradition or other related approaches. Indeed, as is demonstrated in the discussion of studies that apply activity theory to learning and teaching, virtual realities fall well within their scope of investigation.

Spagnolli, Luciano and Daniele (2002), for instance, have applied the concepts of activity theory to the analysis of breakdowns in a virtual library. Guribye and Wasson (1999) use them to evaluate collaborative telelearning scenarios and Northedge from the British Open University (2002) argues that, for distance learning, new forms of social and emotional support are required to assist students in their learning endeavours.

8.3   Methodological tools of activity theory

Various checklists have been suggested for presenting the theoretical structure of activities in an operational form and for moving from theory to practice. The checklists are practical tools to provide guidance and structure for empirical work that take account of context. Kaptelinin and Nardi (1999) distinguish between checklists for design and checklists for evaluation, providing a common preamble to both and sample questions for use in each of the checklists. They cover four basic principles of activity theory, namely:

1. hierarchical structure of activity, which includes identifying the goals of actions,
2. object-orientedness or environment-activities are seen as directed towards an object,
3. internalisation/externalisation – activities include both internal (mental) and external components which can transform into each other, and
4. mediation and development. (p. 33)

The first section, "Means/ends (hierarchical structure of activity)", covers the means and ends of the use of the 'target technology', i.e. the extent to which the technology facilitates and/or constrains the achievement of a users' goals and its impact on provoking or resolving conflicts between different goals.

The second section, "Environment (object-orientedness)", identifies the objects involved in target activities and encompasses the social, cultural and physical aspects of the environment in which the technology is used.

The third section, "Learning, cognition, and articulation (internalisation/ externalisation)", addresses the fact that computer systems should support both the internalisation of new ways of action and the articulation of mental processes, when necessary, to facilitate problem solving and social coordination.

The last principle, "Development", is concerned with the transformations of the foregoing components. It refers to the mediation carried out by a tool, which can be both material (e.g. a computer) and mental (e.g. a tool for thinking) in nature. It includes an analysis of the history of the relationship between subject and object, which in turn can help to reveal the main factors influencing the transformation process or development and thus anticipate their effect on the structure of target activities.

The checklists are a conceptual tool for identifying the most important factors influencing the use of computer technologies in a particular setting. They can help to relate experiences in the field to activity theory concepts, think about the kinds of data to be gathered and formulate the questions to be asked. Key concepts are illustrated by sample questions suggesting avenues for thought and exploration.

According to the creators of the checklists, the application process can be organised into three phases:

1. Analysis of observational data, i.e., to indicate potential problems, formulate requests for further analysis and provide some suggestions on how the problem can be solved.

2. Introduction of the checklists. Their general structure corresponds to the four main perspectives on the use of the technology to be evaluated:

    - focus on the structure of the user's activities
    - focus on the structure of environment -- integration of target technology with requirements, tools, resources and social norms of the environment;
    - focus on the structure and dynamics of interaction - internal *versus* external components of activity and support of their mutual transformations with the target technology;
    - focus on development - developmental transformation of the above components as a whole.

3. Adjusting of the checklists to the specific purposes of the analysis and selection of an appropriate methodology for conducting empirical research.

When applying the checklists to data already gathered in the course of the research – as was the case in this study – they can help structure the observations made. They can also serve as a tool for reflection by counteracting any personal or professional bias which might lead to overlooking certain issues.

Kaptelinin and Nardi emphasise that their checklists should be used in combination with other techniques. These can thus be rendered more effective because the checklists help to identify the relevant issues that need to be covered in an interview or to make sure that important problems are not overlooked.

The following sections discuss some of the methods and techniques that can be used in combination with activity theory:

1. for capturing the context or the environment in which the target technologies are to be applied and
2. for usability testing.

In the first case, the methodology consists mainly of ethnographic methods such as interviews and participant observation or field work. In the second case, it is made up mainly of expert reviews and end-user tests. Focus group discussions were carried out throughout the duration of the Project both to elucidate particular aspects of the environment and to validate the results of the user testing.

8.4 Ethnographic research in an activity theory framework

Ethnographic research is rooted in the discipline of social and cultural anthropology. Here, ethnographers are required to spend a significant amount of time in the field, immersing themselves in the lives of the people they study (Lewis 1985). There are many different schools or types of ethnography e.g. the holistic school that regards empathy and identification with the social grouping under study as a necessity, the semiotic school of thought (see e.g. Geertz 1966) that emphasises the search for symbolic forms and an understanding of the 'webs of significance' which people weave within a cultural context, or 'critical ethnography', which sees ethnographic research as an emergent process, involving a dialogue between the ethnographer and the people in the research setting.

Vygotsky (1978), Engeström and Escalante (1996), Bødker (1991) and other advocates of activity theory have argued that the ideal data for an application of activity theory consist of longitudinal ethnographic observation, interviews and discussion in real-life settings, supplemented by experiments.

More recently, ethnographic research has even become an accepted method in the field of information systems, where information systems research is increasingly focusing on the social and organisational contexts of information systems (e.g. Avison and Myers 1995 or Myers 1997). As far as HCI studies are concerned, some of the early groundbreaking work was carried out by Suchman (1987) in her study of the problems of human-machine communications.

Since then, ethnographic methods have become more widely recognised and used in the study of information systems in organisations, including the development and management of information systems (e.g. Orlikowski 1991; Randall and Bentley 1994). Ethnography is also discussed as a method whereby multiple perspectives can be incorporated in systems design (Holzblatt and Beyer 1993).

Studies inspired by an ethnographic orientation focus on building up an understanding of work or activity as it occurs *in situ*. This orientation eschews employing a prior theoretical stance to the subject of study, preferring to focus instead on the details of the situation-specific practices through which participants achieve their work (or activity).

Nardi (1996), also advocates conducting ethnographic studies to investigate problems of HCI in the social matrix in which they occur, provided such studies are underpinned conceptually by activity theory. In her article "Reflections on the Application of Activity Theory", she discusses how she and her colleague gained valuable insights into the use of slide-making software by means of ethnographic research, but how the lack of a suitable conceptual vocabulary cost them unnecessary time and effort.

> We struggled to find a means of expressing and explaining what was emerging in the slide data, when all along the data would have made immediate sense if we had applied the notions of subject, object, action, and goal from activity theory. (p. 244)

8.4.1 Problems with ethnographic research

Among the common criticisms levelled against ethnographic research are:

- lack of generalisability
- personal bias of the researcher
- difficulty in data formalisation.

8.4.1.1 Lack of generalisability

Ethnography assumes no *a priori* framework that orders data. As a result, we are faced with a lack of cumulative research results which could translate into best practice models or concrete guidelines. This is a common criticism of ethnographic research and situated action approaches, also voiced by Nardi (1996). Although Nardi believes that ethnographic studies are well suited to capturing the context of activities, she argues that they lead to in-depth knowledge only of particular contexts and situations. In her view, the move towards ethnographic and participatory design methods to discover and capture real, everyday activity risks yields ad hoc descriptions cast in situation-specific terms.

> Abstraction, generalization and comparison become problematic. An ethnographic description, although it may contain much information of direct value for design and evaluation, remains a narrative account structured according to the author's own personal vocabulary, largely unconstrained and arbitrary... This leads to a disappointing lack of cumulative research results. (Nardi 1996: 10-11)

Some critics go even further and argue that it is impossible to develop more general models from just one ethnographic study.
Whilst I can appreciate the difficulties mentioned above, I disagree with the view that ethnographic data resist any generalisation. The lack of generalisability is probably more of a limitation due to the novelty of this approach in the field of HCI or information system research than as a limitation per se. Over time, as more ethnographic studies are completed in the HCI field, it should become possible to build up a repository of design knowledge based on extraction and comparison of findings across studies. But, as already pointed out by Honold (2000), the underlying structures have to be made transparent.

8.4.1.2 Researcher bias

Every researcher approaches his or her topic with a particular set of preconceptions and inclinations, which tend to be influenced by his social, cultural and educational background, professional experience and a host of other factors that might be relevant in the particular environment in which the research is conducted and to the issues under investigation. The researcher's own computer usage or attitude to modern technologies, for instance, might play a role when exploring usability aspects or collaborative work in a virtual environment.

Proneness to subjectivity, however, can be offset by safeguards such as audit trails, peer group reviews or involvement of external observers. In the framework of my research, one way of counteracting bias or distortion was to discuss and crosscheck findings with other experts, e.g. interpreters or colleagues who had been exposed to both cultural environments. They can serve as a useful correcting agent and help throw light on puzzling data.

8.4.1.3 Formalisation of data

Ethnographic research relies on the researcher immersing him or herself in the work and the environment in which the study is situated. As a consequence, the resulting data tends to be both copious and unstructured. Some authors even claim (e.g. Randall and Bentley 1994) that data thus acquired resists formalisation.

This difficulty, however, can be overcome by appropriate procedures of documentation such as taking notes, writing up field notes and interview responses, preparing data for analysis etc. as will be discussed in the following chapter. Thus, it becomes possible to provide a structured description of the work which might lend itself to a variety of uses including the requirements definition. To achieve this, all that is required is a powerful, richly descriptive organisational framework with links to the systems design process.

Each of the methods of ethnographic research mentioned so far – interviews with individuals, focus groups, participant observation or field research – have their benefits and shortcomings, as is illustrated in the following table:

	Interview	**Focus group**	**Participant observation**
Naturalness of setting	Low: structured by interviewer	Medium: structured by moderator, but group interaction reflects normal social situations	High: Some data, however, are difficult to collect in the field.
Choice of topic	Interviewer determines topic.	Moderator determines topic which is usu. modified through group interaction.	Not relevant for the individuals/groups or situations under study.
Interpretation of data	After data collection; contradictions / different views become visible only afterwards.	Contradictive views are voiced and validated through group interaction. Data are interpreted in the course of and after being collected.	Data collected are interpreted afterwards independent of people observed.

Table 2: Comparison of ethnographic research methods

There is no single best way of collecting data and each method of course aims at obtaining valid and reliable data. The actual method chosen will depend on the nature of the research questions posed and the specific questions to be asked of respondents. Interviews can be highly structured, following strict interview schedules or self-administered questionnaires, or they can be less structured and designed to resemble natural conversations. In both cases, the interviewer must avoid being directive or judgmental.

8.5 Usability testing

Before discussing the different methods and techniques, I would like to describe the different possibilities of interaction between artefacts and human beings. The following scenarios of inter- and cross-cultural interaction can be distinguished:

1. A technical product or application is used by people from different cultural backgrounds.
2. A technical product or application is defined and developed within a particular culture and used in another.
3. Focus on man-machine interaction in different cultures followed by a comparison (comparative cultural study) of results.

In my own research, scenario one is most relevant as both the KM and the eLearning system were to be used by people from a range of different cultural backgrounds. Scenario two is also of interest, since the applications are to be developed largely by a French/German company, but will then be used worldwide. Scenario three basically aims at a comparison of the different cultural approaches to user interface design, which was not one of the objectives of this study.

For practical reasons, the usability tests – both with experts (e.g. instructors, designers) and end-users (i.e. the trainees) – related to scenario one because it was not feasible within in the framework of the Project to conduct tests outside the Training Campus in France.

8.5.1 General principles of usability

The ISO Standard concerning usability (9241-11:1998 Ergonomic requirements for office work with visual display terminals (VDTs) – Part 11) defines it as "the extent to which a product can be used by specified users to achieve specific goals with effectiveness, efficiency, and satisfaction in a specified context of use". Effectiveness is defined as the extent to which a goal or task is achieved. Efficiency corresponds to the amount of effort required to accomplish a goal. Satisfaction is described as the level of comfort that users feel when using a product and the acceptability of the product to users as a vehicle for achieving their goals. In other words, a product or service can be considered highly usable if it can be used as a tool to accomplish a set of defined tasks easily and with a minimum of frustration.

As already discussed in the chapters Literature Survey and Recent Developments and Theories and Models in Human-Computer-Interaction, a common consensus now seems to exist in usability testing whereby target user groups should be involved in the development process at all stages. Users have come to occupy the central ground in the planning and designing of an application.

The purpose of usability testing in software applications is to evaluate user interfaces by simulating concrete usage. The tests can focus either on measurable performance (time needed for particular tasks, frequency of errors etc.) or on identifying the mental models underlying any difficulties and misunderstandings that can occur in the use of a product or application. Such difficulties can relate both to the design of an interface and the functionality of an application.

The following usability guidelines have been recommended by Nielsen, one of the major experts in this field, and have been largely adopted for the Project:

Visibility of system status	The system should always keep users informed about what is going on, through appropriate feedback within reasonable time
Match between system and the real world	The system should speak the users' language, with words, phrases and concepts familiar to the user, rather than system-oriented terms. Follow real-world conventions, making information appear in a natural and logical order.
User control and freedom	Users often choose system functions by mistake and will need a clearly marked 'emergency exit' to leave the unwanted state without having to go through an extended dialogue. Support undo and redo.
Consistency and standards	Users should not have to wonder whether different words, situations, or actions mean the same thing. Follow platform conventions.
Error prevention	Even better than good error messages is a careful design which prevents a problem from occurring in the first place.

Methodology

Recognition rather than recall	Make objects, actions, and options visible. The user should not have to remember information from one part of the dialogue to another. Instructions for use of the system should be visible or easily retrievable whenever appropriate.
Flexibility and efficiency of use	Accelerators -- unseen by the novice user -- may often speed up the interaction for the expert user such that the system can cater to both inexperienced and experienced users. Allow users to tailor frequent actions.
Aesthetic and minimalist design	Dialogues should not contain information which is irrelevant or rarely needed. Every extra unit of information in a dialogue competes with the relevant units of information and diminishes their relative visibility.
Help users recognise, diagnose and recover from errors	Error messages should be expressed in plain language (no codes), precisely indicate the problem, and constructively suggest a solution.
Help and documentation	Even though it is better if the system can be used without documentation, it may be necessary to provide help and documentation. Any such information should be easy to search, focused on the user's task, list concrete steps to be carried out, and not be too large.

Table 3: General usability guidelines by Nielsen[15]

8.5.2 Usability testing methods and techniques

Various methods have been proposed to ascertain whether or not the above guidelines have been followed. These include expert reviews, end-user tests, systematic reviews, focus group discussions etc. Some experts, for example Honold (2000), distinguish between formative and summative testing, while others differentiate between process- and product-oriented evaluation or design and evaluation-oriented guidelines. The choice of method depends largely on the purpose or objective of the actual testing, (e.g. product certification or understanding mental models/expectations underlying breakdowns), as well as on the time and budget available.

One of the assumptions of this study was that cultural differences affecting usability and design were mainly representational and that a culturally determined usability problem can be characterised as a user's difficulty in understanding the meaning of representations. Therefore, the research focus was on testing the interface design with particular emphasis on breakdowns or critical incidents to identify differences which might be due to cultural factors.

For the purposes of this study, the discussion has been limited to the methods actually applied in the Project, i.e.

1. Heuristic evaluation or expert reviews
2. End-user tests or user-focused testing
3. Focus group discussions

---

[15] Source: http://www.useit.com/papers/heuristic/heuristic_list.html

8.5.2.1 Heuristic evaluation

One of the most prolific writers on usability is Nielsen. He coined the term 'heuristic evaluation' (1994), a method originally developed for the evaluation of software user interfaces. The heuristic evaluation procedure is normally as follows:

Evaluators in spect the interface or a design prototype of the interface, guided by a list of principles – the heuristics – that help them discover design violations and flaws. The difference between heuristics and other forms of expert or usability review is that the heuristics applied by the experts in the evaluation of an interface are made explicit.

When it comes to the value of heuristic evaluation as opposed to testing with end-users Spyridakis et al. (2000:302) argue that "careful and systematic reviews that are guided by heuristics should precede and complement user-focused testing in the design process." Other experts suggest skipping heuristic evaluation altogether if user-focused testing is planned, because the first five users will discover most of the usability problems.

Although this argument cannot be resolved due to the lack of a sound foundation for discussing the value of heuristic evaluation, the common consensus among experts appears to be that there is a place for both evaluation approaches in the design process. The framework developed by van der Geest and Spyridakis (2000) has also revealed the most important success factors for heuristics:

- With regard to coverage and validity, heuristics should not consist of arbitrary items and the rationale behind them should be clear.

With regard to presentation and use they stipulate three requirements:

1. The possibility to 'read between the lines' aided by a meaningful structure and an adequate mix of high-level and low-level items.
2. Users should be able to evaluate the applicability by giving supporting evidence.
3. Their nature and formulation should be tailored to the ways they are to be used in the Web design process. (pp. 323).

The authors argue that more research has to be done into the ways heuristics are actually used by designers and evaluators in relation to their presentation format (manuals, thinking-aloud,...), i.e. practitioners' reports on what the heuristics actually achieved for the Web designers.

The most convincing proof of the benefits of heuristic evaluation would be a demonstration that a site designed with a set of heuristics is better than one designed without heuristics. Gerhardt-Powals (1996) conducted such a study in the domain of interface design in which she was able to demonstrate that an interface designed according to her cognitive Engineering Principles proved to be superior in use situations.

8.5.2.2 End-user tests

End-user tests are often conducted in special usability labs. These tend to be equipped with eye-tracking equipment for recording users' eye movements when carrying out specified tasks or scenarios with products such as mobile phones or software applications. Usability labs also tend to have special audio and video recording equipment, as well as – in the case of computer-based systems – devices that are able to record users' keystrokes. In addition, log files of users' computer transactions can be evaluated. The above-mentioned techniques are normally accompanied by questionnaires to elicit users' opinions on the usefulness of a product or application.

On the whole, these techniques take place outside the normal usage environment. Even if efforts are undertaken to design task scenarios that correspond to real-life situations, the fact remains that contextual factors are largely disregarded. They tend to yield results that say something about the performance of a system according to pre-specified and measurable criteria, e.g. '85% of users were able to carry out
60% of tasks within a pre-determined timeframe without encountering major usability problems', or 'The error rate related to usage scenario X was 30% lower with Product A than Product B'.

This type of tests can be useful, or even necessary, to obtain a particular certification or for comparing two technical systems. However, they will not help understand any misunderstandings or misinterpretations connected with representational problems.

8.5.2.3 Focus group discussions

Focus group discussions are widely used to obtain insights into culture-specific requirements. They have been defined as "a research technique that collects data through group interaction on a topic determined by the researchers" (Morgan 1997:6). They involve group discussions that centre on a particular topic and are given structure by a discussion leader.

Before conducting focus group discussions, the questions to be investigated and the composition of user groups have to be defined. With international user groups, we can normally observe similarities, e.g. due to similar teaching traditions (e.g. countries with strongly hierarchical traditions *versus* countries with more egalitarian systems) or similar use contexts (e.g. similar professional background). The concept of cultural dimensions as developed by Hofstede can be quite useful for an initial classification of user groups and their allocation to groups and sub-groups . Experts such as Honold (2000) and Marcus (2000) insist that they should be as homogeneous as possible with regard to both cultural and professional background and level of know-how/expertise to ensure that the participants 'speak the same language'.

Hofstede's national scores on Power Distance served as a starting point in the consideration of the didactic approach to be integrated in the prototype eLearning module. His tables can be adapted as follows:

Small Power Distance societies	Large Power Distance societies
Student-centred education – premium on initiative	Teacher-centred education (premium on order)
Teacher expects students to initiate communication	Students expect teacher to initiate communication
Teacher expects students to find their own paths	Students expect teacher to outline paths to follow
Students may speak up spontaneously in class	Teacher is never contradicted nor publicly criticised
Effectiveness of learning related to amount of two-way communication in class	Effectiveness of learning related to excellence of the teacher

Table 4: Adaptation of Hofstede's cultural dimension of Power Distance to instructor – trainee relations

In addition to having good communication skills and an understanding of group dynamics, the researcher who acts as a moderator should also know the product or application well and have a knowledge of the context in which it will be used. He/she should speak the 'language' of the participants to enable him/her to assess the relevance of statements immediately and react accordingly.

Quite often, moderation tasks are split between two people, with one in charge of guiding and structuring the discussion, while the other is an expert in the particular domain. Ideally, the analysis of the data gathered in the course of the focus group discussions should be done together. This will help to clarify issues and also allow a weighting of any technical questions which might have been raised.

It is generally agreed that qualitative procedures such as focus group discussions to determine a set of use requirements have to be adapted to meet culture-specific communication behaviour. Beu, Honold and Yuan (2000) list a number of barriers which might hinder discussions in a Chinese context, e.g.

- Modesty and reserve with regard to one's achievements.
- Fear of losing face.
- Standardisation of language usage with differentiated speech and action depending on hierarchies and situations. (p. 356)

They report that behaviour in the focus group in a Chinese context tends to aim at achieving a common consensus and shirks away from voicing direct criticism of others or products.

Their suggestions regarding appropriate ways of leading focus group discussions proved very useful in the current research, even though the contextual features and the professional background of the participants in the present study were probably far more homogeneous than in the cases on which their suggestions were based. They recommend among other things:

- Discussions should focus on specific examples.
- Participants should not limit their comments to their own experiences but include their work environment.
- Participants should always be allowed to 'withdraw' to save face.
- Criticism of the product/design should be presented as an opportunity for the company to learn.
- The discussion leader should take an active role, steering and encouraging discussion.
- Heavy structuring and active control of the focus group are required.
- Enlist the support of the leader of the group, i.e. the person with the highest rank in the hierarchy.

Ideally, discussions would be conducted in all the countries where potential or future user groups can be found. Because of the high costs involved, the difficulties in organising focus group discussions and the lack of infrastructure and equipment, many companies opt for less costly solutions, which can, however, raise another set of problems.

Beu, Honold and Yuan (2000), for instance, report that the Siemens Department for User Interface Design in Munich soon came to the conclusion that the Chinese living in Germany had lost touch with their original culture and could therefore not be regarded as representative of the Chinese context. Among the other problems encountered by the Siemens usability experts were:

- Finding and training native speakers to act as discussion leaders and conduct usability tests.
- Fundamental differences in the way of working, e.g. flexible open solutions of greater complexity which require more training *versus* restrictions in flexibility for the sake of an easy start and instant success and hardly any formal training but learning on the job.

Not all the issues raised in the literature were applicable to my own research. As far as focus groups are concerned, for instance, choice of setting, recruitment of suitable participants, the question of whether to use pecuniary incentives or finding a competent moderator in another culture were irrelevant in the research context of this study or determined by the circumstances, i.e. by the course programme on the Campus.

8.6 Methods for data analysis

The analysis of data gathered using qualitative methods should also rely on qualitative methods, i.e. we cannot simply count the number of statements made about a particular topic and then draw conclusions on the basis of frequency. The fact that a topic is raised several times in the course of discussions might testify to its relevance, but it has also been shown that – especially when focus groups are conducted in foreign cultures – few participants ever make comments on their basic motives or values because this kind of tacit knowledge is assumed to be shared by their interlocutors and therefore does need not be discussed or negotiated (see Honold 2000).

To counteract the subjectivity implied by interpretative methods of analysing data, the procedure must be made transparent and carried out, if possible, by more than one evaluator to allow the results to be verified. The 'Grounded Theory' proposed by Glaser and Strauss (Glaser and Strauss 1967; Strauss 1994) provides a good foundation. It aims less at verifying existing hypotheses and more at conceiving new models or approaches which can be derived from the available data.

8.6.1.1 Grounded theory

Empirical data are seen as indicators of concepts a researcher can derive from the data, provisionally at first, but then with increasing certainty. By comparing the indicators, certain concepts can be verified and confirmed and others modified.

Data which can be considered indicators for basic concepts are 'coded/codified', i.e. they are conceptualised and can be attributed to certain categories, which, in turn, can be put into relation with each other. It does not suffice, however, to identify or discover categories, the researcher also has to try and discern the underlying structure and classify the data according to their relevance to the phenomena referred to a particular category. For this purpose, Strauss suggests classifying data according to

- Conditions
- Interaction between actors
- Strategies and tactics
- Consequences. (Strauss 1994:57)

With grounded theory, the above-mentioned measures accompany the iterative gathering of the data, thus enabling the results to be fed back into the process of data collection and the discovery of any lacunae which have to be filled.

The question remains at what stage a researcher decides to terminate the study because he/she feels that the underlying structure has been sufficiently corroborated. Critics of grounded theory point to the subjectivity involved in the process of conceptualisation. However, since the process of interpretation is rooted in the empirical data, it is fairly transparent and its conclusions can be traced along the line.

8.7 Summary

The answers to the methodological questions posed in the introduction to this chapter, namely:

- To what extent can activity theory serve as an analytical tool for the empirical data gathered?
- To what extent can activity theory integrate the role of cultural factors in the development of computer-based information or eLearning systems?
- To what extent can activity theory cope with contextual and collaborative aspects in such systems?
- How well can activity theory be combined with other methods to deal with these issues?

can be summarised as follows:

As already pointed out in the Introduction, the increasing familiarity with the context combined with the need to find answers and solutions to the practical questions and difficulties encountered in the course of the Project work eventually led to a shift of focus. The quest for a unifying theoretical framework that could be applied to both industry applications of the Project and could accommodate all the diverse aspects of the research involved came to assume a central role.

In many ways, this resulted in an asynchronous process between practice and theory. Or rather, practice became the driving force behind theory and served to provide information for the theoretical investigations. As a result, the activity checklists served primarily as a tool for analysing, interpreting and reflecting on the empirical data rather than as a tool for orienting and guiding research, which is demonstrated in the following chapter.

As far as cultural factors are concerned, the cultural models derived from Hofstede and other interculturalists still dominate the methodological attempts to define culture-specific requirements, but have proved to have little explanatory value for this study. Furthermore, the discussion in this chapter has also shown that the results from studies that have applied them do not corroborate the hypotheses derived from them.

In activity theory, cultural factors are seen as an integral part of the environment and therefore need not be identified separately from the overall contextual investigation. But since activity theory as applied in HCI studies has adopted a somewhat narrow focus of culture, it is suggested to offset this limitation by the Vygotskian tradition as it is manifested in the sociocultural approaches that have been explored in the previous chapter. The treatment of cultural factors can be further enriched by applying Holden's concept of culture as an object of KM.

Contextual and collaborative aspects are easy to accommodate in an activity theory framework because of its emphasis on the embeddedness of all activity in a wider cultural and social context. In this study, ethnographic methods such as participant observation, interviews and focus group discussions have been used for capturing the context or the environment in which the target technologies are (to be) applied. Ethnographic methods have become widely recognised as an appropriate way to study information systems in organisations, including the development and management of information systems.

The following figure illustrates the adaptation of the extended activity triangle developed by Engeström (1987) to the topic under study, i.e. training with its various actions such as course organisation and development.

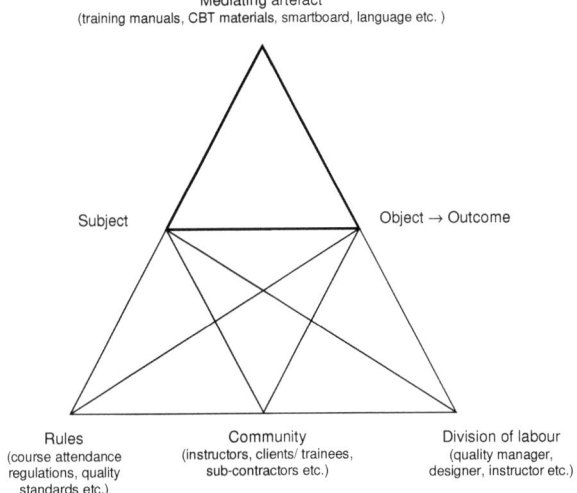

Figure 2: Extended Activity Triangle (adapted)

The activity of training involves a community consisting of instructors, clients, designers, course administrators and others such as interpreters and various sub-contractors. The community lives by a set of rules, both explicit and implicit, that govern the individuals in it, for example rules concerning course attendance, the behaviour of instructors, certification requirements, quality standards etc. The division of labour reflects the different roles individuals play (see, for example, Table 5: Roles and tasks involved in course development).

The objective ('object' in activity theory parlance) of the activity system is the training of clients. This objective is mediated by a variety of artefacts: training manuals, product specifications, computer-aided instruction materials, video sequences etc. and eventually, by the KM and eLearning systems developed in the course of the Project. The outcome of this activity is well-trained clients.

As community forms part of the extended activity 'triangle', it is recognised that an activity is affected by the individual's participation within a community. The contextual research has shown the importance of collaboration in the organising and developing of courses including the tasks and roles distributed among the members of the community This division of labour occurs because in order for a community to achieve a common objective, activities of the individuals in it must be organised, and the paths of communication coordinated, so that together they form the set of actions that will achieve the common objective.

If one intends to develop and introduce new technologies such as a KM and eLearning efficiently and in a user-friendly way, it is not only a question of extending the repertoire of tools to include eLearning modules (as opposed to just computer-based materials to support face-to-face instruction). Rather, any analysis must consider the whole complex of the training activity. Given the bidirectional nature of mediation, the effect of a new technology on training is influenced as much by individuals' mediating their objectives through the technology as by the existing tools and community structures.

The following chapter –Practical Implementation – will show how the different methods and techniques were applied in the concrete research context.

9 Practical Implementation

In this chapter, I describe the ethnographic methods applied to gain an understanding of the environment in which the KM and eLearning systems were to be developed as part of the EU Project. At the time, the research conducted to capture the context surrounding the training activities went under the Project heading of 'capturing the tacit knowledge' necessary for implementing a system that would be accepted by its future users.

The chapter begins with a description of the organisational context in which I conducted my research. As explained in the previous chapter, qualitative methods such as participant observation and interviews were considered most appropriate for investigating the environment in which training courses were organised and developed. I discuss how I gathered the empirical data on course development mostly through attending courses myself and interviewing key actors involved in this activity.

I then describe how I planned and carried out the usability tests including the questionnaires and focus group discussions that were organised to clarify issues raised by the tests.

9.1 Organisational context for the empirical study

As mentioned previously, the research for this thesis was conducted within the framework of a transnational European project called Enhancing Knowledge Management in Enterprises (ENKE). The Project placed a particular emphasis on the human, social and cultural issues that need to be addressed to ensure the success of complex KM applications. Within the Consortium, the partner organisation on whose behalf I carried out the research had been allocated the task of ensuring that these factors would be duly taken into account.

As far as the validation of the functional requirements was concerned, the academic partner in the Consortium was expected to suggest the non-technical measures, including ergonomic, cognitive or social measures, which were to accompany the implementation of the KM tool(s) at the partners' sites. In addition, we defined the features required for the KM tools in terms of usability.

Eventually, the focus of the research, however, came to concentrate on the question of if and to what extent cultural factors would play a role in the design of the KM and eLearning systems. The eLearning platform which would contain the eLearning modules and was to be developed in the framework of the Project, had to cater for a culturally very diverse range of customers from more than a hundred countries. The integration of cultural diversity into knowledge capture and transfer activities was considered an important innovative contribution that this Project and the research associated with it could deliver for the advancement of both KM and eLearning.

The introduction of a KM system was regarded as a prerequisite for the eLearning initiative to succeed. The KM system was to be installed on the server of the Training Academy and contain all the information and documents necessary for course building. The Learning Management System was to store and manage user data, question responses, tests, course structures and access statistics. The actual content of the courses, however, would be located on the KM system. As far as course content was concerned, it was envisaged that the existing instruction materials used in the classroom would form the basis for the Web-based training materials.

The following excerpt from one of the Project reports on the link between eLearning and KM illustrates that even though the original research for the Project was KM-oriented, the observations made and results gained from interviews and group focus discussions are equally relevant to both fields.

Link between eLearning and knowledge management (KM)

The fact that there is a conceptual link between the two fields is increasingly being noticed by experts in both areas. Vendors of eLearning products have started to add KM capabilities to their products, while KM tools have largely fallen short of their ambitious goals and vendors as well as KM practitioners have started to explore other technologies to enhance and/or complement their approach. A working group of Price Waterhouse-Coopers, for instance, has produced the report "Beyond knowledge management: New Ways to Work and Learn". It showed that many organisations with KM efforts under way had also developed substantial eLearning architectures. In general, it is the use of Web technologies for both eLearning and KM that provides a common medium to combine practices.

The Eurocopter application represents a good example for harnessing KM for eLearning purposes. Designing training modules requires a huge joint effort between Web designers, training specialists, KM practitioners, subject matter experts, R&D personnel as well as instructors and interpreters. Knowledge has to be captured in the way it is communicated, i.e. by the instructors who have been responsible so far for conveying the knowledge and skills required for handling new equipment, i.e. helicopters. Linking their experience and – largely tacit - knowledge to the information contained in files, documents, graphics, simulations and existing learning materials was the major challenge. In a mature eLearning and KM implementation, knowledge workers can tap the same knowledge sources for targeted eLearning, unstructured information, in-house experts and instructors and outside resources such as clients' cultural values and learning habits.

Technologies from the KM field such as threaded discussion groups, chat rooms, synchronous meeting tools and other collaborative tools which facilitate knowledge sharing can be adopted in eLearning settings. More sophisticated tools such as knowledge databases that archive unstructured information resources in ways that relevant information can quickly be found through keyword searches, form the next step in integrating eLearning and KM. As eLearning developers work out ways to store and manage learning content in modular, object-based formats, learning content could be served to users together with other knowledge resources from the same information repository.

However, there was never any doubt among the Project participants that despite the advances in eLearning technologies, applications and tools, the best learning still occurs in exchanges between people. The company has never planned to replace direct communication between instructors and students but supplement them.

Given the fact that their clients come from a wide variety of cultural backgrounds and experience the instructors have always had to address their specific needs. Consequently, eLearning components, too, have to boast a high degree of flexibility so as to be adaptable to different user requirements. Two technologies were considered useful in this endeavour: XML and learning object-based content design. XML allows detailed labelling and mark-up of content, thus making it possible to customise eLearning content for the individual client. Object-based learning is a more ambitious scheme to manage learning with independent, reusable learning objects that can be combined to provide mass-customised learning.

9.2 Ethnographic research related to training

The ethnographic approach has informed all research stages including the choice of data collection, analysis of user requirements and evaluation of the results of the usability testing by means of focus group discussions. Most contextual data were collected through participant observation supplemented by semi-structured interviews with a wide variety of actors involved in training, documentary evidence such as annual reports or minutes of meetings, and focus group discussions.

The description and analysis of contextual factors such as corporate environment and strategies, organisational culture and business processes in the company also draw on interviews with key figures involved in and/or affected by course development, i.e. instructors, course authors and designers, sub-contractors such as interpreters, partners and customers/trainees of the Training Center at Marignane, headquarters of Eurocopter France.

The information about current course organisation and implementation was collected through observation arising from participation in a varied series of courses for groups of mechanics, pilots and avionic engineers and from interviews with instructors and staff involved in the planning, scheduling and organisation of courses.
As already mentioned, some demographic data on the trainees, such as country of origin, gender or approximate age, were gathered during attendance, but other data, such as professional background, status (e.g. in the military hierarchy) and level of experience, were normally obtained from those responsible for course planning. In addition, discussions with the Project leader at Eurocopter as well as employees responsible for quality management, course organisation and planning and support staff (secretaries, receptionists etc.) helped to clarify many of the questions which emerged in the course of this work.
The ethnographic research was supplemented by consulting a number of internal documents such as company brochures, business plans, seminar notes, leaflets distributed by the different trade unions as well as information found on the company Intranet.

I was given the status of 'stagiaire' (corporate trainee) at the Training Academy, which gave me access to most of the facilities on the Campus. As was to be expected from an organisation active in the defence industry, certain limitations were imposed with regard to access to documentation – be it on paper or on the Intranet. Any access to classified materials required in the course of the research was only granted under the condition that these would not be taken out of the company or published. For this reason, the analysis and discussion of my observations and interviews do not contain details of the exact course composition in terms of nationalities, helicopter types, strategic business plans and other confidential information.

However, I do not believe that these constraints detract in any way from the findings of this study. After all, its focus is on the role played by cultural factors in the exchange, transfer and presentation of information and knowledge, not on developments in the European defence and helicopter industry.

9.2.1 Investigating course organisation and development

A large part of the knowledge on course organisation and development is tacit and had to be captured by participant observation and in-depth interviews. Although there is no formal information exchange, the trainers are happy to swap stories, discuss course development and ask each other's advice. Apart from a few exceptions, the trainers work in two open space offices, one for light helicopter trainers, the other for heavy helicopter trainers, which facilitates the exchange of information and experiences and is an arrangement which the instructors themselves see as conducive to knowledge exchange.

Apart from attending various courses and observing how instructors organised their work, for example how they went about gathering and exchanging information or liaising with experts from other departments, I interviewed about one third of the instructors during the period of my stay. The interviews were conducted informally, whenever an opportunity arose, and lasted between 30 to 60 minutes.

The following questionnaire was used as a guideline to help ensure a certain measure of consistency and completeness across these interviews:

Instructor - details:
Specialisation:
Mechanic   ☐
Pilot   ☐
Avionics   ☐

Practical Implementation

Background:
    Military   ☐
    Civil   ☐

Type of helicopter:

Information retrieval scenarios - status quo
- On-site
- From abroad

Which information sources do you consult?

Internal server/Intranet	☐
Internal documents (written)	☐
Instructor(s) at Marignane	☐
EC Colleague at Marignane (e.g. in the R&D Dept.)	☐
EC Colleague outside Marignane	☐
Other (please specify)	

How long does it take you - on average –
- to develop a new course?
- to revise a course?

Once the KM server is installed and all the documents, images, videos etc. relevant for course development have been well described, organised and transferred to the server,
- will developing / revising a course be quicker?
- And if so, by what percentage (estimate) ?

Would it be useful do have Yellow Pages with all the contact details, skills and experience of

all instructors (incl. offices abroad)	☐
R&D experts	☐
interpreters	☐
documentation specialists	☐
experts in the field of standards	☐
course designers	☐
others (please specify)	
Student Profiles	

Which factors are most influential for the success of a course?

Students have the same level of know-how	☐
Students have the same country of origin	☐
Students are highly motivated	☐

Practical Implementation

> If you could organise your group according to level of know-how, how much time would you gain?
>
> **Open Questions**
>
> In your opinion what else (tools / work environment...) would facilitate your work in general?
>
> What other factors / tools ... could accelerate the development / revision of a course (module)?
>
> What other factors / tools ... could improve the quality of a course?

Figure 3: Interview questions for instructors

As far as information retrieval from abroad was concerned, I asked the same questions but focused on information sources since time differences generally make personal contact with international colleagues difficult.

I attended a total of 16 courses over a period of about seven months: a four-week preliminary visit in autumn 2002 which included a Project meeting, four months in the spring of 2003 and a further two months in the autumn of the same year. Usually, I spent at least half a day, i.e. three hours, with a group and, wherever possible, would also join them for lunch. During course time, the instructor has lunch with the trainees in the visitors' restaurant instead of the canteen where staff normally eat.

About two thirds of the courses attended were targeted at mechanics, the remaining third at pilots, while one course covered logistics. The class size ranged from one student to 12. In five cases, the class was homogeneous in terms of country of origin, the rest of the classes were mixed, with a maximum of five nationalities in one course. All instructors and trainees were male, except for one company employee from the marketing department who sat in one of the classes to familiarise herself with the subject matter, while five (of six) interpreters encountered were female.

In six of the classes an interpreter was present, who, with the exception of one group which insisted on providing their own interpreter, was hired from one of Eurocopter's two regular agencies. Some of the interpreters had years of experience working for the company and were able to explain the subject matter very well and even point out inconsistencies or infelicities in the documentation.

In ten of the sixteen courses, the language of instruction was English, the rest were held in French. All instructors are expected to be able to teach in French and English; one of the instructors is also qualified to teach in Spanish. Their command of English, however, varies considerably, ranging from near-native fluency to a reasonable command of the language. However, they all are thoroughly familiar with the technical vocabulary associated with the topics they have to teach and, in that respect, speak 'the same language' as their trainees. With regard to the selection of interpreters, it is actually considered more important that they have 'un sens aeronautique', i.e. be familiar with the topic, rather than be 'perfect' linguists.

Before attending any classes, permission was obtained from the instructors, who on the whole proved very welcoming and keen to share their experiences. When I met a group for the first time, I introduced myself and the objectives of the EU Project. I always stressed that I was not an expert in helicopter flying or maintenance, but was interested in the learning and teaching approaches adopted in class with a view to building an eLearning platform.

During attendance, I took notes on general aspects (size/composition of class, atmosphere etc.), but concentrated my attention above all on the level and forms of interaction between the teacher and students and the interaction among students. For example:

- Could any patterns be observed as far as the willingness to ask questions was concerned?
- How did the presence of an interpreter affect the situation?
- Did it matter whether the instructor was talking in English or French?
- Did the students' command of English influence the frequency of questions?
- How did misunderstandings or lack of understanding manifest themselves? How did the instructors deal with such situations?
- How and to what extent did the instructors use the written documentation and the computer-based training materials shown on the smartboard?

Whilst attending the various classes notes were taken and special consideration given to occurrences or statements relating to
- Interaction
- Additional information not contained in written sources
- References to (inter)cultural factors
- References to documentation

In line with the objectives of the Project, the following larger research issues were always at the back of my mind when participating in the courses and interviewing people connected with training activities:

- To what extent does culture (national, organisational, domain) influence the way people seek and use information?

- Culture is mediated by many factors including contextual factors (e.g. training or work environment), individual factors such as gender, age, professional experience, computer usage etc. which all have an impact on information use and knowledge exchange. How – if at all - do these change the effect of cultural background on information use?

9.2.2 Description of case study – the VEMD prototype

In conjunction with the instructors and the Project management, the decision was taken to develop a prototype application, namely a Web-based training module of the VEMD (Vehicle and Engine Multifunctional Display). This prototype would allow future or potential customers, especially those who had been trained on aircraft without more advanced or sophisticated semi-automatic indicating and recording systems, to acquire a basic knowledge of the VEMD before they came to the Campus and therefore enable them to start their training course on an equal footing with their fellow students.

Before the Project team could commence with the development of the VEMD module, certain preparatory measures had to be undertaken:

- Observe how the module is taught in a classroom environment.
- Identify the relevant information sources
- Agree on a common terminology
- Compare the different approaches according to the type of qualification (mechanics, pilots).
- Compare the different approaches according to the level of experience and theoretical knowledge of trainees.
- Collect scenarios and examples used by instructors to illustrate the VEMD.
- Ascertain if teaching methods vary according to cultural background of trainees.

I attended an on-site course on the VEMD which lasted about six hours to see how the information on this topic was transmitted in the classroom. This was followed by an interview with the instructor to clarify and supplement the information gathered during the course with a focus on

- information supplied by the instructor yet not included in any of the information sources.
- information/knowledge acquired as a result of discussion and/or interaction between instructor and trainees or between trainees
- examples given to illustrate particular topics which could later be used for the development of scenarios for the eLearning modules.

Practical Implementation

The first prototype of the VEMD was to consist of a basic learning module for mechanics. They constitute a less homogeneous group than the pilots, especially as far as the level of know-how and experience is concerned. Whereas some have received extensive training including both theoretical foundations and practical skills, others have acquired their skills on the job, but they might have considerable practical experience. This is why in the case of mechanics we distinguish between three levels of know-how, namely basic, advanced and expert.

The basic structure for the prototype was adopted from the Training Manual (THM), which forms the basis both of the actual training courses in the classroom and a CD-ROM produced about the VEMD. Since the eLearning module would be directed at students who had no previous knowledge of the VEMD, the information contained in the THM had to be expanded considerably to include:

- Basic objectives/functions of the VEMD
- A general description of the VEMD
- Explanation of the various control switches
- Description and explanation of indicators
- Explanation of the various modes (operational *versus* maintenance mode)
- Explanation of the various stati (flight *versus* ground) and menus

The information architecture is based on a progressive learning approach from beginners to expert level: Each learning level module is composed of several knowledge blocks or learning objects linked to the other modules and followed by a quiz to test whether the trainee has understood the contents provided. Apart from text, technical drawings and illustrations, video sequences and digital images are used to transfer the information required to familiarise oneself with the basic functions of the VEMD. When appropriate, sound warning signals are inserted. At a later stage voice comments related to specific images can be added in different languages to improve the reading and understanding of the English text. The students will also be able to look up additional information such as charts and diagrams if they wish by following hyperlinks.

After collecting the relevant materials – manuals, product specifications, technical drawings and illustrations, images and videos etc. – both in paper and electronic format – the Project team was faced with the big challenge to agree on a common terminology. The various sources of information were found to differ considerably with regard to the terms used, the amount of detail given and the type (British *versus* American English) and register of English used. Discrepancies were even found with regard to the basic operation modes of the VEMD. The lack of consistency is partly due to the fact that military usage differs from civil usage and at times the terminology even varies between different types of helicopter.

Since in the online environment, the use of unambiguous and clear terminology is of prime importance, it was necessary to agree on an 'authorised' version. It was decided that the terms as used in the Illustrated Parts Catalogue can be considered authoritative – at least as far as physical items are concerned. Ideally, one would include a thesaurus which allows cross-references to alternative terms, but since no such facility was anticipated for the near future, the possibility to create hyperlinks to glossary items/ index terms including alternative terms was considered. Furthermore, it was decided to include a list of abbreviations or acronyms and cross-reference them.

The next challenge was posed by the allocation of metadata to the information to be integrated into the new KMS. When choosing key words it makes sense to use terms already in use in the company. This is why the Project team elected to adopt the metadata used in Eurocopter's image database which is accessible to all Eurocopter employees and is available in both English and French.

The biggest challenge, of course, concerned the transfer of knowledge for eLearning purposes, i.e. how – if at all - can the tacit knowledge 'owned' by an experienced instructor be transferred to a Web-based training module? And how can the information resulting from interaction between instructor and trainees or between trainees be captured and transferred in Web-based training modules?

These issues will be discussed in the next chapter which analyses and describes the results of this research.

9.3 Usability testing

The purpose of usability testing is to evaluate user interfaces by simulating concrete usage. Before conducting the tests with end-users, i.e. Eurocopter clients who attend the courses in the Training Centre, the composition of user groups had to be defined. On the one hand, they should be representative of the overall customer base, yet, on the other, they had to be as homogeneous as possible with regard to both cultural and professional background and level of know-how and expertise to ensure that the participants did indeed 'speak the same language'.

The validation and testing of the prototype VEMD module was conducted mainly via expert reviews or heuristic evaluation. The end-user tests were restricted to a quiz which had been designed in PowerPoint to test the interactive features of the future eLearning module. Actually, the two processes – expert reviews and user tests – took place more or less simultaneously. This was largely due to the fact that developing the eLearning prototype proved to be an extremely time-consuming process. Another consideration was the fact that the development of eLearning materials would eventually be subcontracted to a specialised company, which is why the emphasis of the testing and validation had to be on the provision of guidelines and recommendations rather than the actual design of internationally aware training materials.

9.3.1 Heuristic evaluation through experts

Heuristic evaluation, a method originally developed for the evaluation of software user interfaces, was used for assessing the usability of the interface design of the prototype eLearning module of the VEMD. The procedure was as follows:

Six experts inspected the VEMD module's interface, guided by a list of principles – the heuristics – to help them discover design violations and flaws. The difference between heuristics and other forms of expert or usability review is that the heuristics applied by the experts in the evaluation of an interface are made explicit.

The heuristics applied have been developed in the course of a systematic research and development process by the *Society of Technical Communication*[16]. They coincide largely with WAI WC3 accessibility guidelines[17], focus on the informational elements of Websites and cover five aspects of Web design and evaluation:

- The rhetorical situation
- Navigation as a means to signal the information structure of a site
- Presentation of verbal information
- Visual display and presentation of information
- The involvement of users in the design and evaluation

In addition to the prototype VEMD module, the experts were asked to evaluate a quiz which had been designed in PowerPoint to test the interactive features of the future eLearning module. The questions contained in the multiple-choice questionnaire were taken from real-life exams. The quiz served to ascertain the requirements for interactive features which were considered an essential part of any eLearning application, but which are currently absent in existing computer-based training modules, since these are always used in conjunction with an instructor.

Unlike most test review reports consulted at the preparatory stage, there was no need to ask reviewers to identify and describe the intended audience and purpose of the Web pages or eLearning modules since they were all familiar with the topic and already well-informed about the aims of the Project and the application.

Another step commonly found in usability research is an assessment of users' overall attitudes to and perceptions on using heuristics for the purpose of evaluating Website quality or gathering data

---

[16] In *Technical Communication: Journal of the Society for Technical Communication 47* (2000) 3 (special issue).
[17] WC3's Web Accessibility Initiative has an extensive site of accessible Web design information: http://www.w3.org/WAI.

about their experience with usability evaluation methods. These steps were also skipped because this research has already been done elsewhere and the findings would neither have thrown light on nor contributed to the important research questions such as intercultural or contextual aspects.

The six experts were selected to be representative of the future user groups, i.e. consisting mainly of instructors and trainees, yet also including experts in design and information management. The final make-up of the expert group therefore comprised two instructors (one for pilots, the other one for mechanics), a trainee (pilot), an information management expert and linguist, a design specialist at Eurocopter and the EU Project leader at the French partner site.

The expert reviews lasted around two to three hours each. After a brief introduction to the general usability guidelines and the heuristics developed for informational Websites, the experts were asked to 'think aloud' when navigating through and looking for information in the VEMD prototype module. Was the presentation of information clear and consistent? Was it easy to grasp its structure or architecture? Did the graphics and diagrams enhance and add value to the information?

After a short break, I showed them the quiz questions and emphasised that expressing how they felt about the interactive aspects, e.g. the way feedback was given, the form of address and the overall look and feel. Again, they were asked to 'think aloud' rather than to fill in a questionnaire as was the case with the end-users. was far more important than giving the correct answers.

9.3.2 End-user tests

As already mentioned, for the integration of interactive aspects a quiz was developed in PowerPoint. This allowed us to investigate whether students preferred:

- Immediate responses or a summary – online - response at the end of the test
- Evaluation by instructor sent via e-mail
- Feedback accompanied by icons (e.g. crumbling PC) or simple right/wrong response
- Simple right/wrong compared to extended feedback with explanation

The results should show whether trainees' preferences and expectations regarding interactivity can be correlated with factors such as professional background (e.g. mechanics *versus* pilots), age or cultural origin.

9.3.2.1 Planning and procedure

The planning of the end-user tests had to be done in conjunction with the instructors and course organisers. Since the decision had already been taken to carry out the testing (including the focus group discussions) within the framework of the courses taking place in the Training Campus, the scheduling and group composition as well as group size were very much dependent on external factors.

It had also originally been planned to conduct the tests in the classroom; but it subsequently transpired that the VEMD prototype could not be loaded onto the server dedicated to classroom use (or at least only with great difficulty). Consequently, it was decided to conduct them in the visitors' room, which was at least equipped with both the necessary connection and access facilities as well as a whiteboard. The room did not contain any of the sophisticated observation equipment, such as video cameras or eye-tracking devices, normally found in usability labs. But, as already explained (see Chapter 7.2.2), this was not considered important for the type of usability aspects addressed by the research.

The users were not offered any financial incentives. Apart from the fact that these can actually distort the outcome of the tests (see Honold 2000) no budget had been foreseen for this type of expense. The test participants were motivated primarily by the idea that they would be making an active contribution to the development of more user-friendly training materials. In addition, they were pleased that their views as users were being taken seriously and would be taken into account in the development process.

The atmosphere was relaxed and convivial, but nevertheless conducive to concentrated work. After a brief introduction to general usability guidelines and the questionnaire (see below), the participants were asked to study the quiz questions and fill in the questionnaire. But, as with the prior expert reviews, the emphasis lay primarily on finding out how they felt about the methods used to provide feedback, the form of address (formal *versus* informal) and the overall look and feel, not on giving the correct answers.

How do you perceive being addressed personally?	
Agreeable ☐	
Annoying ☐	
What do you prefer ?	
Regular alternation between short training units and exercises within a single lesson	☐
Test at the end of each lesson or in a separate appendix	☐
What do you prefer ?	
Detailed instructions about how to answer exam questions	☐
Few, but concise instructions	☐
What type of exam questions do you consider most suitable in this context, i.e. a course for helicopter technicians?	
Yes/No questions	☐
Multiple Choice	☐

Practical Implementation

Case Studies/Scenarios	☐
Free text entry (complex questions to test comprehension)	☐
Use of simulation for experimental purposes	☐
Feedback	
Right/wrong	☐
Additional explanations if answer is wrong	☐
Would you like to be guided through the course by a voice or virtual person (avatar) ?	
Yes, it would be helpful ☐	
No, it would only distract ☐	

Figure 4: Evaluation of interactive aspects

The most essential prerequisites for conducting the tests were the support of the instructors and the interest of the trainees. Of course, official permission was also required from the Campus management, but without the active support of the instructors and the willingness of the students to 'sacrifice' about an hour of their time, the tests could not have been conducted.

9.4 Preparation of empirical data for analysis

Before analysing the master document which brings together all the notes taken during the discussions and interviews I attempted to clarify or formulate once again the questions I was seeking to investigate. With these questions in mind, I then marked the passages which related to particular questions. Quite often I encountered paraphrased statements about the same topic made by different participants.

The notes taken whilst attending the various classes and conducting the interviews were examined and relevant passages relating to

- Interaction
- Additional information not contained in written sources
- References to (inter)cultural factors
- References to documentation

were highlighted and colour-coded.

Special attention was given to statements which seemed to be contradictory. How can contradictions be accounted for? Did the participants differ with regard to their role (e.g. captain/test pilot *versus* co-pilot), their age, their professional background (military *versus* civil training)? If possible, the answers were already obtained in the course of the discussions, but for the questions that still remained open I had to draw on my own or the instructor's contextual knowledge.

Even though this eLearning application relates primarily to the professional context, the living environment of the end-users might have an impact on use, especially since in the long run it is anticipated that students should be able to use the eLearning modules from home rather than in the Training Centre. Do they have a room of their own in which to do so, or do they have to share this room with other members of their household?

9.5 Summary

The mix of methods, namely participant observation, interviews both with individuals and groups as well as different methods of usability testing, proved to be the most suitable and effective approach to examining the complex issues in this study. In retrospect, this approach also proved very much in line with the methodological implications of activity theory. Together, ethnographic methods, usability tests and documentary research helped to produce a well-rounded and comprehensive picture of the human, social and cultural environment in which the computer-based systems to be developed would operate.

I began by introducing the organisational context in which I conducted my research. The contextual aspects refer both to the physical and organisational surroundings. I described how I gathered the empirical data on course development (mostly through attending courses and interviewing key actors involved in this activity). As a result of my immersion in the training environment a comprehensive picture of the training activities emerged over time, including the external and internal factors that have an impact on course organisation and development.

This was followed by a discussion of how I actually planned and carried out the usability tests including the questionnaires and the focus group discussions organised to clarify issues raised by the tests with end-users. Expert reviews were conducted with the prototype eLearning module, whereas usability testing with end-users was restricted to a quiz with exam questions, designed to embody the interactive features of the future eLearning module.

In the next chapter, I will analyse the empirical data gathered by means of the different methods. With the help of grounded theory and the activity checklists, these data will be structured and organised and eventually integrated into a wider activity theory framework.

10 Analysis

In this chapter, I analyse the findings gained from conducting the ethnographic research and the usability tests. As described in the previous chapters, most of the contextual data were collected through participant observation and interviews. The empirical data gathered by means of these methods were complemented with usability testing and various documentary/desk research.

I discuss how my perspective on culture changed as a result of immersing myself in the research environment and how my various attempts at classifying the students' behaviour in the classroom according to prevailing cultural models based on national identity proved unsatisfactory.

I try to identify the contextual factors that are relevant for the introduction and operation of KM and eLearning systems. In addition to the characteristics of target groups, infrastructure and organisational aspects such as division of labour are among the more important factors which have an impact on training.

The results of the usability tests are analysed with a view to determining the factors that have an impact on the requirements for the development of eLearning materials. Whereas the expert reviews focused on the informational aspects of instructional materials, the end-user tests with pilots and mechanics focused on interactive features, because these were considered essential for an eLearning application.

In both cases, i.e. the ethnographic data and the results from the usability tests, I derive categories and concepts from the data collected (as proposed by grounded theory). Since the Project was oriented towards information and KM concerns, it is not surprising that the categories and concepts should be influenced by the terminology of these fields.

I make use of the checklist for evaluation developed by Kaptelinin and Nardi (1999) to structure and organise the contextual data and integrate them into an activity theory framework. The 'space of context', as they call it, is represented by four areas, namely:

- Strategies and goals of training
- Organisational context of training
- Learning, cognition and interaction
- Transformation and development

The following section deals with the role of cultural factors in the activity of training. Do they have an influence on training and, if so, how are they presently accommodated? Is it possible and/or necessary to accommodate them in future eLearning and KM systems?

Analysis

In the context of this study, cultural factors turn out to be more closely associated with professional and organisational cultures than with national identity or language. Since culture is considered an integral part of all activities, it represents a horizontal theme and plays a role in all four of the above-mentioned areas.

Finally, I discuss the contradictions that can be observed in the training system, which in activity theory are seen as a source of development and change. As far as the development of the eLearning materials is concerned, the discussion deal with a series of themes that might be relevant in the transfer of the existing materials into an online environment.

10.1 An activity theoretical analysis

At the centre of this structured description of the training activity is the activity 'triangle' developed by Engeström (1987), who extended the basic triangle consisting of Subject – Object and Artefact (see upper highlighted triangle in Figure 1: Extended Activity Triangle on page 104) to recognise that it occurs in the context of a community, praxis (formal and informal rules) and division of labour.

The nodes of the triangle act as points of interface with the larger issues in activity theory such as the sociocultural history of an activity, the role of transformation or development, the role of learning and the internalisation – externalisation dialectic. Thus an activity is a nexus with an internal structure and a location in a cultural-historical continuum wherein it developed and evolved.

10.1.1 The internal structure of the activity

An activity is realised by a set of actions which are directed at achieving a goal (as distinct from the overall objective). Thus, the activity of this study, i.e. training, is composed of a set of actions, such as course organisation or course development, which can in turn be further sub-divided into the actions of gathering the information required for a particular course and entering it into the KM system.

An activity is determined by the particular motive to be fulfilled by performing that activity, i.e. it is directed at an objective (or 'object' in activity theory parlance) which motivates activity and gives it a specific direction. The over-all object of training is the transfer of knowledge. The aim of the Project was to facilitate this transfer by improving access to course-relevant information and developing a KM system and eLearning platform which was to be accessible and acceptable to trainees from different cultural and professional backgrounds and with different levels of skills.

The third element of the basic activity is artefacts or tools, which in this study are represented by the computer-based systems for KM and eLearning. According to Vygotsky (1978), all human actions are mediated by tools. Tools or artefacts refer to culturally produced means of changing the environment and achieving goals. The role of artefacts is to mediate the relationships between subject and object and between subject and community and, as such, they have a history of that relationship embedded in them.

In analysing artefact development, i.e. the KM and eLearning systems to be introduced at the site of the French consortium partner, the goal was to gain insight into the issues of artefact creation, evolution and appropriation by users, e.g. instructors and trainees.

Activity theory emphasises context and therefore insists that we study the whole activity system, not just the actual artefact. In other words, we have to look at training as it occurs in its particular environment, rather than restrict our attention to the eLearning platform to be developed. This also implies that we should study the other artefacts that are used in mediating the relationships.

The following section deals with the contextual data gathered through ethnographic research methods, i.e. participant observation, interviews and group discussions. It is followed by the analysis of the results from the usability tests.

10.2 Results of ethnographic research

This study set out with the assumption that the planning, development and design of computer-based systems or applications is always informed by culturally influenced expectations and assumptions about future user groups and use contexts. However, as already mentioned before, defining the concept of culture is a notoriously difficult matter. Therefore, rather than look for a universally valid definition, it was considered more important to look for the aspects that are relevant to the issues involved in this study.

The observations in the classroom and the many interviews conducted with both instructors and trainees showed that professional and organisational culture had more explanatory value for explaining differences in behaviour, expectations or cognitive approach than culture as a national attribute.

10.2.1 The importance of professional culture

In the course of my field research and interviews, it gradually emerged that organisational and professional cultures played a more important role in training than ethnic or national background. For instance, pilots' expectations and needs regarding the user-friendliness of computer interfaces differed from those of mechanics. They also had different learning styles, interaction patterns and information retrieval and processing behaviour.

Thus, a different perspective on cultural factors emerged which is more closely associated with organisational culture (e.g. military *versus* civil background) and profession (mechanics *versus* pilots) than with national identity. Of course, the country of origin does play a role in classroom behaviour, but as far as its impact on expectations and patterns of interaction and communication is concerned, its weight is on a par with age or experience.

If we use Holden's (2002) definition of culture, namely "varieties of common knowledge; infinitely overlapping and perpetually redistributable habitats of common knowledge and shared meanings", it is the communities of mechanics and pilots respectively that represent the habitats of common knowledge and shared meanings.

After examining the various approaches on how to identify and communicate the influence of cultural factors on usability and eLearning and the way these can be taken into account in the design of computer-based systems, I finally reached the conclusion that – at least as far as the objectives and target groups in our Project were concerned – the hypotheses derived from the various cultural models, especially the cultural dimension model of Hofstede, were not confirmed by the real-life situation.

10.3 Structured description of training

As outlined in Chapter 8, the activity checklists proposed by Kaptelinin and Nardi (1999) can be used as conceptual tools for identifying the most important factors influencing the use of computer technologies in a particular setting. As explained in the introduction to this chapter, I have adopted, and slightly adapted, their evaluation checklist (henceforth referred to as 'the Checklist') for structuring the observations and results that can be gathered from the empirical data.

The Checklist covers four sections based on the basic dimensions of activity theory (the original terms from the Checklist are given in brackets):

- Strategies and goals of training (Means/ends)
- Organisational context of training (Environment)
- Learning, cognition and interaction (Learning/cognition/articulation)
- Transformation and development (Development)

Each section is preceded by a selection of items or questions from the Checklist which seem relevant to the issues of this study. In line with the principles of grounded theory, the concepts and categories used in the discussion are rooted in the data gathered through the various methods. Thus, the factors that influence course development, for example, are described in terms of the participants' language.

10.3.1 Strategies and goals of training

The first section covers the means and ends of the use of the 'target technology', i.e. the KM and eLearning systems to be developed. It also deals with the extent to which this technology facilitates

Analysis

and constrains the achievement of users' goals and its impact on provoking or resolving conflicts between different goals.

The following items have been selected from the Checklist and adapted to orient the analysis of the results:

- Setting of target goals and sub-goals
- Target groups of training activities
- Criteria for success and failure in achieving target goals
- Constraints imposed by higher-level goals on the choice and use of training systems

10.3.1.1 Setting of target goals and sub-goals

Innovation, customer orientation and harmonisation are among the most important objectives of the enterprise as a whole. At Campus level, the company-wide strategies are translated or adapted to training issues. For instance, management is anxious to harmonise all aspects of training across its network of thirteen training centres worldwide. This is to be achieved by issuing common guidelines on - among other issues - the number of training hours allocated to particular modules, the exact content of modules or student tests.

The reasons behind this drive for harmonisation lie primarily in concerns related to quality and liability. Whenever a pilot or technician trained by Eurocopter is involved in an accident, Eurocopter has to be able to prove that this person was adequately trained to fly that aircraft in accordance with any applicable aeronautical, safety and quality regulations.
Although the Eurocopter brand image and certification plays an important role in their business, some individual training centres have gone their own way when it comes to using training procedures and materials. This is partly due to incompatibilities with their own hardware and software systems, but also to reservations regarding procedure, e.g. lack of communication about updates, no modification facilities for subsidiaries, no master files for local printing, etc.

As far as the company's emphasis on innovation is concerned, the Project team felt that other departments would benefit from improved access to and exchange of training information and knowledge and that this would increase the intellectual capital of the company as a whole. For example, sales staff could benefit from the instructors' experience of dealing with different client groups, whilst engineers in the R&D department might benefit from clients' experience with a particular aircraft, a frequent point of discussion in the classroom.

Customer satisfaction is given the highest priority and quality of training is regarded as a key success factor for attracting new and retaining existing customers. Being in a position to offer computer-based training support is increasingly seen as an essential part of the training 'package', and most customers have come to expect it. Some client companies and competitors are already successfully employing eLearning, mostly for refresher courses required to comply with certain certification regulations.

10.3.1.2 Target groups of training activities

Apart from the instructors, the main users or beneficiaries of the eLearning platform to be developed are the pilots, mechanics and avionic specialists employed by Eurocopter's.

Mechanics constitute a less homogeneous group than pilots, especially as far as their levels of know-how and professional experience are concerned. Whereas some mechanics might already have received extensive training on both the theoretical and practical aspects of an aircraft, others will have acquired their skills almost exclusively on the job.

Generally, instructors find it easier to teach a group that is homogenous in terms of know-how, since any problems tend to arise when the levels diverge. A class might comprise students from five different countries of origin, but as long as their expertise and professional backgrounds are similar, this kind of diversity does not seem to have a significant impact on knowledge transfer.

The training of pilots is much more standardised and is the output of a complex selection process. This includes fitness standards, which have to be checked periodically. A pilot's competence and know-how are linked to his or her flight hour records.

These differences have to be taken into account in the design of the eLearning materials. In the case of mechanics, the Project team distinguished between three levels of how-how (basic, advanced and expert), whereas in the case of pilots, two categories (junior and senior pilots) were considered sufficient. The allocation to one of these two categories was based on the number of flight hours.

On the whole, pilots tend to focus on the essential points of a particular topic, whereas mechanics are more interested in, and indeed need, very detailed information to perform maintenance jobs, especially on existing aircraft. When it comes to new helicopters, however, it is sometimes the pilots who are better informed because they are the first to be confronted with them.

In the training of pilots, emergency procedures are accorded great importance. This fact was emphasised by the instructors: "They have to know by heart what they have to do. In an emergency, they won't have time to look anything up in a manual. By then, the helicopter might have crashed."

Pilots receive a training handbook containing a selection of chapters with a minimum of text. They are expected to make lots of notes, adapt the content to their own needs and memorise the salient facts. The text has usually been lifted from the training manual addressed at the mechanics, which is very detailed, and is supplemented with slides prepared by the pilot instructors. They sift through the documentation available with a view to identifying the points relevant to pilots.

The Flight Manual is considered 'the Bible' for pilots. They have to know exactly where to find information on particular procedures. The training as a whole is geared to quick decision-taking. Although mechanics also have to know which procedures to apply in the case of trouble-shooting, they can often choose between several alternatives in a pool of possibilities. Furthermore, when mechanics have to take decisions or find a solution to a particular problem, they often discuss the different strategies possible with their colleagues, whereas pilots, especially those flying light helicopters (where there is generally no co-pilot) are on their own and have no one else to count on.

The differences between these two target groups also manifest themselves in their respective expectations regarding the design of instruction materials, whether in printed or computer-based form. This will be discussed in the section on Learning, cognition and interaction.

10.3.1.3 Criteria for success or failure in achieving target goals

At present, the quality of training is measured by means of an evaluation form. At the end of each course, the trainees are asked not only whether the course fulfilled their expectations and whether the programme was adequately covered, but also about the equipment used for the practical phases, the lecture rooms and logistical issues. They are also asked to mark both the theoretical and practical parts of the course and assess the instructor himself. Although these suggestions and comments are taken very seriously, there is no systematic feedback mechanism in place with regard to course development, let alone to other departments.

The declared aim of Eurocopter according to the Description of Work of the EU-funded Project was to reduce course preparation time by 40%. This was to be achieved mainly by installing a KM system, which would contain all the information required for course development and modification in a well-structured, organised and therefore easily retrievable form. In turn, the KM system would serve as the basis for developing Web-based training modules.

The Project team therefore investigated how to establish an appropriate way of measuring the time spent on course development to assess the time that would be gained through implementing KM tools and measures. Since course preparation and updating takes place all the time, it proved very difficult to devise suitable indicators for measuring the impact of introducing the new applications put into place for this purpose.
Conventional performance measurements (e.g. number of page visits) could not be used because, although the KM system had been installed and data entered, it had not yet been rolled-out, mainly as a result of security concerns. This is why its eventual benefits were measured largely by presenting various scenarios to future/potential users and experts, as well as by conducting interviews with the staff involved in course preparation.

In order to obtain concrete values for the measurement indicators, test scenarios or cases were defined and presented to a series of experts including instructors for pilots and technicians at Marignane, instructors in a subsidiary, as well as staff involved in course organisation and planning.

Analysis

The test scenarios concern a variety of tasks or actions such as course development and modification or alert services that should be made easier by the new technology.

As far as time savings are concerned, the interviews and the discussions based on the test scenarios showed that instructors tend to underestimate the time they spend on course preparation. Indeed, it was only when their estimates were compared with the log sheets kept by the main course planner and the sub-contractors involved in the revision of documentation for training purposes that it became clear that the actual time spent was at least twice, if not three times as much as estimated!

The analysis of both the test scenarios and the interviews also showed that a well-structured and maintained KM system can help reduce the time spent on course preparation by about one third. Most experts/instructors estimate that time savings of between 30 and 50% could be achieved through the availability of a well-organised, comprehensive KM system containing all the relevant documents, illustrations, diagrams, technical specifications, images etc. and with appropriate version management and/or contact details of author(s).

The time and cost savings will also depend largely on the extent to which the company succeeds in installing coherent, reliable and long-term procedures and organisational measures to ensure maintenance of the content of the KM system. The constant updating of the database is a *sine qua non* for its use and acceptance by its users.

Finally, a number of Project goals such as improving the quality of training courses, strengthening the instructors' community of practice or increasing customer satisfaction are difficult to measure. Many KM issues, especially those which involve human and cultural factors or organisational culture, are intangibles unsuited to traditional measurement methods.

10.3.1.4 Constraints imposed on the choice and use of training systems

By the time the Project team started its work, the management of the Training Centre, had already selected Learning Space 4 (LS4) as the learning management system on which the eLearning platform was going to be implemented. According to the evaluation sheets of Web-based course environments carried out by Edutech in Switzerland[18], LS4 boasts a wide range of features to allow participants to interact and exchange information, e.g. mailing lists, discussion fora, teamwork tools, chatrooms, shared whiteboards, audio and videoconferencing functions. Since the other learning management systems also offer a similar array of functions and features, this pre-selection did not represent a limiting factor.

What might turn out to be more of a problem, especially with a view to harmonisation, is the fact that partners and subsidiaries might use different operating systems or learning management systems. Although theoretically the exchange of learning objects is supposed to work across

---

[18] See http://www.edutech.ch/edutech/tools/comparison_e.asp

different software platforms, in reality the exchange is hampered by the use of different operating system (e.g. if one partner's IT system runs on Linux, while the other uses Microsoft) or by the use of different learning management systems. The problem lies not as much in any technical incompatibility – there are ways around that - but in the reluctance of people to get involved with a new system.

10.3.2 Organisational context of training activity

The area concerning the organisational context identifies the social, cultural and physical aspects of the environment in which the technology will be used. The following points have been taken from the Checklist to orient the analysis:

- Role of target technologies (i.e. KM/eLearning systems) in producing the outcome of target actions (e.g. course organisation and development)
- Access to tools and materials necessary to perform training
- Spatial layout and temporal organisation of the working environment
- Division of labour in course development
- Regulations, standards and procedures regulating training

10.3.2.1 Role of target technologies in course organisation and development

The contextual research to identify the factors that influence training most yielded the finding that the homogeneous composition of a class in terms of know-how or experience makes the greatest contribution to the success of a course.

This is why the Project team decided to develop a student profiling tool which could be used for eliciting the entry level of trainees before prior to their arrival at the Training Center. This tool uses a software program which allows the creation of an intelligent questionnaire with different paths depending on the answers given by the students.

Before the arrival of the trainees, instructors specify the requirements for a particular course and select the relevant documentation and teaching aids to be used. The IT administrator then loads the information and tools required onto the network in the classroom where the course is to take place.

The instructors themselves do not have access to the file servers on which the documentation or training manuals and teaching aids are stored (mostly in the form of PowerPoint, Flash or Toolbook files). Only the IT administrator has access and editing rights.

The naming of the files on the server that contains the depository of training manuals corresponds roughly to the present course organisation, i.e. the main folders tend to refer to the type of helicopter and type of course (mechanics, avionics, pilots, regulations, composites) and are broken down into helicopter sub-types, e.g. B2 or B3, chapters of the training manual (THM) or even individual pages.

The file structure on the server that contains the depository of the teaching aids is linked to the classroom network and is a mixture of folders named after helicopter types, instructors, modules etc., as well as a host of other file folders difficult to attribute to any one particular course. The new KM system will facilitate access by organising and classifying course-relevant data, attaching keywords and harmonising terminology.

In terms of tools for training and mediating their relationships with their customers, instructors use a touch-sensitive smartboard, computer-aided instruction materials for use with the smartboard, various training documents and their own personal notes, but also rely on discussions with their colleagues etc.

The outline and structure of the eLearning prototype module is based on the existing Training Manual for a particular class of aircraft. Hyperlinks are provided to more detailed information on the various items, as well as to related documents such as product specifications. Eventually, the eLearning platform is expected to integrate a discussion forum for facilitating the exchange both between instructors and trainees as well as among trainees.

By installing a KM system which contains all the information required for course development and modification in a well-structured, organised and therefore easily retrievable form, the instructors and others parties involved in course preparation will be able to focus on more important issues such as conceptual development and the adaptation of content and methods to meet the needs of different target groups. It should also free up time for developing new ideas and concepts for training, experimenting with new didactic methods, professional development and the exchange of information and experiences.

10.3.2.2 Division of labour in course development

The following table illustrates the different roles and tasks involved in the process of course development that emerged from the observations and discussions held with those involved in course development:

Role	Course tasks	Comments
Instructor	Determine initial level of trainees	To follow a specific training course, a certain level of know-how is required. At present, no *ab initio* courses are offered.
	Implement pilot application / prototype	Training content has to be organised into meaningful Learning Objects (LO) which allow sequencing according to different variables (prior knowledge, experience, type of qualification, country of origin, ...)

	Evaluate pilot application incl. pedagogic experimentation	Obtain feedback from colleagues and trainees through use of LO in real-life courses. Feedback can be both verbal and non-verbal (body language).
	Carry out modifications	Modify course structure and/or composition taking into consideration the results of evaluation.
	Develop customised versions by means of modifying parameters	Customisation of courses can be based on special requirements as a result of: - professional qualification (mechanics, pilots, avionics, logistics, ...) - type of aircraft (old *versus* new versions) - cultural background.
	Determine final level of trainees	Carry out exams to test trainees' understanding of the subject and ascertain if they have achieved the objectives of the course. Issue a certificate as proof of qualification.
	Accumulate intellectual capital	Instructors gain knowledge and experience both with regard to their professional expertise and didactic skills, which - when exchanged with colleagues - will lead to an increase in the intellectual capital of the Training Academy and the company as a whole.
Course author	Collect information	Based on experience, the course author will gather information (documents, images, specifications, files, ...) and access the KMS to select items relevant for a particular course.
	Specify course content and structure	Organise and structure information according to course requirements (e.g. type of qualification, entry level of trainees etc.).
	Development and/or evaluation of course with colleagues	Course authors usually consult their colleagues before using a course in the classroom. Sometimes courses are produced by several authors who contribute different chapters.
	Evaluate pilot application incl. pedagogic experimentation	Obtain feedback from trainees, both verbal and non-verbal.
	Carry out modifications	Modify course structure and/or composition taking into consideration the results of feedback.
	Develop customised versions	Customisation of courses can be based on special requirements as a result of: - professional background (mechanics, pilots, avionics, ...) - type of aircraft (old *versus* new versions) - cultural background
	Internationalisation	When producing course materials, authors have to be aware of any different cultural requirements and therefore avoid ethnocentric design, language or examples.

Course planner	Course specification	Takes into consideration the Eurocopter philosophy/corporate image. Verifies the courses with a view to adherence to common guidelines and company philosophy.
	Implement prototype	Grants permission for exploitation and manages implementation of prototypes.
	Pedagogic experimentation Modifications and adaptations Customisation and internationalisation	All these tasks are taken into account for the integration of the information management and training management systems.
Training systems responsible	Quality control and validation of courses	Examines 'training course comments sheets' filled in by clients, as well as any comments made by instructors. Discusses problems with instructors and authors. Verifies quality of course by evaluating clients' comments.
Trainees	Provide feedback	Trainees give feedback on both the content and quality of training, including the performance of instructor.

Table 5: Roles and tasks involved in course development

In reality, the roles of instructor and course author often overlap. As already mentioned, pilot instructors tend to develop course materials themselves based on the documentation available.

Furthermore, some instructors are adept at using software tools such as Toolbook and Flash and are quite capable of producing computer-based materials without having to resort to professional designers. Actually, one of the best course designers was originally an instructor, who later became involved in the developing of course materials.

Other instructors prefer to delegate this task to professional designers, who normally work on a freelance basis or are sub-contracted from specialist agencies. For the sake of continuity and efficiency, they prefer to work with the same experts, who ideally – like the interpreters – will also have 'an aeronautic spirit'. Furthermore, instructors tend to insist that designers come into the Eurocopter office from time to time, so they can monitor their work and clarify open questions.

The distribution of roles is therefore in constant flux and depends to a great extent on the skills and attitudes of the individual actors.

10.3.2.3 Regulations, standards and procedures

Training activities in the aviation field are subject to national and international regulations. The Civil Aviation Regulations in force in France and in Germany now have to be compliant with the new European Joint Aviation Requirements (JAR) and helicopter training regulations known as Flight Crew Licensing (FCL2).

All training centres have to be approved and registered as a Type Rating Training Organisation. Their performance is checked and audited regularly by European inspectors. Amongst other things, the inspectors attach great importance to the availability and accessibility of the latest versions of training documentation and the mechanisms in place for updating this documentation.

The company's Quality Department also organises audits several times a year. The professional achievements of instructors are reviewed once a year and a written plan with performance targets drawn up. The qualifications of instructors for pilots and technicians are carefully checked and different seminars for professional development are offered throughout the year (including seminars on cultural or human factors).

As far as computer-based instruction materials are concerned, the recommendations issued by the international Aviation Industry CBT Committee (AICC) also have to be taken into account. Their goal is to ensure the aviation industry receives the best possible training value from vendors and they cooperate with several organisations involved in the development of standards and specifications, including:
- Advanced Distributed Learning (ADL),
- Institute of Electrical and Electronic Engineers / Learning Technology Standards Committee (IEEE/LTSC) and
- Instructional Management System (IMS) Global Learning Consortium.

AICC has compiled a series of technical recommendations providing guidance on specific areas, e.g.
- Acquisition of courseware delivery stations,
- Interoperability of Computer-Managed Instruction systems,
- Exchange of courseware elements such as text and graphics,
- Use of digital video in courseware,
- Creation of learner courseware interface and
- Interoperability of Web-based computer-managed instruction systems.

The last of these areas is of particular importance, since it is designed to provide a standard approach to:

- Lesson initiation,
- Storing learner data,
- Defining the data that are passed between lessons,
- Defining the data that are passed between lessons and CMI systems,
- Defining the data passed between computer-managed instruction systems,

- Course structure and
- Lesson evaluation data.

Since Eurocopter intends to extend its eLearning initiative to its subsidiary training centres worldwide, it is important to enable the interchange of eLearning modules. This is why AGR 007 (AICC Guidelines and Recommendations on Courseware Interchange), which defines guidelines for data formats to facilitate the exchange of courseware elements, has to be taken into account.[19]

10.3.3 Learning, cognition and interaction

The area of learning, cognition and interaction is central to this investigation. It addresses the fact that computer systems should, when necessary, support both the internalisation of new ways of action and the articulation of mental processes to facilitate problem solving and social coordination.

The following items in the Checklist appear to be most relevant to training:

- Components of target actions which are internalised
- Knowledge about target technology that resides in the environment and the way this knowledge is distributed and accessed. Is externally distributed knowledge easily accessible when necessary?
- Use of target technology for simulating target actions before their actual implementation
- Coordination of individual and group activities through externalisation
- Use of shared representations to support collaborative work
- Individual contributions to shared resources of group or organisation

10.3.3.1 The capturing of tacit knowledge

This heading actually covers the first two items in the above list and is concerned with the activity theory principle of the unity of cognition and external practical behaviour, i.e. the interdependence of (internal) cognitions and (external) activities.

The tacit knowledge to be captured refers, on the one hand, to the experience of the instructors in conducting courses for a multicultural clientele. On the other hand, it also refers to all the informal procedures and contacts involved, as well as to any external knowledge networks which can be tapped for training purposes.

A great deal of the participant observation focused on the transfer of knowledge within the classroom to identify:

---

[19] More information on AICC, including the current versions of the AGRs, can be found on their website at www.aicc.org.

- any information/knowledge supplied by instructors, yet not included in any of the formal information sources;
- the information/knowledge acquired as a result of discussion or interaction between instructor and trainees or between trainees.

The question of how – if at all – the tacit knowledge 'owned' by an experienced instructor could be transferred to a computer-based system lay at the heart of the Project. The aim was, ultimately, to integrate the didactic and pedagogic approaches adopted by the instructors to respond to the expectations and requirements of the different target groups into the design of the course.

As discussed in the chapter on eLearning, this is not an easy goal and might even, in the end, prove impossible to achieve. The pedagogically rich learning objects so favoured by contemporary learning theorists with their emphasis on the situated nature of learning cannot be re-used in a different context.

One way to overcome this dilemma is to produce good quality content, i.e. content that is accurate, well-structured and interactive, and make it available to instructors who – provided they receive appropriate guidance on how to construct a suitable pedagogy for eLearning – should then be able to put together good learning situations.

A further core question for the Project was if, or how, the information that resulted from any interaction between the instructor and the trainees or between the trainees themselves could be captured and transferred to the new, virtual environment. In the course of attending various classes, it became clear that a considerable amount of the information transmitted was contained neither in the written sources provided nor in the computer-based teaching materials, for example:

- Cross-references to other machines,
- Advice on how to replace certain parts, e.g. the VEMD unit,
- Advice on how and where to obtain spare parts and
- Certain trouble-shooting scenarios.

Interactivity is considered a great benefit of multimedia learning environments (Schulmeister 1997). However, at least as far as the interaction between instructor and trainees or between trainees is concerned, it would seem to be impossible to really integrate this type of information/knowledge into a Web-based training course. The main reason for this is that this type of information tends to be so unpredictable and depends largely on a number of arbitrary factors such as the composition of a class, the personality of an instructor, the presence of an interpreter, the command of English of both the instructors and the students, the atmosphere in a particular class, etc.

The only way to somehow mirror this form of interaction in the virtual world is to introduce a discussion forum on the eLearning platform which facilitates and encourages the exchange between instructor and students as well as among students. This is why features that foster and strengthen virtual communities or communities of practice are so essential in a learning environment.

However, there is another aspect of interactivity that can be covered and, to a certain extent, enhanced by computer-based systems, namely:

10.3.3.2 Relating learning simulations to real-world experiences

The importance of this aspect became obvious right from the start of the Project when the first expert reviews were carried out with the instructors. They immediately focused their attention on the exact agreement between what takes on a real-life VEMD screen and the simulated processes on the VEMD learning tool. They insisted that the sounds, needle position and colours used for particular components should simulate the real thing as closely as possible.

This emphasis on an exact replica of the object as it occurs in the real world also applies to events. It is therefore of utmost importance to devise scenarios that actually reflect real-life situations or problems. At the same time, the instructors pointed out that herein lies one of the major strengths of computer-based training systems: they enable us to devise scenarios which would be too dangerous to implement in real-life. With the help of simulation, the potentially disastrous consequences of a wrong decision or interpretation of indicators on the screen can be demonstrated. If the helicopter explodes, no lives are put at risk.

The cognitive aspects of the learning area are dealt with under the following heading:

10.3.3.3 Different approaches to learning and teaching

It became clear at an early stage in the ethnographic research that most instructors showed a high degree of awareness of cultural differences and were quite capable of articulating or 'externalising' their knowledge and understanding of cultural differences. At the same time, they warned against stereotyping. National clichés would only act as barriers and prevent them from engaging their minds and hearts – a prerequisite for successful training.

A first investigation of student behaviour on-site showed that two main approaches could be discerned:

- trainees who frequently ask questions and engage in dialogue with the instructor and other students (interactive, problem and task-oriented approach) and
- trainees who prefer to keep quiet and rarely interact with the instructor or other students, but tend to assimilate new topics and know-how through systematic, step-by-step individual learning.

Using Hofstede's cultural model, the first approach corresponds to the type of student-teacher interaction one would expect in societies with small power distance and individualist traditions, whereas the second corresponds to the interaction patterns more likely to be found in societies with large power distance and collectivist orientation (see Table 4: Adaptation of Hofstede's cultural dimension of Power Distance to instructor – trainee relations).

However, the observations made in the classroom did not tally with Hofstede's country scores on these dimensions. As mentioned earlier, professional background had a greater impact on classroom behaviour than country of origin. With regard to style of interaction, pilots lean more towards the first behaviour model, whereas mechanics as a group, and especially those who originate in countries with authoritarian traditions, are more likely to exhibit the patterns characteristic of the second style.

The instructors adapt to the different behaviour patterns by adopting different didactic methods. In the first case, they tend to act more as coaches and are happy to engage in discussion, recognising the students as peers and experts. In the second case, they make an effort – through close observation of trainees' non-verbal behaviour – to gauge the degree of comprehension and respond accordingly.

Other factors that play a role are language, hierarchy and age (the latter are usually closely connected). It is not surprising that students with a poor (active) command of the language of instruction are usually hesitant to ask questions. In most groups with non-European native languages, there tends to be at least one person – usually of senior rank – who is more fluent in either French or English than the others and is able to act as an interpreter; those who are less fluent then address their queries to this person.

The presence of an interpreter also influences the style of interaction. On the whole, his or her presence hampers the immediate exchange and direct dialogue between instructor and trainees. However, whether or not this barrier can be overcome depends very much on the personality and subject knowledge of the interpreter. In some cases, the interpreter is so familiar with the topic and so steeped in the two cultures that he/she will assume the role of cross-cultural communicator in addition to his/her interpreting role.

As is to be expected, in groups with strongly hierarchical structures and traditions, (military) rank is an important factor in classroom behaviour. However, whereas in some groups the presence of senior rank officers more or less had the effect of silencing trainees of lesser ranks, it proved less intimidating in other groups.

Although no systematic investigation has been made into this difference in impact, it can be assumed that in cultures – both organisational (e.g. the military) and national (e.g. Asian countries such as Japan and Korea) – that exhibit a higher degree of power distance, junior personnel will be more likely to feel intimidated by senior people.

In the course of the interviews, it also emerged that as far as the role of the instructor is concerned, attitudes have changed considerably over time. Whereas 15 years ago the instructor was generally expected to act as the 'sage on the stage' and adopt a rather authoritarian teaching approach, in recent years a more egalitarian attitude has found its way into the classroom, and the instructor is seen more as a peer among peers.

10.3.3.4 Collaborative work

Under this heading, I have subsumed the last three items of the Checklist, i.e.

- Coordination of individual and group activities through externalisation,
- Individual contributions to shared resources of group or organisation and
- Use of shared representations to support collaborative work.

As discussed in previous chapters, collaboration is essential to all aspects of KM. Collaboration is also increasingly seen as an important element in learning and teaching and plays a major role in most contemporary pedagogic models such as Problem-Based Learning, Progressive Inquiry Learning and, of course, Collaborative Learning.

On the whole, the instructors are quite aware of the importance of collaboration and do their best to create a team spirit in the group. It may take a few days to break the ice, especially in groups whose members have never previously met, but the instructors pride themselves on the fact that they usually succeed. Some organise joint outings or visits to the construction or assembly plants on the company site, but above all they are convinced that actual hands-on teamwork is the most conducive way of producing group feeling. Indeed, by the end of a course, many groups have been transformed into a sort of community of practice, where pools of knowledge overlap freely and members not only exchange experience and know-how, but also swap 'insider' jokes.

Group and interpersonal interactions involve the use of language, which implies a social process. It is considered absolutely essential to employ consistent, precise and unambiguous language in the eLearning materials. Whilst the instructors can clarify terms or explain obscure phraseology in the existing computer-based teaching aids, online training lacks this disambiguating mechanism.

Before any course-relevant data can be entered into the KM system, differences in terminology have to be resolved. For the purposes of the development of the prototype, an 'authorised version' had to be agreed upon. To our surprise, there seemed to be no agreed terminology regarding the basic layout or general description of the VEMD unit. In various discussions with experts, i.e. instructors and quality managers, it emerged that these discrepancies could be attributed to several factors:

- Actual every-day use deviates from 'official' terms – many of the alternative terms were actually used in the practical work by the instructors and/or the trainees,
- Inference from French in the English-language documentation and
- Bad translations.

It was decided that the terms used in the Illustrated Parts Catalogue could be considered authoritative – at least as far as physical items are concerned. Concepts, procedures or different modes of the instruments (e.g. flight *versus* ground mode) posed more of a problem and no real solution could be found because it turned out that in most cases the terms were originally coined by the Design Office and then adopted by the instructors. This lack of consistency can also be attributed to the fact that military usage differs from civil usage and, at times, the terminology even varies between the different types of helicopter.

Given that in several instances no generally accepted term could be found, it was decided that a thesaurus which provides cross-references to alternative terms should be integrated into the KMS. Furthermore, the possibility of creating hyperlinks to glossary items or index terms including alternative terms was explored. The final system would also have to include a list of abbreviations and acronyms.

Another aspect of collaboration is associated with the entering of the data. Allocating metadata to make the data easier to find and retrieve also requires a cooperative effort. Even if a centralised system is envisaged, i.e. administered and controlled by a particular person or group of people, the instructors will have to agree on and be familiar with the categories and keywords to be used, to ensure that the system finds acceptance.

Furthermore, in the interviews, all the instructors emphasised that course development is and should be teamwork. The spatial layout of their offices – two connected offices, one for instructors dealing with heavy helicopters, the other for those specialising in light helicopters – actually encourages the exchange of information. Even though each instructor has his own customary desk, they move around freely and often sit down with a colleague or with a small group to discuss a particular problem or work on course materials. Although, on the whole, the instructors appreciate the open plan offices, they feel that there should also be a room where they can retreat if they need peace and quiet for concentrated work.

As a group, the instructors exhibit many of the characteristics of a community of practice as defined by Wenger, such as:

- Sustained mutual relationships

- absence of introductory preambles, as if conversations and interactions were merely the continuation of an ongoing process
- very quick set-up of a problem to be discussed
- knowing what others know, what they can do, and how they can contribute to an enterprise
- specific tools, representations and other artefacts
- local lore, shared stories, inside jokes, knowing laughter, jargon and shortcuts to communication as well as the ease of producing new ones (Wenger 1998:125).

The new technology intends to extend this community of practice to include the instructors in the company's subsidiaries around the world. The employees responsible for course planning, scheduling and organisation, as well as the designers and sub-contractors involved in developing training materials, also share in the collaborative effort and exchange of knowledge, but they constitute more of an outer layer, whereas the instructors represent the core layer of this community of practice.

Instructors also seek advice from colleagues in other departments, for example, engineers in the Design Office. They deplore the fact that there is no established procedure to automatically pass on information (e.g. about modifications) to the Campus, but that they instead have to rely on informal contacts to obtain such information. Since such contacts are often tied to particular individuals, the whole system is somewhat precarious and arbitrary.

In the interviews, all the instructors insisted that the Yellow Pages to be developed as part of the KM system should include information not only about instructors in the various subsidiaries, but also contact details and skills profiles of experts in other departments such as the Design Office or Client Support.

When introducing the computer-based systems, one should therefore try to implement automatic procedures for data entry from a variety of sources rather than simply rely on the goodwill of the information holders. This, however, requires cross-departmental coordination and collaboration, which in turn is not possible without the support of management.

The last item of the Checklist concerns the use of shared representations to support collaborative work. As discussed in the Methodology chapter, cultural differences affecting usability and design are mainly representational, i.e. any aspect of the system conveying or intended to convey meaning. As the meaning of a representation is determined by its context of use, it could be expected that the meaning of terms or symbols which relate to the professional context was clear. Regardless their country of origin or cultural background, the future users of the eLearning materials all have a great deal of experience either of helicopter flying, maintenance or of avionics.

Misunderstandings are more likely to occur in connection with the interactive and community functions of the eLearning tool, e.g. functions involving feedback, communication etc. This issue will be discussed in the analysis of the usability tests.

10.3.4 Transformation and development

The last contextual area, "Transformation and development", is concerned with the transformation of the foregoing components. It includes an analysis of the history of target activities, which in turn can help to reveal the main factors influencing the transformation process or development and, thus, anticipate their effect on the structure of target activities.

The following items from the Checklist are considered most relevant:

- Use of target technology or tools at various stages of target action 'life cycles' – from goal setting to outcomes,
- Transformation of existing activities into future activities supported with the system,
- Users' attitudes towards target technology (e.g. resistance) and changes over time and
- Anticipated changes in the environment and the level of activity they directly influence (operations, actions or activities).

From an activity theory perspective, computer-based technologies – including KM systems, eLearning systems or the internet – are regarded as tools. Using the concepts of tool mediation and transformation, it is possible to focus on those parts of course development concerned with transforming (i.e. extending, improving, ...) the existing training system, which is the goal of the action. Re-examination of the corpus of data shows that this transformation proceeds along a number of different dimensions:

- Distributed – Centralised (connected with the role of internalisation and externalisation)
- Provisional /Ephemeral – Decided / Persistent
- Local artefact – Boundary object

There is no doubt that other dimensions could also be identified, but, as will be seen, the above-mentioned dimensions prove to be the most useful.

10.3.4.1 Distributed - centralised

The Distributed *versus* Centralised dimension is closely linked with the role of internalisation and externalisation, i.e. capturing the tacit knowledge that resides in the environment and in the instructors' community of practice. By making it explicit, it is transformed into a centralised, unified form as the basis of an agreed understanding. One of the main tasks of the Project consisted in gathering the information required for course development, agreeing on a common terminology and selecting appropriate keywords or metadata.

The work to be done for the introduction of the target technology, i.e. the computer-based KM and eLearning systems, was broken down into the following steps and measures:

- Investigate users' attitudes to target technology.
- Identify the sources of information for eLearning modules.
- Identify the differences e.g. in terminology and agree on an 'authorised version'.
- Enter information relevant to course development into the KM system and attach keywords.
- Develop a basic storyboard for the pilot application.
- Investigate training processes in the classroom that focus on interactive and community features not included in formal training materials or teaching aids.

The first step – investigate users' attitudes – is of primary importance because the success of KM depends to a great extent on the support and participation of people affected by it. Any KM initiative – even if it has top-management support – will be met with a certain measure of resistance or at least caution. One way of dealing with people's reservations is to involve them right from the start.

Participatory design approaches are characterised by similar concerns. They stipulate that it is essential to involve real users right from the outset of the design process, since this results in an iterative design process in which users' comments are fed back into the design process. Such an approach might be more time-consuming in the early phases, but pays off at a later stage. A comprehensive development process will not only improve the quality of the eLearning product and the user experience, it will also save time and money in the long run as there will be less need for costly redesign measures.

The fear that the instructors might be opposed to the whole idea of eLearning proved unjustified. They know that any form of computer-based training system can only complement their work, but never replace it. Both helicopter flying and helicopter maintenance are skills that require face-to-face training. Furthermore, many machines are customised according to specific client wishes or needs, which, in turn, requires specialised training.

10.3.4.2 Provisional – decided/persistent

Changes in the technology are connected with the provisional *versus* decided/persistent dimension. This dimension refers to the transformation of the design from a provisional stage into one which has the agreement of the team. As the Project progressed, the tasks involved in implementing a KM system and developing eLearning modules gradually crystallised.

Analysis

As described earlier, the Project team devised a KM framework consisting of eight interlinked modules, which was then analysed in detail and guidelines produced for its application in a business environment. Comparable to the Activity checklists, the framework helped the research team to identify the key issues that needed to be addressed in the two industrial applications and suggest appropriate methods and tools. In the process, the team aimed to strike a balance between IT and non-IT elements and provide the industrial partners (and any subsequent users of the framework) with practical guidelines on how to use the framework and implement a KM project.

This process, which starts out with suggestions and proposals and ends with recommendations and guidelines that go beyond the individual case studies, is typical of the development of computer-based systems. The actual design process happened more or less in parallel, with different parts of the design at different stages of maturity at any particular time.

10.3.4.3 Local – Boundary object

This dimension concerns the transformation of the training system from an artefact that is either local or restricted to the Project team into one for external consumption by the wider Campus community and, eventually, for the worldwide network of training centres.

Such transformations result in the creation of so-called 'boundary objects', i.e. shared work objects, which cross the boundaries of different workgroups, departments or organisations and as such act as vehicles for communication. This process usually requires putting ideas into writing and phrasing them in such a way that they can be understood by people outside the immediate Project team or community of practice.

For instance, in the communications directed at the management of the Training Center, the Project team stressed the anticipated changes in the environment and the benefits these would bring in terms of time and cost savings. In the reports addressed to the European Commission, the emphasis was on the relevance of the Project work for the wider research community.

In the field of KM, one talks of the necessity of finding 'champions' to promote a KM initiative. These champions can be regarded as the human equivalent of boundary objects. They cross departmental boundaries to promote the idea of KM and motivate others to get involved in the endeavour.

Organisations also need to mobilise the tacit knowledge held by outside stakeholders such as customers, suppliers, competitors, the regional community and the Government through social interactions. To tap these sources, it is necessary to move beyond the organisational boundaries.

This dimension often involves specifying criteria for measuring the benefits of a target technology since the value of a new technology might not be so obvious to people outside the community or people not familiar with the advantages of KM or eLearning.

10.4 The role of cultural factors

This section discusses the results of expert reviews, end-user tests and focus group discussions with a view to the role of cultural factors in the development and evaluation of eLearning materials.

As mentioned earlier, a major challenge faced by the helicopter manufacturer was the need to recognise and integrate the different requirements and expectations of its culturally diverse customer base into its training activities. Although all trainees are expected to be proficient in English and share the same professional context, it was assumed that their varied cultural values, traditions and attitudes would have an influence on their understanding of the content and their cognitive approach to its presentation.

Since the focus of the usability testing was on the influence of cultural factors rather than on general usability issues, the analysis is primarily concerned with the role of cultural factors in the development of computer-based systems.

In activity theory, cultural factors are considered an integral part of any activity and therefore represent a horizontal theme across all four areas addressed by the Checklist, namely:

- Strategies and goals,
- Organisational context,
- Learning, cognition and interaction and
- Transformation and development.

Because of practical constraints, it was not possible to conduct the usability tests to the extent and with the numbers of participants originally planned. The main reason for this was the fact that the development of the prototype took much longer than expected, forcing us to resort to a quiz produced in PowerPoint to simulate the interactive features. Consequently, the end-user tests could not be carried out with a fully-fledged eLearning training module.

Secondly, the delays in development meant that the testing period coincided with the final stage of the Project , during which various reports had to be drafted and the Project team had to prepare for the Final Review of the Project by the European Commission.

Finally, but equally importantly, a breakdown of results according to nationality would have violated the confidentiality agreement with the company.

Since only 18 trainees participated in the end-user tests, the results cannot be regarded as statistically significant. In addition, the majority of participants were mechanics (16 of 18) and two thirds came from the same country of origin. The remaining third were of different nationalities with a fairly even spread across the continents. Thus, the sample cannot be considered representative of the student population as a whole, and the results of the end-user tests should be regarded more as indicators of tendencies and pointers for further research.

10.4.1 Strategies and goals

Because of the cultural diversity of its clients, which come from more than one hundred different countries, the company aimed to produce so-called 'internationalised' products, i.e. modules which have been stripped of any culture-specific content, and can be customised or localised comparatively easily at a later stage, if required. To cope with this eventuality, Eurocopter also wanted to have guidelines on how to produce customised modules for different target groups (including guidelines for usability testing for culturally diverse user groups).

As a result of observing the training process *in situ* and analysing the results of the usability tests, the Project team eventually reached the conclusion that the cultural differences between the professional target groups were greater than those between the different nationalities.

In addition, far more importance was attributed to the content than to its presentation. The efforts of the designers to produce colourful, entertaining user interfaces were largely wasted. The attention and emphasis of both the subject experts, i.e. the instructors, and the end-users, i.e. the customers, was on the accuracy, correctness and reliability of the information presented; graphical design and other surface features were seen as an issue of minor concern.

Consequently, information organisation came to replace the development of eLearning modules as the primary goal to facilitate and improve the transfer of knowledge. Structuring and organising the information required for the courses and agreeing on the terminology and metadata to describe the content, took precedence over the design of user interfaces for eLearning modules.

10.4.2 Organisational context

The staff responsible for planning and scheduling courses use the following criteria for allocating students to a particular class:

- Professional experience
- Language
- Religion /Culture/ History

This ranking was confirmed in the interviews with instructors. As mentioned earlier, the composition of a class plays a decisive role for the success of a course. The more homogeneous a class is in terms of prior knowledge and experience, the more efficient the training.

Whereas for pilots, level can be ascertained comparatively easily on the basis of the number of flight hours, this is more complicated in the case of mechanics because of the differences in training traditions and career paths. The standard forms to be completed by the trainees when applying for a course do not do justice to this state of affairs.

This is why the Project team decided to develop a student profiling tool which can be used for eliciting the entry level of trainees before they arrive at the Training Center. In cooperation with the instructors, a series of questions were put together which would give the instructor a clearer idea of both the practical experience and the theoretical expertise of prospective students.

From experience, and as a result of feedback from instructors, the people responsible for course planning know that clients from certain countries take longer to assimilate the course contents. They attribute this to differences in training systems or traditions, cognitive approach and contextual factors, for example, the fact that in most countries formerly under Soviet hegemony, maintenance tasks were carried out by Russian technicians.

They also avoid mixing clients from countries with acrimonious relations to prevent potential difficulties or tensions which might have a negative impact on the atmosphere.

10.4.3 Learning, cognition and interaction

The two major themes in this area are:
- Usability issues in eLearning
- Interactivity and eLearning

10.4.3.1 Usability issues relevant to eLearning

For practical purposes, i.e. in designing the questionnaire for the usability studies to be carried out in connection with the VEMD pilot course, we decided to focus on issues which had already been identified by the usability community as being particularly relevant in relation to an eLearning context.

As mentioned above, it was assumed that cultural differences affecting usability and design were mainly representational and that the meaning of representations depended largely on their context of use. Given the shared professional background of the trainees, the Project team felt that, at least as far as the information transfer part was concerned, it should be possible to design culturally 'neutral' modules since the target groups were thoroughly familiar with the subject matter.

This assumption was largely born out by the results of both the expert reviews and end-user tests. The mechanics and pilots who participated in the tests had no difficulty in understanding the text, graphics or icons related to the subject matter.

For orientation purposes, we adopted the following table from Kamentz and Womser-Hacker (2003), which illustrates cultural differences with regard to interface design and usability issues. It is based on a comparison of German and American learning software programs carried out by the authors. Type A was found to be prevalent in American programs, whereas Type B was typical of German learning software.

In line with the cultural models of Galtung (1981), Clyne (1994) and Hofstede (1986), Kamentz and Womser-Hacker assume that Type A is generally preferred not only by users from Germany, but also by learners from Scandinavian and Asian countries, whereas Type B is expected to be more popular with learners from Latin countries (France, Spain, Latin America).

Type A	Type B
Graphical design	
Ca. 60% of screen empty, short lines	Screen almost full, long lines
Simple screen layout	Complex, but clearly structured layout
Short paragraphs, many list items	Long text passages
Frequent use of multimedia	Most information is presented as text
Graphics and animations used for illustration and entertainment	Graphics and simulations used as teaching aids
Lots of contrasting colours and highlighting	Contrasting colours mainly used to differentiate different screen components (e.g. navigation buttons, contents,..)
Interaction and navigation	
Greater choice of interactive features with exercises: simulations, drag and drop, multimedia elements for case study templates	High interactivity through use of simulation. With exercises: multiple choice, free text entry. Overall, frequent use of pop-up windows
Content	
Detailed objectives and intensive use of advance organizers to introduce lessons	Detailed introduction to subject, survey and general learning objectives at beginning
Facts, examples, case studies; problem solving strategies and checklists	Theory, facts, examples; historical background at beginning
Personal dialogue with learners	Largely impersonal presentation of information
Concise presentation of information	Detailed presentation of information
Linear information structure with flat hierarchy	Deeply hierarchical

Lessons not interrelated	Lessons build on each other
Didactic approach	
Regular alternation between short training units and exercises within a single lesson	Exercises at the end of each lesson or in a separate appendix
Exercises: yes/no, multiple choice, case studies	Multiple choice, free text, complex questions testing people's comprehension; use of simulations for experimental purposes
Detailed instructions for answering questions	Few, but concise instructions
Feedback: right/wrong, additional explanations	Feedback: right/wrong, revision of teaching material
Emphasis on values such as performance, material advantages, practical application (extrinsic motivation)	Emphasis on acquisition of knowledge, understanding, fun (intrinsic motivation)

Table 6: Cultural differences with regard to user interface design

When applied to the user groups in this study, the preferences for Type A and B co-related with professional culture rather than with national culture. The majority of pilots leaned towards Type A, whereas mechanics tended to opt for Type B. Nonetheless, the following detailed analysis shows that these co-relations are nothing more than tendencies and that many responses to the individual questions do not correspond to the schema at all.

Both subject experts and end-users regarded graphical design, including the use of icons, colours or images, layout of text, size of font, etc., as far less important than the fact that the information conveyed should be absolutely accurate, reliable and correspond to real-life conditions. The majority of participants felt that 'gimmicks' such as flashing icons, animated graphics or even exclamation marks to indicate whether an answer was right or wrong were inappropriate or "over the top" and only distracted from the tasks in question. "Better use the memory for technical information", was a frequently heard comment. Only non-subject experts seemed to attribute any importance to such "surface" details.

In any case, these two types can be regarded as the two poles or extremes on a wide spectrum of preferences, conventions and expectations, all of which can be influenced by a variety of factors such as teaching and learning traditions, age, national or ethnic heritage and professional background.

As far as the last point in the Kamentz and Womser-Hacker table is concerned, with most trainees the sources of motivation are a mixture of both intrinsic and extrinsic reasons, the latter because all students – with the exception of the occasional 'guest' – have to take an exam at the end of the course. If they do not pass this exam, this might have a negative impact on their future careers, especially in the case of junior personnel. For senior-rank personnel, the final certificate is of less importance, but a really bad result would nonetheless be a stain.

But whatever the significance of the certificate, virtually all trainees are highly motivated, eager to absorb new knowledge and share their experience with their course colleagues. In a few rare instances, trainees seemed to view the course primarily as an incentive trip or as a reward for something. In such cases, they were more oriented towards enjoying the pleasures of Southern France.

Another interesting factor that could be noted, however, is that, by and large, mechanics emphasise values such as acquisition of (detailed) knowledge, understanding and solving problems, whereas with pilots the emphasis was on performance and quick decision-taking, especially in emergency situations. Furthermore, the atmosphere among pilots tends to more competitive.

10.4.3.2 eLearning and interactivity

As mentioned in the last chapter, the end-user tests were restricted to a quiz which had been designed in PowerPoint to test the interactive features of the future eLearning module. The emphasis in these tests lay primarily on finding out how trainees felt about the methods used to provide feedback, the form of address (formal *versus* informal) and the overall look and feel.

On the whole, all trainees preferred being addressed personally. Although wide-spread German cultural models or standards might lead one to assume that they would show a preference for an impersonal neutral style, even the German technicians were in favour of the more personal form of address. The respondents, however, were divided on the issue of whether they wanted to be guided through the program by a human voice or avatar. Some suggested that a female voice be used for emergency messages (comparable to the voice of 'Red Rita' for MIG 25 pilots) since this is said to trigger an immediate response from the overwhelmingly male pilot population.

The majority of respondents opted for the option "Regular alternation between short training units and exercises within a single lesson" as opposed to "Exercises at the end of each lesson or in a separate appendix" and for "Few, but concise instructions" to precede exam questions.

With regard to the type of question, no clear preference could be discerned and, at times, the answers given in the questionnaire even contradicted the opinions voiced in the group discussions. About half of participants opted for multiple-choice questions, but then conceded to their colleagues that these were somewhat arbitrary and that free text entry was a better way for finding out whether trainees had really understood a topic.

As far as feedback is concerned, most prefer to receive additional explanations if they give a wrong answer. On the whole, they do not appreciate the use of particular sounds in the quiz to indicate a right or wrong answer. This is particularly relevant for Asian students, who would lose face if others in the room were to know that they had given an incorrect answer.

The respondents were divided on whether or not they should be given the possibility to try again immediately after giving a wrong answer and receiving a summary of results at the end of the test. Some respondents suggested that the system should log any wrong answers and present them again after completion of the test together with additional information.

At present, the test results and the certificate are handed to the trainees in a closed envelope and not usually discussed further – neither with the instructor nor among the trainees. In discussions with instructors it emerged that even trainees from countries where it is common to display results publicly (e.g. some Anglo Saxon countries) are quite happy with this regime.

The instructors are of the opinion that the general reluctance towards the publishing of test results might be due to the following reasons:
- a very competitive atmosphere (especially in the case of pilots),
- the hierarchical structure in the military (e.g. problems can occur if the ranking of test results does not coincide with the ranking in the military hierarchy) and
- loss of face.

10.4.4 Transformation and development

When transferring training materials from the printed format to a computer-based or Web-based system, these have to undergo certain transformations to make them more suited to the new medium. It is certainly not sufficient or satisfactory just to run them through an HTML editor and place them onto the eLearning platform.

At present, training in the classroom is supported not only by printed documents (including training manuals, product specifications and even vendor-specific information, e.g. about engines), but also by so-called 'CAI materials', the computer-aided materials normally produced with Toolbook or Flash. These are mounted on the server in the classroom and projected onto the smartboard.

The smartboard is an interactive whiteboard, which can turn a computer and projector into a tool for teaching, collaborating and presenting. The computer image is projected onto the board and the user simply presses on its touch-sensitive surface to access and control the application. Using a special pen, an instructor can write notes, draw diagrams and highlight important information with electronic ink.

The CAI materials are used exclusively in the classroom where they support and accompany teaching, but they are not intended for use without an instructor. However, they can serve as the foundation for the eLearning materials. The various steps and measures taken in the development of eLearning materials have been described in Chapter 9.2.2. They include organising and structuring the relevant information, agreeing on a common terminology and basically supplying all the explanations, background knowledge, trouble-shooting scenarios, etc. that form part of face-to-face instruction.

10.4.4.1 Users' attitudes to eLearning

End-users attitudes' to and expectations of eLearning modules as tools for training were largely identified by means of group discussions. Although they are quite aware of the advantages of eLearning, such as independence of time and place, working at one's own pace, etc. most users felt that the applicability of eLearning in their field of action is fairly limited. They regard it as useful for preparing certain well-defined topics (such as the VEMD), revision or follow-up purposes. All are adamant that face-to-face training is more effective because so much learning occurs as a result of interaction and collaboration, and these can never be adequately integrated in computer-based systems.

Those who had been exposed to computer-based programs in the training centres of other vendors expressed their dislike of individualised training by means of computer- or Web-based modules. In their opinion, the role of computer-mediated instruction materials is to support face-to-face training, as practised in the Eurocopter Campus. This wide-spread scepticism can be found regardless of whether clients have had prior experience with eLearning or not. In addition, most clients feel that eLearning is not suited for certification purposes, mainly because of the problem of authentification.

A note of clarification seems necessary here with regard to the term 'clients' to account for certain discrepancies in attitude. Particularly in the case of light helicopters, clients may be private individuals who receive training as part of the purchase contract. Most heavy helicopters, however, are purchased by the military, the police, oil-exploring companies or organisations in charge of rescue missions. Here, the clients who actually purchase the aircraft are not to be equated with the trainees. This is where a conflict of interests can arise: (paying) clients might want to cut down on training costs and demand an expansion of the eLearning programme, whereas the trainees themselves on the whole prefer (more expensive) face-to-face training.

10.4.4.2 Emerging themes in the development of eLearning materials

Given the small sample in the end-user tests and the fact that the eLearning prototype was still under development, it is not possible to draw any definite conclusions about how best to transform the existing training materials and procedures into training supported by computer-based systems. However, based on both the group discussions and the usability tests, as well as on literature sources (especially Chase et al 2002), certain themes with intercultural implications appear to be relevant for the development of eLearning materials.

The following list of themes is rather tentative and far from final or exhaustive, but nonetheless provides orientation for similar research.

Attitudes towards authority

These may have an impact on participant expectations regarding the role of online moderators or facilitators, e.g. with regard to the degree of guidance through the course or to resolving technical problems.

Intellectual style or discourse

Different learning and teaching traditions may influence whether trainees expect a formal, sober style focused on their professional role or if they feel more at ease with an informal and personal style. Some trainees might prefer to have information presented to them by way of stories, case studies or scenarios. Some find extensive theoretical passages tedious and long run-on paragraphs difficult to read, whereas others are happy with solid blocks of text.

Attitudes toward time

Most people have explicit and implicit assumptions about 'time' and what constitutes punctuality. Certain cultures show little tolerance with delay and expect immediate responses. When it comes to communicating results, they would not be prepared to wait until the end of an online test to find out if their answers were right or wrong.

Group versus individual focus

In some cultures, students are used to learning in a group environment which is why, for example, the use of sound might not be advisable, since it could disturb other group members. It might also be better to avoid the use of sounds to indicate if an answer is right or wrong, because in some cultures this might result in a loss of face in front of colleagues or superiors.

Furthermore, in some professional cultures, e.g. mechanics responsible for the maintenance of aircraft, many problems are solved as a team, and any system introduced would have to facilitate the exchange between course participants, whereas in other professional cultures, e.g. pilots, most decision-making and problem-solving takes place on an individual basis.

High versus low context communication patterns

When trainees share the same professional background, the requirements for contextual information regarding the subject matter are lower than for training programs directed at a general, more heterogeneous public.

However, contextual information might be relevant regarding any interactive features involving communication patterns, which can differ between cultures. Whereas some trainees expect short, precise instructions on how to answer exam questions, others might feel lost without very detailed instructions. Similarly, the rating or ranking scales for test results vary between cultures and will need to be explained.

Another aspect that deserves closer consideration here is the communication patterns involved in collaborative computer-supported work and problem-solving.

Task versus relationship focus

Tensions between relationship building communication and 'on-task' communication might emerge in the interaction between instructor and trainees. According to the instructors, establishing a good 'rapport' is a key factor for a successful course with most groups, especially those with trainees from Asian or Arab countries.

Attempts to transfer relationship building to a virtual environment will affect – above all – the interactive aspects of eLearning, for example, e-mail correspondence between instructor and trainees or among trainees or exchange in a discussion forum.

Cyberculture

The final theme is related to the medium, which has its own cultural implications in the sense that it is associated with mental models, expectations and practices. Cyberculture is not neutral or value-free, but reflects the values of its (original) developers and is thus a carrier of the culture that prevails in that particular community.

It is overtly maintained by guideline creation, covertly by facilitators and participants. Features include rules of formality/informality, flexibility, interaction style (including greetings/farewells, use of apology) expectations of response speed and work ethics. As we have seen, differences in attitudes to work can lead to tensions between communications aimed at relationship building and 'on-task' communications.

In an online course environment, significant cultural 'gaps' can result out of role differences, e.g. between junior and senior people, experience, perceptions of academic ability, gender, perceptions of time, professional status, tolerance for criticism and debate.

Many communication technologies lack elements inherent in face-to-face communication, e.g. context perception, dynamic real-time repair mechanisms, a parallel visual channel, eye contact, gesture information and the flexibility we normally expect to obtain or emerge between conversational partners.

The online environment also limits the ways in which participants can utilise face-saving strategies. Attitudes towards person-to-person communication using information and communication technologies can vary greatly between cultures, organisations, lines of business, academic disciplines or professions. Individual discomfort or ease with the 'anonymity' of online discourse also depends strongly on factors such as gender or age.

Significant cultural differences have been observed in the ways participants write about their own identity and the degree of 'self-revelation' they display (see e.g. Chase et al 2002). These can range from very formal exchange focusing on the participants' professional roles to 'chatty' conversation and discussions of family matters.

Technical and formatting issues influence effective communications. The more adept a person is at using a computer, the less likely it is that he/she will become frustrated with such issues. Familiarity with computer usage can therefore have a significant impact on people's perceptions of eLearning materials.

All the above-mentioned themes should be considered in the development of eLearning materials or environments for multicultural target groups.

10.5 Contradictions

According to activity theory, contradictions refer to difficulties or weaknesses in the existing system. However, these should not be viewed as negative, but as the driving force behind development and transformation. As discussed in the chapter on activity theory Framework, the concept of contradiction is closely related to the concept of critical incidents proposed by Thomas and is sometimes also described as 'breakdowns' (e.g. Spagnolli, Gamberini and Gasparini 2002).

The Project itself owes its conception to weaknesses perceived in the training system. It was initiated because the management at the time was aware of certain inadequacies with regard to the exchange, use and transfer of information and knowledge and was looking for solutions to address these issues. The measures proposed by the Project team aimed to overcome the barriers to efficient knowledge exchange and develop new technologies that would enhance access to and retrieval of information. This, in turn, was considered a prerequisite for setting up an eLearning system.

In this section, I try to answer the question raised at the beginning of this chapter, namely what kinds of contradictions can be observed in the training system and what are the reasons behind them? The description follows the same structure as the previous sections, i.e. the four areas outlined by the Checklist.

10.5.1 Strategies and goals of training

At the higher strategic level, the contradictions identified concerned the somewhat half-hearted support and commitment of management, the organisational barriers between different divisions that prevented the effortless flow of information relevant to course development and the lack of an integrated approach to KM and eLearning.

As far as the training activity is concerned, the drive for customer satisfaction, on the one hand, and the wish to save money, on the other, represent another contradiction difficult to resolve. Although it is recognised that the quality of training is a key factor in creating customer satisfaction, management was nonetheless reluctant to allocate additional resources.

On the end-user front, a similar contradiction can be observed: the majority of clients are aware of the fact that highly specialised skills require constant updating and attribute great importance to the professional development of pilots and technicians. However, they are also anxious to reduce costs. Even though the actual training costs are included in the purchase price of an aircraft, attending a course on Campus incurs considerable travelling expenses and living costs. The demand for the provision of eLearning materials on the part of clients is often rooted in their wish to cut down on the number of days spent on site.

Since solving the conflict between achieving cost savings and investing in training, was beyond the control of the Project team, its efforts focused on those contradictions or weaknesses in the training system that were within its reach.

In the interviews, the instructors were encouraged to make suggestions about how to improve the existing training system. Many clients, too, voiced opinions about the present training system and training materials, including the computer-based material. This consultation process is the best strategy to counteract the contradictions that lurk in a process that does not involve the people who (will) use the target technologies.

The suggestions made both by the instructors and the clients can be summarised and subsumed under several categories described in the following sections.

10.5.2 Strategies and goals

A wide-spread contradiction lies in the erroneous belief that the development of eLearning modules is best left to the experts, i.e. designers or IT personnel. Without close collaboration with subject experts, the outcome of such an endeavour is likely to be unsatisfactory.

This was confirmed when investigating the history of the training activity. It emerged that ours was not the first eLearning module to be produced, and that a specialised agency had previously been commissioned to develop an eLearning module demonstrating the benefits of this progressive form of training. However, the product was never actually used in the classroom. The main reason given for this was – apart from insufficiencies associated with the product itself – a lack of involvement of instructors and end-users, and, as a result, lack of acceptance.

The instructors have very clear ideas of the topics where the development of eLearning training modules makes sense. They are able to pin-point areas and topics that are relatively self-contained and suited for individualised training. They are also aware of the areas where it makes economic sense to develop eLearning materials, since they can help level out differences in *a priori* knowledge and thus lead to more homogeneous groups.

The decision by the Project team to produce the eLearning prototype on the VEMD was actually the result of many discussions with the instructors, who were in the best position to distinguish between essential and less important features as well as the best sequence in which to present the content.

10.5.3 Organisational context

In this area, contradictions can be found above all in the recognition of the importance of cross-departmental collaboration, yet lack of procedures or mechanisms to facilitate it. As mentioned earlier, instructors often seek advice from colleagues in other divisions, especially engineers in the Design Office or colleagues in the Client Support division.

When introducing the computer-based systems, one should therefore try to implement automatic procedures for data entry from a variety of sources including those outside the Campus. This, however, requires cross-departmental coordination and collaboration, which, in turn, is not possible without the support of decision-makers in the upper echelons of the company.

A similar contradiction can be observed in the fact that while the importance of client feedback is appreciated, it is not systematically fed into the design and production process. This also applies to other people in the system such as interpreters, suppliers, sub-contractors, etc. whose knowledge is potentially very valuable to the company.

Last but not least, the status and recognition given to the instructors does not always reflect the official company recognition of training as a key factor in customer satisfaction and customer loyalty. It was only recently that all instructors were awarded a status more in line with their responsibilities and skills. However, many still feel that their work is not always appreciated by their superiors. If their intrinsic motivation and commitment to their students were not so great, this might be a highly damaging factor.

10.5.4 Learning, cognition and interaction

The main contradiction in this area concerns information and knowledge organisation. It is generally recognised that a well-structured repository of course-relevant information is a *sine qua non* for producing and developing high-quality training courses as efficiently as possible. However, when gathering the information required for course development, the Project team was faced with a lack of common and/or consistent terminology, lack of metadata to describe the information and make it easier to retrieve and data repositories full of obscure file names and intransparent structures.

These deficiencies can also partly be found in the printed documentation. The production of technical documentation and communication products is a highly skilled and complex process, especially when it involves different language versions. Increasingly, some of the tasks associated with this are being outsourced, which requires efficient mechanisms for coordination and quality control. Unfortunately, these processes are not always managed as efficiently as they should be. The introduction of a KM system therefore presents an excellent opportunity to alleviate these weaknesses in the present system.

The majority of instructors stress that course development is a teamwork task. Although they are in favour of centralised control of the KM server, they argue that the input of data should be organised by groups, for example, a group of instructors working on a particular helicopter type. At present, collaboration does takes place, but not in a systematic manner. The lack of established collaborative procedures and mechanisms makes it more difficult and time-consuming for new employees to familiarise themselves with the system.

10.5.5 Transformation and development

Since the transfer of existing instruction materials was not completed in the course of the Project, it was only possible to outline the themes that appear to be relevant for the development of eLearning materials. It is in connection with these themes that contradictions are likely to occur.

The effect of introducing eLearning modules as part of the training will only become clear when the implementation has progressed further. However, by making people aware of the areas of possible contradictions, it is hoped that these can be counteracted or resolved at an early stage.

11 Conclusions

In the previous chapter, I have demonstrated that activity theoretical concepts can be used to structure and organise the wealth of ethnographically acquired data, thereby achieving a greater understanding of the processes and dynamics of an activity such as training. To move from theory to practice, activity checklists can serve as a tool for analysing and structuring the empirical data.

The empirical data were gathered mainly by means of ethnographic methods such as interviews, participant observation and focus group discussions. These have come to be recognised as the most appropriate methods of gaining an in-depth understanding of the context in which an activity occurs. In the case of this study, this includes not only existing tools and materials for training purposes, but also strategies and goals at organisational level, rules and regulations concerning training as well as mental models such as expectations and attitudes of users.

In this final chapter, the findings of the ethnographic research and usability tests are summarised and translated into a series of recommendations and guidelines for usability testing, accommodating cultural factors, developing eLearning materials and methodology. Although so-called 'adaptive' user interfaces are considered the ultimate solution to successful and efficient cultural adaptation, the recommendations are based on a more pragmatic and realistic approach.

Though the main focus of this study is on training and course development, its scope goes well beyond the development of eLearning training materials to encompass the exchange and transfer of knowledge and information as a whole, with training being just one aspect of this.

I conclude that activity theory is an extremely flexible framework that can be combined with concepts and models derived from other approaches depending on the particular environment or organisational context in which activities take place. For the purposes of this investigation, Holden's approach to culture as an object of KM and Wenger's concept of communities of practice, proved to be the most appropriate complements to activity theory.

11.1 Why activity theory?

The main contribution of this study lies in showing how activity theory can serve as a framework for the complex issues involved in developing and introducing new technologies such as computer-based KM and/or eLearning systems. The challenge of finding a theoretical framework that can embrace all the diverse aspects, guide the researcher when investigating requirements for computer-mediated training in an inter- and cross-cultural environment and provide suitable tools for analysing the empirical data became the main research focus and finally led to the adopting of activity theory.

The design of any new interactive system, be it for the purposes of learning, training or information management, involves the design of a new activity – individual or organisational. Activity theory can be used to develop a representational framework that will help designers to capture current practice and build predictive models of activity dynamics. In particular in the early phases of design, such conceptual tools could assist designers to achieve appropriate design solutions.

Before developing new technologies for enhancing the transfer and exchange of information and knowledge, it is important to identify the factors in the environment that have an impact on the activity as a whole and on its component actions such as course organisation or development (e.g. the division of labour, the characteristics of target groups). This is considered a prerequisite for the successful introduction and implementation of a new computer system or application such as an eLearning platform.

In addition, activity theory looks capable of coping with subject matters that undergo rapid change. When the current methods, styles and standards in HCI or eLearning are used, the results are inevitably obsolete soon after they are formulated. Activity theory puts them both into the context of the basic, invariant principles underlying human activity and thus provides a better opportunity for creating a theoretical framework that has predictive potential.

Activity theory prevents researchers in HCI and eLearning from adopting too narrow a focus and thus responds to the move toward context and extending units of analysis. In both fields, there has been a shift of focus from interaction between the user and the computer to a larger context of interaction of human beings with their environment, i.e. transcending the user interface to reality beyond the human-computer dyad.

Given these reasons, activity theory appears to be the most comprehensive framework for tackling the issues connected with this research. From it, we can derive models and concepts for analysing social and cultural structures and processes in usability engineering as well as computer-mediated learning and teaching. It offers us a unified framework for looking at the use of computers as tools to achieve certain goals and for exploring issues connected with these activities. Furthermore, it is not restricted to activities performed by individuals, but also includes those carried out by groups and organisations.

11.2 Recommendations and guidelines

Recommendations and guidelines are the result of a process of generalisation and abstraction, i.e. they go beyond a narrative account of a particular case study. This process has been made possible by the application of the activity checklists to structure and organise the empirical data collected through ethnographic methods. The author's personal bias and vocabulary is thus replaced by activity theory concepts supplemented by concepts and models from other approaches such as Holden's concept of culture and Wenger's communities of practice.

Analysis

As already noted in the Methodology chapter, the (supposed) lack of generalisability of ethnographic data is seen more as a limitation due to the novelty of this approach in the field of HCI or information systems research than as a limitation per se. Over time, as more ethnographic studies are completed in the HCI and eLearning fields, the cumulative research results will help build up a repository of design knowledge based on extraction and comparison of findings across studies.

The recommendations and guidelines presented in the following section are based on a pragmatic and realistic approach that takes into account the constraints to which most organisations are subjected. They have been derived from the analysis of the results in the previous chapter and are subsumed under several categories:

1. Usability testing
2. Developing eLearning materials
3. Accommodation of cultural factors
4. Methodology.

11.2.1 Guidelines for usability testing

General usability guidelines such as those developed by Nielsen (see Table 3: General usability guidelines by Nielsen) can serve as a good starting point. The guidelines proposed by Hoft (1995) or Marcus (2000) focus on the intercultural aspects of technical communication and Web design, respectively. Both authors refer to the cultural models of Hofstede and other intercultural theorists who espouse an essentialist view of culture as mental software. Nonetheless, much of their advice is sound, rooted in practical experience and observation and can therefore be used as a source of inspiration independent of cultural categories.

Various attempts to define criteria for good usability design in accordance with various cultural models have proved unsatisfactory or simply confirmed that users from all cultural backgrounds agree on what constitutes good design, i.e. clear navigation, constant visibility of system status, emphasis on recognition rather than recall and aesthetic minimalist design. The last point implies the avoidance of 'gimmicks' such as animated graphics, which tend to distract from rather than enhance understanding.

The above observation applies in particular to Websites whose main intention is to inform and instruct (as opposed to Websites that, for example, want to market something or induce users to play games). This means that they do not need to attract their users' attention, but can instead count on a captive audience. The design and evaluation criteria therefore focus on navigation as a means to signal the information structure of a site, the clear and consistent presentation of verbal information and – very important to the target group in this study – the exact correspondence of simulated events to real-life scenarios.

Above all, the system should speak the users' language, using words, phrases and concepts familiar to the user, rather than system-oriented terms. For this reason, the Project team spent a considerable time improving the information infrastructure. This included agreeing on a joint terminology, attaching metadata or keywords to the information and organising it in a manner that followed real-world conventions.

Among the three solutions proposed for international Web design – internationally aware Websites, translated Websites and fully internationalised Websites – the first (and most economical) of these solutions, i.e. internationally aware Websites, would seem to be adequate if the target group – as was the case in this Project – is characterised by great cultural diversity yet professional homogeneity and has a command of a common language (usually English). This type of use scenario is becoming increasingly common in today's world of multicultural teams, virtual communities of practice and globally operating companies.

To ensure the highest possible acceptance around the world, it helps to use simple language (English), restrict the use of graphics to those that assist during navigation and indicate the flow of information by means of arrows or other directional indicators. When designing for an international clientele, it is particularly important to avoid the idiomatic, jargon-rich language usually cherished by Website designers. It is also absolutely essential to employ consistent, precise and unambiguous terminology.

Creating internationally aware Websites does not rule out the possibility of fully internationalised versions at a later stage, if this should prove desirable or if new markets open up where a command of the original language cannot be taken for granted. Web designers can consult plenty of guidelines about how to enable customisation. Hoft's (1995) book on *International Technical Communication* has proved particularly useful in this respect.

Of course, use scenarios can also be envisaged where it might be appropriate to translate Websites into various languages and customise their design to address the needs of users in other countries and language communities. There will also be cases where it is necessary to completely redesign Websites for different cultures, changing content, organisation, graphics, colours and so on - the most costly and time-consuming option. This last option tends to be espoused only by large companies with a strong presence in foreign markets and is usually beyond the means of most organisations.

11.2.2 Recommendations for the development of eLearning materials

All the development efforts in the Project followed the principles of participatory design, i.e. to develop computer-based applications or systems not *for*, but *with* the people who use them. Involvement of users right from the outset is a prerequisite for acceptance and, thus, for the efficient use of a system. Closely connected with participatory design is an iterative procedure concerning usability testing. This means that testing of the product, computer system or application does not take place at the end of the development cycle, but instead accompanies it throughout, with users' comments and criticisms fed straight back into the design process.

Participatory design also implies that development engineers and designers should be (made) aware of the fact that technical products are 'cultural carriers'. For this purpose, it is more important to identify the standards and requirements that apply to specific applications or products rather than promote awareness of the influence of cultural factors in general. Because of the multi-facetedness of the term culture, it is only by means of contextual research, however, that such standards can be identified. In the context examined in this study, culture was associated with belonging to a professional group such as designers, mechanics or pilots rather than sharing the same country of origin.

Cultural standards can be identified mainly by investigating critical incidents that occur in the use of a product or application. In activity theory, these are called 'contradictions' and are seen as the main driving force behind development and change. Contradictions can be observed at different levels such as strategies and goals, e.g. aiming at higher customer satisfaction through the provision of high-quality eLearning materials on the one hand, yet showing reluctance to commit more resources to training activities on the other, or be inherent in the work organisation (e.g. course development should be teamwork but the reward system does not encourage collaboration).

As discussed in the chapter on the activity theory framework, the rules and norms (also called praxis) that mediate the relationship between subject and community represent a further node in the extended activity triangle. Praxis denominates the shared collective ensemble of ways, methods and traditions of doing things. Praxis may be transmitted informally or by way of apprenticeship, but can also be written down. Certain lines of business, organisations or associations, for example, issue their own standards and guidelines which have to be observed. In the aviation industry, the recommendations issued by AICC, the Aviation Industry CBT Committee, should be taken into account even though they are not legally binding or compulsory. Adherence to standards or industry guidelines is particularly important for collaboration and exchange of knowledge or courseware elements with other partners.

When it comes to the actual design of eLearning materials, flexibility and adaptability are of primary importance. Within the framework of the Project, these have been achieved by developing a very 'slim' basic module which contains only the basic content relevant to the majority of users. Any additional information can be accessed either by means of hypertext links, e.g. under the heading "Further reading" or "If you want to know more..." or by separate scenarios or tasks addressed to specific target groups such as pilots, mechanics or avionic engineers.

Flexibility and adaptability also apply to sequencing, functionality or feedback mechanisms. Sequencing refers to the order in which learning objects are arranged and delivered. Learning objects, i.e. content broken down into manageable, reusable entities that can be delivered across multiple platforms, are now widely recognised as the most appropriate way of developing and delivering learning content. In practice, however, most eLearning providers and publishers still focus on creating learning content as large 'packaged' or fully integrated courses with limited reusability for other purposes. Some may produce innovative interactive solutions and, in some cases, simulations of experiments or activities (such as flying a helicopter) that allow students to control or manipulate aspects of the activity.

The 'packaged' approach also applies to the eLearning offerings in the aviation field that were examined in the course of the preliminary research for the Project. However, the Project team and the experts consulted eventually decided that it should not be considered a drawback if the pedagogic elements called for by educational scientists were virtually absent. Instructors, for instance, consider it more important to surround learning objects with contextual information, even though this makes them difficult, if not impossible, to re-use in a different context. Both instructors and trainees agree that the content has to be of high quality, i.e. absolutely accurate, well-structured and interactive. 'Interactive' in this context refers particularly to the possibility of simulating scenarios on the screen which the users can manipulate and which would be too risky to enact in real life.

If the online component is to be extended throughout the company, the instructors in the subsidiaries, for example, should receive guidance on how to construct a suitable pedagogy and thus enable them to put together good learning situations. This approach may involve creating tools for teachers and students such as templates that are characteristic of particular pedagogical models (e.g. problem-based learning).

As far as knowledge exchange among students and between the students and instructor in the classroom is concerned, the unpredictability of this type of interaction would seem to make it impossible to simulate this in an eLearning course. It depends largely on arbitrary factors such as the composition of a class, the personality of an instructor, the presence of an interpreter, the command of English of both the instructor and the students or the atmosphere in a particular class.

However, in the course of attending a series of classes, certain topics cropped up repeatedly (e.g. how to obtain spare parts) and should be incorporated in the eLearning materials. Apart from that, the only way to somehow mirror the classroom interaction in the virtual world would be to introduce a discussion forum on the eLearning platform which enables and encourages the exchange between instructors and students as well as among students. However, the introduction of such a forum would have to bear in mind that communication patterns in cyberspace differ from those in face-to-face interaction.

11.2.3 The accommodation of cultural factors

The study started out with the problem of defining culture and the different approaches for determining the influence of cultural factors. Finally, a pragmatic approach was chosen which implied looking for the aspects that were relevant to the issues involved in this particular investigation rather than a universally valid definition.

In activity theory, social and cultural factors are considered an integral part of the context of any activity, regardless of whether the target groups are culturally homogeneous or characterised by great cultural diversity. Once we decide to study an activity in its context and try to identify the factors that influence its use, historical, social and cultural aspects automatically come into play. Depending on the target users and the usage situations, these can manifest themselves in different forms.

The findings of this study challenge the conventional, anthropologically inspired bias towards equating culture with ethnic or national identity. The results of both the ethnographic research and the usability tests have shown that professional background had a higher predictive and explanatory value concerning learning style, interaction patterns or preferences with regard to user interfaces than country of origin or age.

It goes without saying that this finding cannot be generalised given its very specific context. However, there are other professions such as lawyers, doctors or journalists which have a strong sense of tradition or absorb certain attitudes or communication patterns as part of their training which may yield similar results (see e.g. Abramson and Mizrahi 1996). In any case, this once again confirms the importance of immersing oneself into the environment or organisational context to gain a comprehensive and in-depth understanding of an activity.

The analysis also showed that preferences and requirements with regard to usability cover a very wide spectrum. Attempts at rendering them more systematic or pressing them into a particular schema have not met with great success. As a result, the product or computer-mediated system to be developed should be as flexible and adaptable as possible. In the long run, so-called adaptive or personalised systems appear to be the only solution to tailoring user interfaces, functions and the various interactive and collaborative features to an individual or a particular group. They also represent the most promising solution to the contradiction between striving to achieve cost-savings on the one hand and high-quality training and customer satisfaction on the other. By tailoring training to the needs and requirements of clients and giving them more control over the pace and time of study, training becomes more efficient.

However, although the concept of adaptive or personalised computer systems has recently been discussed at many conferences, its actual implementation still looks rather remote. For the time being, customisation and adaptation has to be achieved by other techniques such as parameterisation or systems that allow multidimensional views of the content. As already noted in the usability section, designers should aim for the most flexible design possible. In the field of eLearning, this may involve the development of certain core scenarios supplemented with some culture-specific variations of scenarios of tasks.

Another aspect of culture which has to be considered when developing eLearning materials is the conventions, values and communication practices that prevail in cyberspace. In the environment of an online course, significant cultural 'gaps' can result from role differences, seniority/experience, perceptions of academic ability, gender, perceptions of time, professional status, tolerance for criticism and debate.

These factors have been subsumed under a series of themes with possible intercultural implications, among them attitudes towards authority, group *versus* individual focus, intellectual style or discourse and task *versus* relationship focus. Their relevance for the development of eLearning materials will, however, depend on the target group(s), the context of training, the topic or any other contextual factors that can only be ascertained through examining both the environment in which they will be used and the motives and goals of the future users.

11.2.4 Recommendations concerning methodology

The general methodological implications of applying activity theory as an overarching framework can be summarised as follows:

- Conduct a longitudinal study
- Apply a mix of methods consisting of (semi-)directed interviews, participant observation and focus group discussions
- Try to understand critical incidents in intercultural situations

Although the general principles of activity theory can help orient thought and research, they are nonetheless somewhat abstract when it comes to the actual evaluation of the data. This is why so-called activity checklists have been developed (e.g. by Kaptelinin and Nardi 1999) that can be adapted to the research context under study and used to structure and organise the empirical data usually gathered through ethnographic methods.

With the help of these checklists, a contextual space is laid out which is represented by the most relevant areas. For the purposes of this study, the key areas consisted of strategies and goals, organisational context, learning, cognition and interaction as well as transformation and development. The checklists help make concrete the activity theory conceptual system for specific tasks and elucidate the most important contextual factors in the (computer-mediated) activities under study.

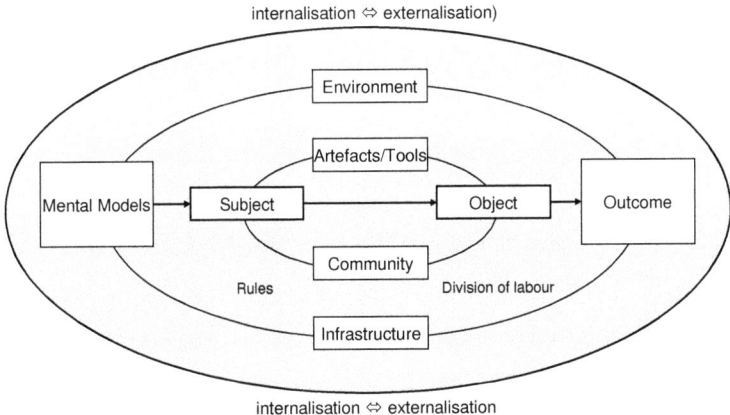

Figure 5: Training Activity System

The diagram above illustrates how the key areas/factors identified in the course of this investigation can be integrated into an activity theory framework. At the centre of the structured description of the training activity is the activity 'triangle'. This goes back to Engeström (1987), who extended the graphical representation of an activity to recognise that it occurs in the context of a community, praxis (formal and informal rules) and division of labour. See also Figure 1: Extended Activity Triangle on page 104 and Figure 2: Extended Activity Triangle (adapted) on page 135.

The Subject denotes the target users (mainly instructors and clients); the Tool refers to the KM system and the eLearning platform (to be) developed in the course of the Project. The model is complemented with the Environment, i.e. the organisational context that influences the training activity, as well as the Infrastructure, which in this case refers less to the hardware and more to the information architecture that lies at the heart of any knowledge transfer and exchange.

Another key area is represented by Mental Models, i.e. the expectations, traditions and behaviour patterns of users. These are acquired through interaction with the environment and are thus rooted primarily in experience and the tacit knowledge resident in the environment and the way it is distributed and accessed. They do not determine the behaviour of individuals but point to probable modes of perception, thought and action.

Mental models also include the human, social and cultural factors that are integrative to any activity. In order to coordinate individual and group activities, this context-specific knowledge has to be externalised, i.e. formalised and communicated.

The interaction between the two types of knowledge – as indicated by the bidirectional arrows - brings about what is referred to as the spiral of knowledge creation and, thus, is closely associated with learning. Learning, cognition and interaction represents *the* key area in this study and encompasses the entire shaded area in the diagram. The arrows indicate that the internalisation – externalisation dialectic drives the development process whilst, at the same time, influencing the mental models. It thus mirrors the fact that computer systems should support both internalisation of new ways of action and articulation of mental processes, when necessary, to facilitate problem solving and social coordination.

The figure brings together the essential elements of the training activity, i.e. the role of cultural factors, the embeddedness of the activity in its organisational context and the importance of community and collaboration in both HCI and eLearning.

The quest for a theoretical framework underlying the discussion of the various theoretical approaches, models and concepts in both fields finds its conclusion – at least for the time being, since any solution or hypothesis is provisional and can, of course, be superseded by a more appropriate, sophisticated novel approach – in the adoption of activity theory.

However, the fact that activity theory is a conceptual tool, which does not exclude other approaches and does not reject the usefulness of other conceptual schemes, will guarantee its applicability and continuity long into the future. After all, no tool, no matter how powerful, can ever serve all needs and help to solve all problems. By drawing together the diverse strands that have sprung from the Vygotskian tradition, we should be able to deal with most – if not all – of the problems that might occur when researching the use of computer-mediated activities.

12 References

12.1 Literature

Abramson, J.S. and Mizrahi, T. (1996). When Social Workers and Physicians Collaborate: Positive and Negative Interdisciplinary Experiences. In: *Social Work*, 41(3), 270-281.

Alexander, J.E. and M.A. Tate (1999). *Web wisdom. How to evaluate information quality on the Web*. Mahwah, NJ: Lawrence Erlbaum.

Angrosino, M.V. and K.A. Mays de Perez (2000). Rethinking observation: From method to context. In: *Handbook of Qualitative Research*, N.K. Denzin and Y.S. Lincoln (eds) Sage Publications. Thousand Oaks, CA, 673-697.

Avison, D.E. and Myers, M.D. (1995). Information Systems and Anthropology: an anthropological perspective in OT and organizational culture. In: *Information Technology & People*, 8, 3, 43-56.

Ballstaedt, S.-P. (1997). *Wissensvermittlung. Die Gestaltung von Lernmaterial*. Weinheim: Psychologie Verlags Union.

Bannon, L. and S. Bødker (1991). Beyond the interface: Encountering artifacts in use. In: J. Carroll (ed.) *Designing Interactions: Psychology at the Human-Computer Interface*. New York: Cambridge University Press.

Baumgartner, P. and Payr, S. (1997). Erfinden lernen. In: K.H. Müller and F. Stadler (eds) *Konstruktivismus und Kognitionswissenschaft. Kulturelle Wurzeln und Ergebnisse*. Vienna et al.: Springer, 89-106.

Bedny, G., and Meister, D. (1997). *The Russian theory of activity: Current applications to design and learning*. Mahwah, NJ: Lawrence Erlbaum.

Bellamy, R.K.E. (1996). Designing Educational Technology: Computer-Mediated Change. In: B.A. Nardi (ed.) *Context and consciousness: Activity theory and human-computer interaction* (pp. 123-146). Cambridge, MA: MIT Press.

Bereiter, C. and Scardamalia, M. (1993). *The Psychology of Written Composition*. Hillsdale, NJ: Lawrence Erlbaum.

Beu, A., P. Honold and Yuan, X. (2000). How to Build Up an Infrastructure for Intercultural Usability Engineering. In: *International Journal of Human-Computer Interaction, 12* (3&4), 347-358.

Boesch, E. E. (1991). *Symbolic Action Theory and Cultural Psychology*. Berlin: Springer.

Bødker, S. (1989). A human activity approach to user interfaces. In: *Human Computer Interaction*, 4.

Bødker, S. (1991). *Through the interface: A human activity approach to user interface design*. Hillsdale, NJ: Lawrence Erlbaum.

Bødker K. and Pedersen J S. (1991). Workplace Cultures: Looking at Artifacts, Symbols and Practices. In: J. Greenbaum J and M. Kyng (eds). *Design at Work: Cooperative Design of Computer Systems* (pp121-136). Hillsdale, NJ: Lawrence Erlbaum.

References

Bourges-Waldegg, P. and S.A.R. Scrivener (2000). Applying and testing an approach to design for culturally diverse groups. In: *Interacting with Computers 13*, 111-126.

Brown, B., Green, N. and Harper, R. (eds) (2001). *Wireless world: Social and interactional aspects of wireless technology*. London: Springer.

Brown, J.S., Collins, A. and Duguid, P. (1989). Situated cognition and the culture of learning. In: *Educational Researcher*, 18 (1), 32-42.

Carey, Jane M. (1998). Creating global software: a conspectus and review. In: *Interacting with Computers, 9*, 449-465.

Chase, M., L. Macfadyen, K. Reeder and J. Roche (2002). Intercultural Challenges in Networked Learning: Hard Technologies Meet Soft Skills In:. *First Monday*, 7 (8) (August 2002).

Cluts, M. M. (2003). The Evolution of Artifacts in Cooperative Work: Constructing Meaning Through Activity. In: *GROUP'03*, Nov. 9-12, 144-152. ACM Press.

Collins, A., Brown, J. S., and Newman, S. E. (1989). Cognitive apprenticeship: Teaching the crafts of reading, writing and mathematics. In L. Resnick (Ed.), *Knowing, learning, and instruction: Essays in Honor of Robert Glaser*. (pp. 453-494). Hillsdale, NJ: Lawrence Erlbaum.

Cushman, W. H. and Rosenberg, D. J. (1991). *Human Factors in Product Design*. Amsterdam: Elsevier.

Davenport, T. and Prusak, L. (2000). *Working Knowledge. How Organizations Manage What They Know*. Boston: Harvard Business School Press.

Davydov, V.V. (1988). Learning activity: The main problems needing further research. In: *Activity Theory*, 1(1-2), 29-36.

Day, D.L. (1998). Shared values and shared interfaces: The role of culture in the globalisation of human-computer systems. In: *Interacting with Computers*, 9, 269-274.

Del Galdo, M. and Jakob Nielsen (eds) (1996). *International User Interfaces*. New York: Wiley.

Derry, S.J. and Lajoie, S.P. (eds) (1993). *Computers as Cognitive Tools*. Hillsdale, NJ: Lawrence Erlbaum.

Dong. J., and Salvendy, G. (1999). Designing menus for the Chinese population: Horizontal or vertical? In: *Behaviour & Information Technology*, 18, 467-471.

Dubach, E., Jacko, J. and Sears, A. (2000). International Aspects of World Wide Web Usability and the Role of High-End Graphical Enhancements. In: *International Journal of Human-Computer Interaction, 12* (2), 241-261.

Dunckley, L. and Smith, A. (2000). Cultural Dichotomies in User Evaluation of International Software. In: *Designing for Global Markets 2*, IWIPS '00, Baltimore, MD, Backhouse Press.

Engeström, Y. (1987). *Learning by expanding*. Helsinki: Orienta-Konsultit.

Engeström, Y. and Escalante, V. (1996). Mundane Tool or Object of Affection? The Rise and Fall of the Postal Buddy. In: B.A. Nardi (ed.), *Context and consciousness: Activity theory and human-computer interaction* (pp. 325-373). Cambridge, MA: MIT Press.

Engeström, Y., Engeström, R. and Suntio, A. (2002). Can a school community learn to master its own future? An activity-theoretical study of expansive learning among middle school teachers. In: G. Wells and G. Claxton (eds). *Learning for Life in the 21st Century – Sociocultural Perspectives on the Future of Education*. Oxford: Blackwells Publishing.

Erickson, T. (1990). Working with interface metaphors. In B. Laurel (ed.). *The Art of Human-Computer Interface Design* (pp. 65-74). Reading, MA: Addison-Wesley.

Evers, V. (2001). Cultural Aspects of User Interface Understanding: An Empirical Evaluation of an E-Learning Website by International User Groups, University of Amsterdam.

Flor, N. and Hutchins, E. (1991). Analyzing distributed cognition in software teams. A case study of team programming during perfective sofware maintenance. In: J. Koenemann-Belliveau et al. (ed.) *Proceedings of the Fourth Annual Workshop on Empirical Studies of Programmers* (pp. 36-59). Norwood, NJ: Ablex Publishing.

Galtung, J. (1981) :"Structure, culture and intellectual style: An essay comparing saxonix, teutonic, gallic and nipponic approaches". In: *Social Science Formation*. London/Beverly Hills: Sage.

Garfinkel, H. (1967). *Studies in Ethnomethodology*. Englewood Cliffs, NJ: Prentice Hall.

Geertz, C. (1966). The Impact of the Concept of Culture on the Concept of Man. In: J.R. Platt (ed.) *New Views on the Nature of Man*. Chicago: University of Chicago Press.

Gerhardt-Powals, J. (1996). Cognitive Engineering principles for enhancing human-computer performance. In: *International journal of human-computer interaction*, 8 (2), 189-211.

Glaser, B. G. and Strauss, A. L. (1967). *The Discovery of Grounded Theory: Strategies for Qualitative Research*. Chicago: Aldine Publishing Co.

Gobbin, R. (1998). The role of cultural fitness in user resistance of information technology. In: *Interacting with Computers, 9*, 275-285.

Gould, E., Verenikina, I. and Hasan, H. (2000). Activity Theory as a Basis for the Design of a Web Based System of Inquiry for World War 1 Data. In: *Proceedings of IRIS 23*. University of Trollhättan Uddevalla.

Griffith, T. L. (1998). Cross-cultural and cognitive issues in the implementation of new technology: focus on group support systems and Bulgaria. In: *Interacting with Computers 9*, 431-447.

Guribye, F. and Wasson, B. (1999). Evaluating collaborative telelearning scenarios: A sociocultural perspective. In: Collins, B. and Oliver, R. (eds) *Proceedings of Educational Multimedia, Hypermedia / Telecommunications 1999* (EdMedia '99). Charlottesville, VA: AACE.

Hackos, J.T. and D.M. Stevens (1997). *Standards for online communication*. New York, NW: John Wiley & Sons.

Hall, E. T. (1959/1973). *The silent language*. New York: Doubleday.

Hakkarainen, K. and Sintonen, M. (2002). Interrogative Model of Inquiry and Computer-Supported Collaborative Learning. In: *Science & Education*, 11 (1).

References

Hakkarainen, K., Järvelä, S., Lipponen, L. and Lehtinen, E. (1998). Culture of collaboration in computer-supported learning: Finnish perspectives. In: *Journal of Interactive Learning Research*, 9, 271-287.

Hannerz, U. (1996). *Transnational connections: Culture, people, places.* London: Routledge.

Helfrich, H. (1993). Methodologie kulturvergleichender psychologischer Forschung. In: A. Thomas (ed.) *Kulturvergleichende Psychologie: Eine Einführung* (pp. 81-102). Göttingen, Germany: Hofgrefe.

Heron, J. and Reason, P. (2001). The practice of co-operative inquiry: Research 'with' rather than 'on' people. In: P. Reason and H. Bradbury (eds) *Handbook of Action Research*, Sage Publications: Thousand Oaks, CA, 179-188.

Herskovits, M. J. (1965). *Economic anthropology: the economic life of primitive peoples.* New York: Norton.

Hofstede, G. (1986). Cultural Differences in Teaching and Learning. In: *International Journal of Intercultural Relations,* 10, 301-320.

Hofstede, G. (1980/1991). *Culture's consequences: International differences in work-related values.* Beverly Hills, CA: Sage Publications.

Hofstede, G. (1991). *Cultures and Organizations: Software of the Mind.* London: McGraw-Hill.

Hofstede, G. (2001*). Culture's consequences: Comparing values, behaviors, institutions and organizations across nations* (second edition). Thousand Oaks, CA: Sage Publications.

Hoft, N. (1995). *International Technical Communication. How to Export Information about High Technology.* New York: John Wiley & Sons.

Holden, N. (2002). *Cross-Cultural Management – A Knowledge Management Perspective.* Harlow: Prentice Hall.

Hollan, J., Hutchins, E. and Kirsh, D. (2000). Distributed Cognition: Toward a New Foundation for Human-Computer Interaction Research. In: *ACM Transactions on Computer-Human Interaction*, 7 (2), 174-196.

Hollnagel, E. (1997). Cognitive Ergonomics: it's all in the mind. In: *Ergonomics 40* (10), 1170-1182.

Holzblatt, K. and Beyer, H. (1993). Making customer-centered design work for teams. In: *Communications of the ACM*, 36, 10. 93-103.

Honold, P. (1995). "Gesicht-wahren" als zentraler chinesischer Kulturstandard in der Interaktion zwischen deutschen Managern und Taiwanesen. Unpublished doctoral dissertation, University of Regensburg, Germany.

Honold, P. (1999). Learning how to use a cellular phone: Comparison between German and Chinese users. In: *Technical Communication, 46,* 196-205.

Hutchins, E. (1994). *Cognition in the Wild.* Cambridge, MA: MIT Press.

Jahoda, G. (1993). *Crossroads Between Culture and Mind. Continuities and Change in Theories of Human Nature.* Boston: Harvard University Press.

References

Jarvenpaa, S. L. and Leidner, D. E. (1999). Communication and Trust in Global Virtual Teams. In: *Organization Science*, 10 (6), November-December, 791-815.

Jonassen, D.H. (1991). Objectivism versus Constructivism: Do We Need a New Philosophical Paradigm? In: *Educational Technology Research and Development*, 39 (3), 5-14.

Jones, A. and Mercer, N. (1993). Theories of learning and information technology. In: P. Scrimshaw (ed.) *Language, classrooms and computers* (pp.11-26). London: Routledge.

Jones, S. et al (1992). The Digital Guide to Developing International User Information, Digital Press.

Kamentz, E., Schudnagis, M., Womser-Hacker, Ch. (2002). SELIM: Human Computer Interaction in the Context of Multimedia Learning Systems and the Aspect of Adaptivity on the Basis of Cultural Differences. In: Wagner, E., Szücs, A. (eds). *EDEN Second Research Workshop 2002. Research and Policy in Open and Distance Learning* (pp. 211-215). Research Workshop Book. Universität Hildesheim..

Kamentz, E. and Womser-Hacker, Ch. (2003). Kulturbedingte Aspekte als Ausgangspunkt der Entwicklung adaptiver Lernumgebungen. In: U. Reimer et al (ed.). *WM2003. Professionelles Wissensmanagement – Erfahrungen und Visionen*. Bonn: Gesellschaft für Informatik, 213-222.

Kaptelinin, V. (1996). Activity theory: Implications for human-computer interaction. In: B.A. Nardi (ed.), *Context and consciousness: Activity theory and human-computer interaction* (pp. 103-121). Cambridge, MA: MIT Press.

Kaptelinin, V., Nardi, B. and Macaulay, C. (1999). The activity checklist: A tool for representing the "space" of context. In: *Interactions*, July & August, 27-39.

Karakowsky, Leonard (2001). Do We See Eye-to-Eye? Implications of Cultural Differences for Cross-Cultural Management Research and Practice. In: *The Journal of Psychology, 135* (5), 501-517.

Knoll, K. and Jarvenpaa, S. (1995). Learning to Work in Distributed Global Teams. In: *Proceedings of the Twenty-Eighth Hawaii International Conference on System Sciences, IV. Information Systems – Collaboration Systems and Technology/Organizational Systems and Technology* (Wailea, Hawaii, 1995) (pp. 92-101). Los Alamitos: IEEE Computer Society Press.

Kroeber, A. A. and Kluckhohn, C. (1952). *Culture. A critical review of definitions and concepts*. Cambridge, MA: Peabody Museum.

Lave, J. (1988). *Cognition in practice: Mind, mathematics and culture of everyday life*. Cambridge: Cambridge University Press.

Lave, J. and Wenger, E. (1996). Practice, person, social world In: H. Daniels (ed.) *An Introduction to Vygotsky* (pp. 143-159). London: Routledge.

Leontiev, A. N. (1978). *Activity, Consciousness, Personality*. Englewood Cliffs, NJ, Prentice Hall.

Lewis, I. M. (1985). *Social Anthropology in Perspective*. Cambridge: Cambridge University Press.

Liaw, M.-L. and Johnson, R. J. (2001). E-mail writing as a cross-cultural learning experience. In: *System*, 29 (2), 235-251.

References

Limaye, M. R. and Victor, D. A. (1995). Cross-cultural business communication: state of the art and hypotheses for the 1990s. In: Jackson, T. (ed.) *Cross-cultural management* (pp. 217-37). Oxford: Butterworth-Heinemann,.

Luong, T., Lok, J., Lok, S., and Driscoll, K. (1995). *Internationalization: Developing software for global markets*. New York: Wiley.

Mambrey, P. and Robinson, M. (1997). Understanding the role of documents in a hierarchical flow of work. In *Proceedings of Group' 97*, Phoenix, Arizona, November, 119-127.

Mantovani, G. (1996) *New Communication Environments: From Everyday to Virtual*. London: Taylor & Francis Ltd.

Marcus, A. (2000). Cultural Dimensions and Global Web User Interface Design: What So What? What Now? In: *South African Human-Computer Interaction Conference*, May 2000.

McCormick, R. and Scrimshaw, P. (2001) Information and communications technology, knowledge and pedagogy. In: *Education, Communication & Information*, 1 (1), 39-57.

McPhee, W. and C. Nøhr (2000). Globalisation and the cultural impact on distance education. In: *International Journal of Medical Informatics, 58-59*, 291-295.

McSweeney, B. (2002). Hofstede's model of national cultural differences and their consequences: a triumph of faith - a failure of analysis. In: *Human Relations*, 55 (1), 89-118.

Mejias, R. J., Vogel, D.R. and Shepherd, M.M. (1997). GSS Meeting Productivity and Participation Equity: A U.S. and Mexico Cross-Cultural Field Study. *Proceedings of the Thirtieth Hawaii International Conference on System Sciences. Vol. II. Information Systems Track – Collaboration Systems and Technology* (Wailea, Hawaii 1997). pp. 469-478. Los Alamitos: IEEE Computer Society Press.

Morgan, D. L. (1997). *Focus groups as qualitative research*. Thousand Oaks: Sage Publications.

Myers, M.D. (1997). Critical Ethnography in Information Systems. In: A. S. Lee, L. Liebenau and J. I. DeGross, *Information Systems and Qualitative Research* (pp. 276-300). London: Chapman and Hall.

Myers, M. D. and Tan, F. B. (2002). Beyond models of national culture in information systems research. In: *The Journal of Global Information Management*, 10 (1), 14-29.

Najjar, L. J. (1998). Principles of educational multimedia user interface design. In: *Human Factors*, 41(2), 311-323.

Nardi, B. (ed.) (1996). *Context and Consciousness: Activity Theory and Human-Computer Interaction*. Cambridge, MA: MIT Press.

Nardi, B., Whittaker, S. and Bradner, E. (2000). Interaction and outeraction: Instant messaging in action. In: *Proceedings of CSCW '2000*. Philadelphia, PA, 79-88.

Nielsen, J. (1993). *Usability Engineering*. Boston, MA: Academic Press.

Nielsen, J. (2000). *Designing Web Usability: The Practice of Simplicity*. New Riders Publishing.

Nonaka, I. and Takeuchi, H. (1995). *The Knowledge Creating Company*. New York: Oxford University Press.

References

Onibere, E. A., Morgan, S., Bursang, E. M. and Mpoeleng, D. (2001). Human-computer Interface Design Issues for a Multi-cultural and Multi-lingual English-speaking Country – Botswana. In: *Interacting with Computers 13*, 497-512.

Orlikowski, W.J. (1991). Integrated Information Environment or Matrix of Control? The Contradictory Implications of Information Technology. In: *Accounting, Management and Information Technologies*, 1 (1), 9-42.

Paavola, S., Ilomäki, L., Lakkala, M. and Hakkarainen, K. (2003). Evaluating virtual learning materials through the three metaphors of learning. Paper presented in the Symposium *Designing Virtual Learning Material* EARLI 10th Biennial Conference *Improving Learning, Fostering the Will to Learn*, 26-30 September, 2003.

Piamonte, D. P. T., Abeysekera, J. D.A. and Ohlsson, K. (2001). Understanding small graphical symbols: a cross-cultural study. In: *International Journal of Industrial Ergonomics 27*, 399-404.

Piaget, J.(1962). *Play, Dreams and Imitation*. New York: Norton.

Porter, D. (2001). Object lessons from the web: implications for instructional development. In: G.M. Farrell (ed.) *Changing Faces of Virtual Education*, 47-69. Vancouver: Commonwealth of Learning.

Probst, Gilbert, Raub, Steffen and Romhardt, Kai (1999). *Wissen managen*. Wiesbaden: Gabler.

Quinn, A. (2001) Why people can't use eLearning. What the eLearning sector needs to learn about usability. In: *Frontend*, 5th June, 2001.

Randall, D. and Bentley, R. (1994). *Tutorial Notes on Ethnology and Collaborative Systems Development*, HCI'94.

Ratner, C. (1996). Activity as a Key Concept for Cultural Psychology. In: *Culture & Psychology*, 2 (4), 407-434.

Ratner, C. (1997). In Defense of Activity Theory. *Culture & Psychology,* 3 (2), 211-223.

Rieber, L. P. (1994). *Computers, Graphics, and Learning*. Dubuque, Iowa: Wm. D. Brown Communications Inc.

Ringstaff, C., Kelley, L., and Dwyer, D. (1993). Breaking the mold of instruction with technology: Formative case studies of the unit of study process. *ACOT Report* (August).

Russo, P. and Boor, S. (1993). How fluent is your interface? Designing for international users. In: *Proceedings of INTERCHI '93*, 342-347. New York: ACM Press.

Schein, E. H. (1997). *Organizational Culture and Leadership*. San Francisco: Jossey-Bass.

Schofield, J.W. (1993). Generalizability of Qualitative Research. In: M. Hammersley (ed.) *Social Research – Philosophy, Politics and Practice* (pp. 200-225). London: Sage Publications.

Searle, J.R. (1995). *The Construction of Social Reality*. London: Penguin.

Savenye, W.C. and Robinson, R.S. (1996). Qualitative research issues and methods: An introduction for educational technologists. In: D.H. Jonassen (ed.)*Handbook of Research for Educational Communications and Technology*. New York: Simon & Schuster Macmillan, 1171-1195.

References

Schwartz, S. H. (1994). Beyond Individualism/Collectivism: New Cultural Dimensions of Values. In: U. Kim et al (eds) *Individualism and Collectivism: Theory, Methods and Applications* (pp. 85-119). London: Sage.

Sfard, A. (1998). On two metaphors for learning and the dangers of choosing just one. In: *Educational Researcher, 27* (2), 4-13.

Sears, A. (2000). Introduction: Empirical Studies of WWW Usability. In: *International Journal of Human-Computer Interaction*, 12 (2), 167-171.

Shuell, T.J. (1992). Designing Instructional Computing Systems for Meaningful Learning. In: M. Jones and P. Winne (eds). *Adaptive Learning Environments.* NATO ASI Series F., Vol. 85, 19-54. New York: Springer.

Shore, B. (1996). *Culture in Mind. Cognition, Culture, and the Problem of Meaning.* New York: Oxford University Press.

Simon, J. S. (2001). The Impact of Culture and Gender on Web Sites: An Empirical Study. In: *The DATA BASE for Advances in Information Systems*, Winter 2001, 32 (1), 18-37.

Singleton, W. T. (1989). *The mind at work, Psychological ergonomics.* Cambridge: Cambridge University Press.

Soudijn, K. A., Hutschemaekers, G. J. M. and van de Vijver, F. J. R. (1990). The conceptualisation of culture. In: F. J. R. van de Vijver and G. J. M Hutschemaekers (eds). *The Investigation of Culture. Current Issues in Cultural Psychology* (pp. 19-39). Tilburg: Tilburg University Press.

Spagnolli, A., Gamberini, G. and Gasperini, D. (2002). In: *Psychology Journal*, 1 (1), 5-17.

Spyridakis, Jan H. (2000). Guidelines for Authoring Comprehensible Web Pages and Evaluating their Success. In: *Technical Communication*, special issue, 3rd quarter 2000.

Steinwachs, K. (1999). Information and Culture – The Impact of National Culture on Information Processes. In: *Journal of Information Science*, 25 (3), 193-204.

Stewart, T.A. (1996). The Invisible Key to Success. *Fortune, 134*, August 5, 173-175.

Strauss, A. L. (1994). Grundlagen qualitativer Sozialforschung. Munich: Fink.

Suchman, L. A. (1987). *Plans and Situated Actions.* New York: Cambridge University Press.

Sun, H. (2003). Exploring Cultural Usability: A Localization Study of Mobile Text Messaging Use. In: *CHI 2003: New Horizons*, ACM Press, 670-671.

Tan, B.C.Y., Wei, K. K. and Watson, R. T. (1995). National Culture and Group Support Systems: Filtering Communication to Dampen Power Differentials. In: *European Journal of Information Systems*, 4 (2), 82-92.

Thomas, A. (1991). *Kulturstandards in der internationalen Begegnung.* Saarbrücken, Germany: Breitenbach.

Thomas, A. und Helfrich, H. (1993). Wahrnehmungspsychologische Aspekte im Kulturvergleich. In: A. Thomas (ed.) *Kulturvergleichende Psychologie* (pp. 107-135). Göttingen, Germany: Hofgrefe.

Trompenaars, F. (1993). *Riding the Waves of Culture, Understanding Diversity in Global Business.* Burr Ridge (IL)/New York: Irwin Professional Publishing.

Turner, P., Turner, S. and Horton, J. (1999). From description to requirements. an activity theoretic perspective, 286-295. ACM Press.

Tylor, E. B. (1958). *Origins of culture.* (Primitive Culture, Part I.) New York: Harper & Row.

Van der Geest, T. and Spyridakis, J. H. (2000). Developing Heuristics for Web Communication: An Introduction to this Special Issue. In: *Technical communication*, Third Quarter 2000, 301-325.

Victor, D. (1992). *International Business Communications.* New York: Harper Collins.

Vygotsky, L. S. (1978). *Mind and Society.* Cambridge, MA: Harvard University Press.

Wells, G. and Claxton, G. (2002) (eds). *Learning for Life in the 21st Century – Sociocultural Perspectives on the Future of Education.* Oxford: Blackwells Publishing.

Welsch, W. (1998). "Wirklich". Bedeutungsvarianten – Modelle – Wirklichkeit und Virtualität. In: S. Krämer (ed.) *Medien – Computer – Realität. Wirklichkeitsvorstellungen und Neue Medien* (pp. 169-212). Frankfurt: Suhrkamp.

Wenger, E. (1998). *Communities of practice: learning, meaning, and identity.* New York: Cambridge University Press

Wenger, E. (2000) Communities of practice and learning systems. In: *Organization*, 7 (2), 225-246.

Wertsch, J.V. (1994). The primacy of mediated action in sociocultural studies. In: *Mind, Culture and Activity*, 1 (4), 202-208.

Wiley, D. et al (2003). Using 02 to overcome learning objects limitations. In: E. Duval et al (eds) *Learning Objects 2003 Symposium: lessons learned, questions asked* (pp. 61-67). ED-MEDIA 2003, Honolulu, Hawaii, USA.

Yeo, A. (2001). Global-Software Development Lifecycle: An Exploratory Study. In: *Proceedings of the SIGCHI conference on Human factors in computing systems*, March 31-April 4, Seattle, Washington, 4-111. New York: ACM Press.

12.2 Internet Resources

Alexander, J.E. and M.A. Tate (1999). Evaluating Web resources.
http://www2.widener.edu/Wolfgram-Memorial-Library/webevaluation/webeval.htm.
Visited on 15/09/2004.

Alvarez, M.G., L.R. Kasday and S. Todd (1998). How we made the Web site international and accessible: A case study.
http://www.research.att.com/conf/hfweb/proceedings/alvarez/index.html.
Visited on 17/09/2004.

Barber, W. and Badre, A. (1998). Culturability: The Merging of Culture and Usability.
http://www.research.att.com/conf/hfweb/proceedings/barber/index.html.
Visited on 17/09/2004.

Kearsley, G. and Shneiderman, B. (1999). Engagement Theory: A framework for technology-based teaching and learning. http://home.sprynet.com/~gkearsley/engage.htm.

Visited on 19/06/2004.

Koper, R. (2000). *From change to renewal: Educational technology foundations of electronic learning Environments*. Heerlen: Open University of the Netherlands. Web-version: http://eml.ou.nl/introduction/docs/koper-inaugural-address.pdf.
Visited on 17/09/2004

Margules, Di (1996). Instructivism or Constructivism: which end of the continuum? In: *AUC Academic Conference 'From Virtual to Reality.'* The University of Queensland.
http://auc.uow.edu.au/conf/Conf96/Papers/MarguleD.html.
Visited on 15/09/2004.

Nichols, M. (2003). A theory for eLearning. *Educational Technology & Society*, 6(2), 1-10, available at *http://ifets.ieee.org/periodical/6-2/1.html*.
Visited on 17/09/2004.

Nielsen, J. Heuristic Evaluation.
http://www.useit.com/papers/heuristic/
Visited on 17/09/2004.

Nielsen, J. (2000). Why You Only Need to Test With 5 Users.
http://www.useit.com/alertbox/20000319.html
Visited on 17/09/2004.

Ormondroyd, J.M. Engle and T. Cosgrave (1999). "How to critically analyze information resources." http://www.library.cornell.edu/okuref/research/skill26.htm

Orrill, C.H. (2001). Learning objects to support inquiry-based online learning. In: D.A. Wiley (ed.) *The Instructional Use of Learning Objects*. Online at http://www.resuability.org/read/
Visited on 16/09/2004.

Sveiby, Karl-Erik (1996). *What is Knowledge Management?*
(http://www.sveiby.com/articles/KnowledgeManagement.html)
Visited on 17/09/2004.

W3C (World Wide Web Consortium) (1999). Web content accessibility guidelines 1.0 W3C recommendation 5-May-1999.
http://www.w3.org/tr/wai-webcontent/wai-pageauth.html.
Visited on 17/09/2004.

Yeo, A. (1996). World-Wide CHI: Cultural User Interfaces, A Silver Lining in Cultural Diversity. In: *SIGCHI Bulletin*, 28 (3). http://sigchi.org/bulletin/1996.3/international.html.
Visited on 17/09/2004.

Die VDM Verlagsservicegesellschaft sucht für wissenschaftliche Verlage abgeschlossene und herausragende

Dissertationen, Habilitationen, Diplomarbeiten, Master Theses, Magisterarbeiten usw.

für die kostenlose Publikation als Fachbuch.

Sie verfügen über eine Arbeit, die hohen inhaltlichen und formalen Ansprüchen genügt, und haben Interesse an einer honorarvergüteten Publikation?

Dann senden Sie bitte erste Informationen über sich und Ihre Arbeit per Email an *info@vdm-vsg.de*.

Sie erhalten kurzfristig unser Feedback!

VDM Verlagsservicegesellschaft mbH
Dudweiler Landstr. 99   Telefon +49 681 3720 174
D - 66123 Saarbrücken   Fax   +49 681 3720 1749
www.vdm-vsg.de

Die VDM Verlagsservicegesellschaft mbH vertritt

Printed by Books on Demand GmbH, Norderstedt / Germany